The Discourse of Public Participation Media

The Discourse of Public Participation Media takes a fresh look at what 'ordinary' people are doing on air – what they say, and how and where they get to say it.

Using techniques of discourse analysis to explore the construction of participant identities in a range of different public participation genres, Joanna Thornborrow argues that the role of the 'ordinary' person in these media environments is frequently anything but.

Tracing the development of discourses of public participation media, the book focuses particularly on the 1990s onwards, when broadcasting was expanding rapidly: the rise of the TV talk show, increasing formats for public participation in broadcast debate and discussion, and the explosion of reality TV in the first decade of the 21st century. During this period, traditional broadcasting has also had to move with the times and incorporate mobile and web-based communication technologies as new platforms for public access and participation – text and email as well as the telephone – and an audience that moves out of the studio and into the online spaces of chat rooms, comment forums and the 'Twitterverse'.

This original study examines the shifting discourses of public engagement and participation resulting from these new forms of communication, making it an ideal companion for students of communication, media and cultural studies, media discourse, broadcast talk and social interaction.

Joanna Thornborrow is Professor of English Language and Linguistics at the University of Western Brittany. She has published widely on forms of media talk and social interaction in edited books and major international journals, and is the author of *Power Talk: Language and Interaction in Institutional Discourse* (2002).

The Discourse of Public Participation Media

From talk show to Twitter

Joanna Thornborrow

Routledge
Taylor & Francis Group

LONDON AND NEW YORK

First published 2015
by Routledge
2 Park Square, Milton Park, Abingdon, Oxon, OX14 4RN

and by Routledge
711 Third Avenue, New York, NY 10017

Routledge is an imprint of the Taylor & Francis Group, an informa business

British Library Cataloguing in Publication Data
A catalogue record for this book is available from the British Library

Library of Congress Cataloging in Publication Data
Thornborrow, Joanna, 1957-
  The discourse of public participation media : from talk show to twitter /
  Joanna Thornborrow.
  Includes bibliographical references and index.
  1. Mass media and language. 2. Discourse analysis—Social aspects.
  3. Conversation analysis—Social aspects. I. Title.
  P96.L34.T495 2014
  302.2301′41—dc23
                                                        2014021705

ISBN: 978-1-138-02494-6 (hbk)
ISBN: 978-1-138-02495-3 (pbk)
ISBN: 978-1-315-74040-9 (ebk)

Typeset in Sabon
by RefineCatch Limited, Bungay, Suffolk

MIX
Paper from
responsible sources
FSC® C013604

Printed and bound by CPI Group (UK) Ltd, Croydon, CR0 4YY

The book is dedicated to my parents John and June, who would never watch reality television, and to my children Alice and Nicolas, who, one way or another, have grown up with it.

Contents

Acknowledgements

This book has taken quite a few years to write, during which time it has changed shape and direction at least once. I am grateful to my former colleagues and many friends from the Centre for Language and Communication Research at Cardiff University for being there along the way, for all the informal discussions over the years as well as for their useful comments and questions during more formal opportunities to present work in progress at departmental research seminars. Special thanks to Justine Coupland, Nikolas Coupland, Adam Jaworski, Marie-Jet Bekkers, Theo van Leeuwen and David Machin for your support and collaboration on so many occasions.

It could not have been written without the consistently challenging discussions and intellectual company of members of the Ross Priory Group for Research on Broadcast Talk. The meetings of this group have provided an invaluable test bed for most of the ideas in the book, and many of the analyses it contains have originated in papers given at this annual seminar. In amongst the many conversations, I have particularly appreciated the help and encouragement of Steven Clayman, Mats Ekström, Richard Fitzgerald, Louann Haarman, Stephanie Marriott, Martin Montgomery, Greg Myers, Kay Richardson, Angela Smith and Andrew Tolson, who, in various ways, have contributed to the book being what it is today. Thanks to Kay, who was there to talk to during the final stages, and a very huge thank you to Louann Haarman, who agreed to take on the unenviable task of reading the first drafts of the chapters and keeping me on track. *Grazie mille, Trudy!* This is probably the place to say that any remaining problems and shortcomings are entirely my own responsibility. Last, but not least, thanks to Richard for being a great co-author on the *Election Call* projects.

The other group of people who have played a very significant role in the genesis of this book are all the undergraduate students I have taught in various places since 1993; first, at Roehampton, on the Language in the Media module, and, later, at Cardiff, in Media Texts and its subsequent incarnation, The Discourse of Broadcasting. For their enthusiasm, their willingness to participate in seminar discussions, their search for data and their readiness to engage with all aspects of broadcast talk (including, on one occasion, organising a trip to take part in a talk show audience and find out for themselves what was going on), I am extremely grateful. It has been a journey through several genres, and I have appreciated their company along the way. Thanks also to Claire Evans and Stephanie Kautzmann for their help in data collection and transcription, and to Debbie Morris for her collaborative work on *Big Brother*.

I would like to thank the following institutions for their generous support in the form of research leave and funding: the School of English, Communication and Philosophy at Cardiff University for two periods of research leave, one in 2006–2007 and the other in Spring 2011; the UK Arts & Humanities Research Council for its matching funding research award in 2006–2007; and my current institution the University of Western Brittany and research group Héritages et Constructions dans le Texte et l'Image for giving me the space I needed to finally finish the book. I'd like also to say thank you to Louisa Semlyen, Natalie Foster and Sheni Kruger at Routledge who have been very positive from the beginning and throughout the various stages of this project.

1 Introduction
Talking on television and radio

Ordinary people on air

This book is about ordinary people and their forms of engagement with the media through participation in broadcast talk on television and radio. The presence of people known as 'ordinary' on air has increased substantially over the last two decades or so. This increase – the result of shifting contexts for public participation generated by a proliferation of new 'reality' and 'lifestyle' media genres, in addition to the well-established phone-in and talk show programmes, and accompanied by the development of multi-platform interactivity between old broadcast and new digital media – calls for a re-examination of the role of members of the general public on the radio and on television.

Although it is certainly the case that voices of the public have been regularly heard on air since the early days of broadcasting (Scannell and Cardiff 1991; Scannell 1996), the participation of ordinary people – that is to say, people who are neither actors nor media professionals – is now a routine and staple ingredient in the diet of TV programming on all channels, and this is giving rise to new frameworks for public participation in contemporary forms of broadcast talk. The other significant change in public participation media in recent years has been the growth of digitally mediated communication and interactivity between web-based and mobile technology and traditional radio and television broadcasting. This, too, has had an impact on frameworks of participation and interaction in broadcast output, and has shifted relationships between broadcasters, participants and audiences in quite significant ways (Holmes 2004).

In this introductory chapter, I begin with an overview of existing research into public participation broadcasting. The key concepts of expertise and lay participation, as well as the distinction between interaction and interactivity, will be presented here as a frame for subsequent discussions of participation and access relating to public involvement in broadcast media output. I will also briefly introduce the principal environments where ordinary people appear as participants on radio and TV, and outline the main analytic frameworks on which I will be drawing in my analyses of the discursive activities that structure this participation. The central question of what being an 'ordinary' person means in relation to public participation media underpins this discussion here and in subsequent chapters of the book.

For the last 20 years at least, research into forms of broadcasting that involve members of the public in one way or another has distinguished between 'lay' participants and those who are media professionals, or 'experts'. Different kinds of discourses (Fairclough 1995) and footings (Goffman 1981) have typically been associated with each category – with perhaps the most prominent of these being the claim that experts speak for others while lay participants speak for themselves (Livingstone and Lunt 1994). However, this distinction between ordinary people and media professionals is, in many ways, no longer a sufficient or an adequate one in terms of describing the variety of identities and range of performances that constitute public participation in contemporary broadcasting. Because of the changing forms of public participation in the media that have been brought about by developments in radio broadcasting and, particularly, in new television genres, it is time to reassess and re-theorise the very notion of 'ordinary' as a way of talking about people who are non-media professionals and yet who are found in so many different contexts and genres, from the caller to a radio phone-in discussion to a contestant on *X Factor*. One of the central issues I will address in this book, therefore, is what it means to be 'ordinary' on radio and television, and how this concept of ordinariness may relate, or not, to the lay participants who, in various ways, are implicated and involved in the production of broadcast talk.

The first appearances of the ordinary person on radio is documented in Paddy Scannell's (1996) account of sociability in early broadcasting, and the production of 'the social occasion' in BBC radio broadcasts such as *Harry Hopeful* in the mid 1930s.[1] This kind of programme 'brings ordinary people into an unfamiliar and intimidating studio, puts them on stage and expects them to produce performances that are appropriate to the occasion' (Scannell 1996: 29). The social occasions in this case were scripted interviews recorded live in a studio, but which were based on earlier spontaneous talk with the same participants in their own environment (e.g., workplace, village or local community) and re-scripted for the live recordings. In contemporary reality television programmes, while conventional notions of what may be appropriate to the occasion may have changed beyond recognition since the 1930s, as have the available recording and editing technologies, the practices of reshaping, semi-scripting or in some way rehearsing and staging ordinary interactions between ordinary people to produce broadcast talk as a performance for a viewing audience seem to be as pervasive as they ever were.

There are, of course, still occasions and opportunities for members of the public to participate in unscripted, spontaneous forms of broadcast talk. Many media genres such as radio phone-in programmes, political panel discussions with a studio audience and some television talk shows are made up of largely unscripted interactions between presenters, hosts, experts and guests, where the opportunity for audience participation to occur live on-air remains the primary focus. However, many of the participants in such programmes frequently work at establishing a particular identity for themselves which puts an altogether different value on our understanding of the term 'ordinary'. Such identity work is discursively accomplished (Benwell and Stokoe 2006), and this brings us back to the questions of what talking as an ordinary citizen means and how do people do it? As I will show, whether as individuals or as representatives of a specific group, the identities claimed and displayed by lay participants in broadcast interactions seem to be far more complex and fine grained than simply being ordinary.

Ordinary identities and ordinary performances

As I have just noted, in much of the research on audience and public participation broadcasting, whether in relation to talk shows, radio phone-in shows or, more recently, to reality television and lifestyle formats, members of the public who take part in these programmes tend to be referred to as 'ordinary people' (Bonner 2003; Bignell 2005; Turner 2010). This term distinguishes them, as 'lay' participants, from other categories of participant: those who are employed by the media network as hosts or presenters; other media professionals, including journalists and politicians; and those who are labelled as 'experts' and who often represent institutions or organisations of one sort or another. And, as such a distinguishing category, it works – but only up to a certain point. Increasingly, it is being acknowledged that non-media professionals who take part in radio broadcasts and televised debates are often not speaking just for themselves as individuals, but on behalf of broader social constituencies or groups, while those who appear on television, particularly in the context of reality television genres, are people who are doing very specific kinds of being 'ordinary'. And, as Myra Macdonald (2007) has observed, the use of such categories as 'the public' or 'ordinary people' tends to homogenise the differences between them. These ordinary people are not experts speaking on behalf of an institutional organisation or position, nor are they politicians or journalists who have a stake in framing their message in particular institutional ways, but to label them 'ordinary' members of the public does not fully capture the complex local identities and situated expertise that their participation frequently involves. We need therefore to examine much more closely the forms of talk that constitute the discourses of public participation broadcasting in order to understand how participant identities in a range of media contexts are being constructed and displayed, oriented to and performed.

In current research on public participation and the kind of television formats we have come to know as 'reality TV', the notion of ordinary is often closely related to the notion of performance (Bonner 2003; Turner

2010). Since the first series of *Big Brother* was aired in the summer of 2000 (on Channel 4 in the UK and franchised in other countries around the world), reality TV has turned into one of the most significant developments in media formats to involve the participation of ordinary people over the last 15 years or so. Taking up a point made by Frances Bonner (2003), Graeme Turner (2010) notes that 'ordinary people on television are not ordinary like the rest of us; what they possess is the capacity to perform a particularly spectacular version of ordinariness in public', and that 'television is now providing more space for the ordinary person to perform a version of themselves than ever before' (Turner 2010: 43–44). However, Turner goes on to argue that this ordinary identity is increasingly being 'authored' by the media, rather than 'mediated', giving broadcasters a powerful role in the constitution of participant identities for their own ends – that is, the proliferation of profitable formats in what is now a global market. In so doing, television is in the business of com-modifying social identities in order to sell entertainment programmes in which, he says, 'reality is [. . .] satisfactorily performed by the ordinary citizen even when their "ordinariness" is at least debatable' (Turner 2010: 19). This practice of authoring (as compared to mediating) social identity also raises questions about how such performances of ordinary identities are achieved. Although people are no longer placed on an intimidating stage and given a script to rehearse for an interview during which they are required to sound chatty and sociable, as in the *Harry Hopeful* days, what exactly does this participation require and what kind of performances of being ordinary, or, indeed, of being 'not ordinary like the rest of us', do they produce? From a discourse analytic perspective, we might ask: How are participants' social identities being displayed and constructed within the context of reality television? And how are they being produced as a spectacle or performance for audiences?

In order to explore these issues around ordinary performance and identity through the lens of discourse analysis, the discussions in this book will be organised around three principal thematic areas. The first is how members of the public either position themselves within, or are positioned by, the mediated context of interaction in which relevant social identities are at stake. The second is the identification of particular discourses of public participation – where they are located, what they accomplish and how they are being performed, mediated or, indeed, authored. The final thematic area is the impact of interactivity on these identities and per-formances, and an examination of how the relationship between broad-casters, participants and audiences is shifting in a world where the pervasive presence of digital media may be playing its part in reconfiguring these discourses of participation.

In more concrete terms, the aim of this book is to identify and illustrate, through a series of empirical case studies and analyses of forms of mediated interaction, the different discourses of public participation in contemporary broadcast media. Throughout, I will be arguing that the distinction between ordinary people and media professionals is no longer a sufficient or an adequate one in terms of describing the variety of identities and range of performances that we find within these interactions. In addition, I will be exploring the emerging relationship between broadcast talk and developing platforms of digital communication, and how it is articulated with existing frameworks of public participation and participant identities. In the digital age of YouTube, and its invitation to 'broadcast yourself', once again, the traditional distinction between media professionals, experts and lay participants, in terms of production and performance, is effectively becoming more and more blurred (Hartley 2009; Tolson 2010). Furthermore, if we consider the increasingly prominent place and function of web- and text (SMS)-generated forms of participation in current broadcast output, then it really does seem that the relationship between broadcasters, participants and audiences in a world of multi-platform access to the media is radically changing. From a discourse perspective, where and how do we see this change occurring? For example, are digital platforms offering new arenas of public engagement, in terms of discussion and opinion-giving, in relation to traditional broadcast phone-ins or talk shows? How are the modes of mobile and web-based media – chatting, emailing, texting, tweeting – changing these forms of public participation on radio and television, and where are they most in evidence? Again, I will argue that the communicative relationship between traditional forms of broadcasting and the affordances of what used to be called 'new media' technologies is far from being a straightforward one.[2] An emailed question, for example, is not the same thing as a question delivered over the telephone, while a text or a tweet can open up different, new participatory possibilities within the framework of a live broadcast.

What I propose in this book is a re-examination of these discursive relationships in terms of the available access for audience participation through emails, texts and tweets, and how these give rise to different forms of participation within broadcast discourse. This will include looking in detail at the kinds of things that people do and say on air, and the constraints and affordances of how they get to do and say them when new media technologies are involved. How do the traditional forms of talk – including discursive activities such as asking questions and telling stories, opinion-giving and arguing, advice-giving and receiving – become adapted to new modes of communication and access to TV and radio? The contexts for such activities will include phone-in discussions, reality shows, advice-giving on radio shows and political question/answer broadcasts, where we can critically consider the function of email and web forums (Thornborrow and Fitzgerald 2002) as well as the contrasts between participation as interaction and the notion of interactivity (Macdonald 2007).

Here, we should proceed with a note of caution, however. As Jannis Androutsopoulos points out, 'digital data are available in overwhelming amounts, making it difficult to select and focus on one specific sample or site of discourse' (Androutsopoulos 2013: 238). In taking a discourse analytic approach to the seemingly infinite and diffuse world of the web, it is often difficult to establish clear research parameters and to decide where to draw boundaries. Since digital platforms are increasingly connected on multiple levels and content changes moment by moment, pinning down particular phenomena for analytical purposes can be problematic. I intend, therefore, to delimit quite carefully the scope of interactivity under investigation, and focus specifically on examples of the ways in which programmes that include some form of public participation either incorporate or generate digital participation and engagement; for example, how a radio advice-giving programme involves its audience as participants via texting, or how viewers engage with a political debate as a live event online. This thematic sampling will enable selective analysis of some of the discursive practices that are at the interface between broadcast talk and the digital media.

Analysing broadcast talk – method and practice

Talk of various kinds has always been at the core of broadcasting output. There are now many excellent accounts of broadcast talk available that address the particularities of radio and television as contexts for language and interaction, so what follows here is just a brief overview of some of the key work in this field. Back in the early 1990s, the publication of a collection of papers from the disciplinary fields of linguistics, discourse and conversation analysis, sociology, and cultural and media studies (Scannell 1991) played a major part in establishing the specific communicative nature of broadcast talk as a focus for interdisciplinary research. Unlike other forms of media discourse analysis, which tend to focus much more on its institutional power to represent the world in particular ways, including the identities and relationships it sets up for those who are involved in its production (Fairclough 1995; Chouliaraki and Morsing 2010), this research takes a rather different approach to the analysis of the discourses of radio and television. It is an approach based on three closely related premises, which, very broadly, are that:

1. Broadcast talk is produced within and according to a communicative ethos and set of communicative entitlements (Scannell 1996: 20–21) that, in different ways and at different times, pay particular attention to the listening or viewing audience.
2. It is produced within a frame of 'double articulation' (Scannell 1991) – that is to say, it is at the same time designed for immediate, co-present recipients as well as for the non co-present listening and/or viewing audience whom it addresses in identifiable, empirically analysable ways.
3. It can be analysed as a form of institutional discourse that is differentiated through its systematic organisation from conversational or

non-institutional interaction (Drew and Heritage 1992; Thornborrow 2002), yet which frequently exhibits many of the features we associate with ordinary conversation (Tolson 2006).

Above all, this is an empirical approach to the analysis of broadcast talk that is neither 'critical' in the sense that it does not provide particular social interpretations of media discourses as texts, nor 'critical' in the sense of making value judgements regarding the content of its objects of study as high or low culture, as quality or 'trash' TV. Andrew Tolson succinctly sums it up by saying that it is 'the very mundane practices of spoken interaction which occur on radio and television' that are its primary interest and principal focus (Tolson 2006: 22). Examples of some of the research that has been based on this empirical approach to broadcast talk over the last decade or so include conversation analysis work on news interviews with public figures and politicians (Clayman and Heritage 2002) and work on various forms of spoken discourse on TV and radio (Hutchby 2006; Tolson 2006), on news discourse (Montgomery 2007) and on the discourse of television talk shows (Tolson 2001). From a range of analytic perspectives, then, all these studies give us detailed insights into some of the specific features of the organisation and production of talk on radio and television for its audiences.

As we can see from the scope of the above-listed research, the term 'broadcast talk' is generally used here to refer to unscripted, naturally occurring, 'fresh talk' (to use Erving Goffman's (1981) term) produced by participants on air – a form of talk that is very different from the scripted talk and dialogue of, say, actors in TV dramas, soaps or sitcoms.[3] In fresh talk, speakers take up the footings (again, to use another key concept from Goffman) of both animator and author, and also generally of principal of the words they utter. Fresh talk also carries connotations of authenticity and spontaneity (Montgomery 2001) that we associate with the notion of all naturally occurring talk; that is, talk that is spontaneous and unplanned, rather than authored by a researcher or scriptwriter, and produced in and of the moment. There are, however, different levels of planning and semi-scripting apparent in many contexts of broadcast talk, and one must be wary of assuming that all public participation discourse is spontaneously produced. Members of talk show audiences often recount their experiences of unexpected levels of pre-planning and pre-rehearsal of the show before recording; politicians may be interviewed live on radio, but with a prepared set of on-message notes, and interviewers may have a list of potential questions; while participants in reality TV shows talk about how they are often asked to re-enact or repeat several times an original, fresh sequence of conversation that was missed first time around by the camera.[4] The kind of 'authoring' that takes place through production processes of voiceover and editing is also worth consideration. Nevertheless, the interactional talk produced in broadcast encounters between people who are not acting is qualitatively different from talk that is written to be spoken, such as news broadcasts, scripted shows or fictional drama. Talk radio hosts, in particular, are quick to distinguish between fresh talk and scripted talk – callers that appear to be, or, rather, are *heard* to be, reading from a prepared script are quickly taken off-air. Spontaneity on radio is difficult to fake.

The discourse analytical concepts I work with in this book are by now familiar ones to most students and scholars who are interested in media discourse as a form of social interaction, since they are primarily grounded in the well-established fields of conversation analysis, pragmatics and interactional sociolinguistics. The premise that talk is locally and sequentially organised, jointly produced and managed and designed by participants who are orienting to each other as well as to relevant contextual features and categories (Sacks et al. 1974; Levinson 1983) is a cornerstone to this approach. Goffman's seminal work on footing and participation frameworks (1981), as well as on front-stage and backstage behaviours (1959, 1963) and the framing of talk (1983), is also particularly relevant in the discursive analysis of talk show participation and reality television performances (Thornborrow 2001a; Thornborrow and Morris 2004; Lorenzo-Dus 2009). However, I also relate these theoretical approaches and discussions of the discourse of public participation broadcasting to studies in the broader context of mediated discourse, culture and communication, where appropriate. In so doing, the aim is to bridge a gap between the reference to broad-sweep discourses often found in research into contemporary cultures of broadcasting – something akin to what Paul Gee (1990) has referred to as big 'D' discourses, which are to do with socially and culturally conventionalised forms of speaking – and small 'd' discourses, which are the focus of detailed, micro-level analyses of specific situated instances of broadcast talk. And, without the engagement and participation of people who are not media professionals in this talk, much of contemporary broadcasting as we now know it would not happen.

Structure of the book

So far, in this introductory chapter, I have briefly sketched out the key arguments, concepts and methodological approaches to the discourse of public participation media that will be developed throughout the book. Three principal thematic areas have been identified that will be addressed in various ways and through empirical examples: (1) the concept of lay identities, (2) the discourses of public participation as performance and (3) the interface between spoken interaction and interactivity. I have also outlined some of the different genres of broadcast media that I will be using in order to base this discussion in empirically grounded analytical examples. The following two chapters consist of a more in-depth consideration of the limits of 'lay' and 'ordinary' as descriptive categories for public participation, and develop the theoretical frameworks of locally relevant identities and grounded expertise, as well as the notion of performance, in two different kinds of broadcast contexts: (1) political phone-ins and debates and (2) reality TV genres.

Chapter 2, entitled 'Identity and expertise', provides a critique of the expert/lay distinction, and the role of the lay participant in terms of the situated identities they are able to take up across a range of mediated contexts. I will show how these participants construct situated forms of expertise, particularly in environments where they are engaged in questioning, opinion-giving and argument, such as political panel and debate programmes. The data examples are drawn from programmes such as BBC's *Question Time*, political radio phone-ins and television talk show debates. Chapter 3, 'Performance and the mediated "self"', examines the role of ordinary people in tele-factual contexts of reality shows; again, in relation to the types of discursive environments in which such participation is organised. Looking at confessional talk and disclosure (e.g., in the *Big Brother* diary room) and talk direct to camera (e.g., in programmes like *Wife Swap*) as a location for producing what John Corner (2002) terms 'the self-in-performance', I will discuss the ways in which relevant social identities are constructed in these discursive environments, and how 'backstage' talk (Goffman 1959) is transformed through editing and voiceover into mediated, 'front-stage' performances of participant identity.

The focus in the next four chapters will be on a selection of broadcast environments where public participation involves the mediation of specific forms of discursive activities: telling stories, opinion-giving and argument, evaluation and judgement and advice-giving. The participatory frameworks involved in each context are analysed in terms of access to, and organisation of, these activities in a range of different broadcast contexts, from talk shows to makeover and lifestyle programming. Here, I will also examine the specific affordances and constraints of digital technologies and the development of audience interactivity that is increasingly characteristic of many of these media genres. In Chapter 4, 'Telling stories', I address one of the most pervasive discourses of public participation broadcasting: personal narrative. Starting with the production of personal experience narratives in different kinds of talk show, from *Esther* to *Judge Judy*, and moving through the format of host-mediated stories of listeners' experience on radio (from *Our Tune* to *Changing Tracks* on BBC Radio 1), this chapter also examines where and how interactivity through new media platforms is integrated into narrative discourse. It also sets the scene for the subsequent chapter, with an account of the function of mediated narrative discourse in the production of stance. Drawing on examples from radio phone-ins and TV talk shows, stance, opinion-giving and argument are discussed in Chapter 5 ('Opinion and argument'), which begins with an overview of discourses of opinion-giving, then looks at how opinions are produced in broadcast media and used as a resource for debate and argument. I also examine the ways in which web-based participation has been integrated into debate formats (e.g., the prime ministerial debates for the first time on UK television) and the kind of discursive environment that this offers for public engagement.

Building on these discussions of narrative, opinion and argument in the preceding chapters, in Chapter 6 ('Conflict and judgement'), I examine discourses of evaluation and judgement, and how conflict and personal confrontation are being mobilised as performance and spectacle in a range of different reality TV genres. The focus here will be the genres of confrontational talk shows and of reality competition formats, and on the various discourses of conflict, judgement and evaluation that constitute much of the interactional business of lay participation in such programmes. In this chapter, I also examine the ways in which digital platforms such as YouTube and Twitter are functioning to provide new and shifting discursive relationships between these genres of public participation broadcasting and their growing web-based audience.

Chapter 7 ('Advice and makeover') deals with the place of advice-giving as another central discourse of public participation broadcasting, first looking at the radio phone-in and other forms of advice programming, and then at the development of advice-giving in tele-factual formats of makeover and lifestyle transformations. The focus here will be the design and delivery of advice in different contexts, as well as how members of the public are positioned as recipients of advice by the experts; for example, in programmes such as *Super Nanny* or *Little Angels*, which deal with parenting problems and family relationships. Advice-giving in these contexts can often tend towards a discourse of instruction that places the ordinary participant and the expert in an asymmetrical relationship of either compliance or resistance. Here, again, the role of the digital media in opening up new participation frameworks for advice-giving through texting, chat rooms and emails will be examined, showing how access to these frameworks sets up a mediated space for the display of listener expertise. The examples in this chapter are taken from such diverse sources as BBC Radio 4's *Gardener's Question Time* and Radio 1's *Surgery*, Channel 4's *How to Look Good Naked* and BBC Three's *Little Angels*.

The concluding Chapter 8 draws together the different strands of the discussion throughout the book, and the arguments for a critical reconceptualisation of ordinariness in discourses of contemporary public participation broadcasting. These will be centred on the locally situated participatory identities that are closely tied to the discursive practices and locations in which ordinary people participate in mediated interactions, and to the broadcast contexts in which such identities are found 'in performance'. In this final chapter, I also address the extent to which the articulation between broadcast interaction and digital frameworks for interactivity might be opening up new directions for participation in broadcast talk in terms of the constraints and possibilities this relationship now makes available for public participation, and what these shifting interfaces between the broadcast media and the participating public might be offering for broader questions of public engagement with political and social issues.

Some notes on terms, transcripts and data

As will have become clear in this introduction, the data that I use for the analysis and discussion of situated practices and performances of broadcast talk on radio and television are taken from a variety of different sources and time frames. These range from the early days of issue-based talk shows such as *Kilroy* and *Oprah* in the late 1980s and early 1990s, which first drew the attention of media scholars and discourse analysts alike, through to current, 21st-century confrontational talk show formats like *Jeremy Kyle*. The reality TV phenomenon is illustrated through a range of examples from the *Big Brother* UK series and programmes like *Wife Swap* and *Come Dine with Me*, as well as lifestyle advice and makeover programmes such as *Super Nanny* and *The Biggest Loser*. The extracts from radio broadcasts also span over two decades, with examples taken from phone-in advice and discussion programmes as well as popular DJ shows from the mid 1980s to the present day.

The extracts are presented as transcripts of talk that are based on established methods and practices of representing spoken discourse as text. The transcription conventions and symbols that I use are explained in a key in the Appendix at the end of the book. Where appropriate and relevant, non-verbal and visual information is also provided in these transcripts, including particular features of gaze, gesture and intonation, and, in some cases, the specific relationship between the verbal and visual track is indicated. Also, where appropriate, some of the data extracts I discuss are taken from other published work on broadcast talk, and, wherever this is the case, full acknowledgement is made of the transcript's source. Otherwise, all data transcripts are my own.

Through the examination of these extracts as representative examples of key environments for public participation, we will see how some interactional practices have remained the same over time, while others have changed considerably; how broadcasters experiment with interactive, digital forms of participation, moving from the TV studio to the wider, web-based audience and back again; and how different participatory frameworks and formats exploit different kinds of discourses as spectacle and entertainment. In all cases, the objective is to show how members of the public are actively, interactionally and interactively engaged in the production of broadcast talk, and to re-evaluate the notion of 'ordinary' in these contexts.

In my analysis of the data extracts and discussion of the mediated interactions presented in this book, I will still use the label 'ordinary people' as a short and convenient way of differentiating participating speakers who are not media professionals, journalists or publicly known figures from those who are. However, as I will argue in some detail in the next chapter, and continue to illustrate in subsequent chapters throughout the book, the shift from ordinary to 'ordinary' (in quotation marks) indicates my view that this label is increasingly problematic as a way of describing the scope of identities of those people formerly known as 'ordinary' who often appear in contemporary broadcasting as anything but.

Notes

1 *Harry Hopeful* was the BBC's first attempt to produce 'sound pictures' of northern British life (cf. Scannell 1996: 25–26).
2 The concept of 'affordances' that I have found most useful for this book is based on Oliver's (2005) suggestion that an account of the relationship between communication and technology needs 'an approach that involves studying existing repertoires of use and recognising the potential of analogous or newly imagined applications' (Oliver 2005: 411). I therefore use this term very simply to describe the ways in which technologies and frames of participation are interconnected to produce specific discursive activities.
3 See Richardson (2010) for an in-depth discussion of this kind of talk and its relationship to conversation.
4 For example, one former *Come Dine With Me* contestant reports: 'The curtain has been pulled back. I can see the joins. For example, I now clearly see where a bon mot has been told for the second or third time because the camera wasn't focused on the witty guest the first time.' Extract from McCausland, D. (n.d.) '8 things I learnt from appearing on *Come Dine With Me*', *Siren Magazine*. Available at http://sirenmagazine.ie/8-things-i-learnt-from-appearing-on-come-dine-with-me (accessed 18 July 2013).

2 Identity and expertise

Introduction: public identities on air

The focus of this chapter is the discursive construction of participant identity, and a critical examination of the use and scope of the term 'ordinary people' to refer to participating members of the public in audience participation programming on television and radio. This will involve revisiting the traditional distinction between the categories of 'expert' and 'lay' participants, as first defined by Livingstone and Lunt (1994) in their pioneering study of audience participation in UK television talk shows. Through an analysis of interactions between hosts, experts and lay participants in a range of media contexts – talk shows, panel debates, and radio phone-ins – my aim is to show that what 'lay' members of the public do, in participating either as members of a studio audience or as callers to a phone-in, is to engage in a range of discursive activities that are actually not about being ordinary at all. This argument is based on observations of three significant things that speakers tend to do when they talk in such contexts: first, they generally establish a relevant local identity for themselves as speakers at that moment; second, they generally invoke some kind of relevant expertise in relation to whatever topic they are talking about; and, third, they often speak for or on behalf of other people, and not just for themselves.

I begin with an overview of the discourse of lay participants, and focus particularly on the situated identities they take up in their talk across a range of broadcast contexts. However, rather than seeing the characteristic differences between the contributions of lay and expert participants in terms of binary sets of contrasting features originally proposed by Livingstone and Lunt (1994) (e.g., 'hot/cold', 'relevant/irrelevant', or 'authentic/alienated'), I take a somewhat different approach, examining the discursive work that these participants do in order to construct their own locally relevant identities, particularly in those environments where they are engaged in activities such as questioning and arguing, which include talk shows but also political panel debates and many radio phone-in and discussion programmes.

In these environments, who they are matters and is closely related to the questions they raise and the points that they make.

Through this analysis of the way lay participants construct their locally situated identities, I develop the notion of 'situated expertise'. It has been argued that, in contrast to the detached and fragmented discourse of experts, lay contributions to media debates are centrally grounded in the 'lifeworld' (i.e., domains of private, personal experience and commonsense knowledge), and are most often expressed in narrative form (Livingstone and Lunt 1994; Fairclough 1995). However, when we look at interactions between members of the public and the institutionally legitimated voices of media professionals and experts, we find that lay speakers routinely work to display their own knowledge and identity in relation to the questions they ask and the points that they make. The description of lay participants as 'ordinary' does not, therefore, necessarily capture these complex local identities and forms of knowledge that they construct and claim for themselves in the course of their talk.

In broadcast genres that are principally dealing with issues of public interest, it has also been argued that public figures, or experts, provide institutionally legitimised opinions while private (lay) people provide experiences. This view was expressed by Livingstone and Lunt in their claim that 'experts speak for others, the audience speak for themselves' (1992: 24). So, in addition to reconsidering the notion of ordinary lay identity, we will also re-evaluate the idea that lay participants 'speak for themselves'. Again, from a close analysis of data from talk and interaction in TV and radio debates and phone-ins, I will show that contributors are very often 'speaking on behalf of' a particular constituency or social category, and that, therefore, we also need to take into account how participants position themselves as representatives of others, not just as themselves.

Finally, in the light of this discussion of lay participant identity and situated expertise, I will look at how this plays out in the introduction of interactive media into some of these broadcast contexts, in order to see whether the same discursive forms of participation are manifest in the new participative frameworks offered by texting and emailing – and, more recently, tweeting – and, if so, how these might be contributing to wider public access and increased audience participation in broadcast discussion and debate.

'Expert' and 'lay' revisited

In their analysis of audience discussion programmes in the late 1980s and early 1990s, Livingstone and Lunt (1994) described the ways in which these shows privileged discourses of commonsense knowledge and lifeworld experience over institutionalised knowledge and expertise. Talk shows like *Kilroy* and *The Time, The Place*[1] were based on audience participation in televised debates on a wide range of social topics and issues, during which, championed by the host, voices of a 'lay' public were regularly heard challenging and calling to account the 'experts' who represented political positions or academic/scientific, legitimised, institutional knowledge. Livingstone and Lunt argued then that 'the participation of private individuals in public debates, on television or elsewhere, draws upon two key opposition[s]: expert/lay and public/private' and that such contexts for participation 'prioritize the lay over the expert, requiring the expert to talk in lay terms and making the expert accountable to the laity' (1994: 97).

The TV talk show thus stands in contrast to other media genres such as news, current affairs and documentary, where the expert/lay relationship tends to work the other way around, and where 'private' discourses are generally downgraded and devalued in relation to the perceived higher status of rational, objective and often abstract 'public' discourses of science, knowledge and other forms of expertise. Livingstone and Lunt also point out that TV talk shows bring issues that normally belong in the private domain of individual experience into the public domain of the media, arguing that this transformation from private to public involves 'using private individuals to illustrate public issues and demanding that private people be transformed into public citizens' (1994: 97). It is thus through the transformation of private experience into public discourse that ordinary members of the public are able to make relevant, meaningful and authentic contributions to argument and debate.

Since the mid 1990s, one of the concerns of media discourse analysis of broadcast talk has been to undertake a detailed investigation of how this transformation is accomplished by participants, through the institutional interactional frameworks in talk shows and other audience discussion programmes (Thornborrow 1997; Haarman 1999; Tolson 2001; Lorenzo-Dus 2001). However, with the demise of *Kilroy* in 2004, the number of such issue-based discussion talk shows in TV schedules has declined, while programmes that involve a rather different configuration of commonsense knowledge and lifeworld experience have been on the rise. In talk shows like *Jerry Springer* and *Jeremy Kyle*, we are arguably no longer witnessing the transformation of ordinary people into public citizens, but the transformation of ordinary people into public spectacle. I will return to this point in more detail in Chapter 6, when looking at broadcasts that are framed around a different set of discursive practices and interactional frameworks from those at play in an issue-based talk show. My focus for the moment is broadcast contexts where members of the public are brought into direct interaction with experts and public figures – in panel debates, radio phone-ins and talk show discussions – and on the discursive constructions of participant identity and expertise in those contexts. These discourses emerge and are made relevant in interactional environments where legitimated institutional and political positions and arguments are questioned and challenged by participants who are generally described as 'ordinary' members of the public.

What counts as 'ordinary'?

Ordinariness, as Harvey Sacks (1984) convincingly argued, is not such a straightforward matter, and requires a certain amount of interactional work. Although the term 'ordinary people' has been used as a key participant category to identify lay participants throughout much of the research on talk shows and public participation broadcasting, Livingstone and Lunt were right to acknowledge that the terms 'expert' and 'lay' were 'inherently problematic and becoming more so' (1994: 100). The work of Erving Goffman and Harvey Sacks shows us how people routinely engage in particular communicative strategies to be seen as ordinary, unremarkable and not at all different in any noticeable way from the next ordinary person (Goffman 1963; Sacks 1984). To appear on a TV talk show, or to participate in a panel discussion audience or radio phone-in, inherently involves doing things that achieve something other than ordinariness, at least for the duration of the contribution or the call. And this participation requires discursive work in its local accomplishment that is very different from the discursive work required for being ordinary and unremarkable.

First of all, let us look at the spectrum of social identities of participants. People invited or selected to be in a talk show audience are likely to be a mix of volunteers, sometimes responding to an advertisement for the show, often students, people approached at random in the street and even 'regulars': participants who are invited to return to the show, precisely because it turns out that they are not ordinary at all. As one of these regular participants pointed out during an interview with audience members on *Kilroy*:

'[T]hey've got me typed as (a) a new man and (b) as someone who is prepared to open their mouth about their and other people's sex lives.'
(Livingstone and Lunt 1994: 101)

To be a talk show participant, people need to be ready to speak up, to have something to speak up about and, as this man says, to belong to a particular social group or category; in this case, a 'new man'. In the past, some shows were accused of using actors, or members of the production team, as 'fake' audience members to fill empty seats in the studio. Some actually acknowledged doing so, which rather undermines the notion of an authentic, bona fide 'ordinary' person in the audience taking on the 'experts' who have a different kind of institutional status. These cases notwithstanding, and despite being slotted into certain pre-existing social categories such as the 'new man' referred to in the above quote, being a participant in an audience discussion programme, a debate or a radio phone-in crucially involves establishing some locally relevant identity and/or area of knowledge and expertise. As we will see, these situated identities and forms of local expertise emerge and are oriented to by speakers in the course of their interaction with hosts, experts and other participants.

Secondly, and related to this notion of participant identity and status, is the question of how members of the audience get to make a contribution to the discussion and what they say when given the floor. Some participants may be invited or selected precisely because they have a relevant story to tell. These speakers are usually 'prepped', or primed in advance of the show being recorded to say certain things at certain moments and to tell *that* particular story, while others have to bid for a turn to speak. This preparation is sometimes referred to by participants as they take the floor, as in this extract from *Kilroy* where speaker Derek checks with the host that he has to tell his story about 'the cars' at that point in the debate:

Extract 2.i: 'Can you spot a con-man?', *Kilroy*, 2002

1. DER: I got conned
2. KIL: a second time
3. DER: uh yes uh we're going into the um
4. KIL: the cars
5. DER: the cars (.) ok having been –

Each type of participation requires different kinds of access to the floor; either an elicitation from the host to someone already identified as having a story to tell, or a bid from an audience member followed by a host nomination as next speaker. Bidding for a turn to speak on a current topic of debate involves first getting the attention of the host, or a member of the production team with the roving microphone, then, once given the floor, very quickly asking a question or producing a relevant point. We can see examples of this kind of contribution illustrated in the next extracts; the first two are taken from a TV talk show on the effects of divorce on children, and the third on whether women should be allowed to box:

Extract 2.ii: *Esther*, 1997

1. HOST: Sir you wanted to speak
2. MAN: I've just- (.) I'm divorced I- I have uh (.)
3.   a- a child fr- from the divorce and I- I would like to think that (.)
4.   that he has a much wider family now—

Extract 2.iii: *Esther*, 1997

1. HOST: Sir yes
2. MAN: yeah Esther I'm nineteen and (.) I'm quite lucky
3.   my parents have been married for twenty five years—

Extract 2.iv: *Esther, 1997*

1. HOST: the lady back there (.) what do you say
2. WOMAN: um I'm a (Thai) boxer I've been Thai boxing and kick
3.   boxing for ten years (.)
4.   believe me I'm a hundred per cent woman

In each extract here, before going on to make their point, the speakers provide some relevant contextual identity that warrants their upcoming contribution to the debate. They could have many other alternative ways of identifying themselves, but, in their current participant role as a contributor to a talk show debate, it is this particular identity category that is made relevant to the topic under discussion: 'I'm divorced', 'I'm nineteen and I'm quite lucky' or I'm a Thai boxer'. While, on one level, invoking such identities may be considered as constitutive of the kind of discourse of 'lay' authenticity described by Livingstone and Lunt, on another, I would argue that what these speakers are doing in their initial turn is building a locally relevant identity that establishes them not as 'ordinary', but much more specifically as *someone who* is divorced, has parents who have been married for 25 years, is a boxer, and, thus, have a *legitimated* status to speak about such matters on that occasion.

Lastly, although members of the audience may be drawn from a range of constituent publics, as described above, and may be more or less 'ordinary' in the sense that they are not affiliated to an institution or public or political body, many do belong to particular groups of people, local communities, organisations, occupational or other categories, and it is often these identities that emerge as relevant through the interactional framework of the talk show debate. In their discussion of opinion and identity categories in radio phone-in programmes, Fitzgerald and Housley (2002) show how caller identities are closely tied to the kind of things they have to say, and are oriented to by phone-in hosts. We will return to this aspect of caller identity in relation to opinion-giving in Chapter 5, but, for now, the following extract from a call to the radio phone-in *Election Call* illustrates how callers often speak not just as individuals, but as representatives of broader social categories:

Extract 2.v: 'Transport industry', *Election Call*, 2010

1. MK: let's go to Durham now and to Jimmy Sturdy it's your
2.   *Election Call* to Caroline Lucas
3. CALLER: good afternoon.
4. CL: hello [Jimmy]
5. CALLER: [now] I was listening earlier on to your
6.   proposals for the transport industry I'm self-employed
7.   heavy goods vehicle driver (.) and I also have to travel
8.   to work (.) together with the rest of the family

9.	we all travel to work um and I thought
10.	>I don't know who thought of it but< it was <u>totally</u>
11.	ill thought out like pie in the <u>sky</u> stuff (.) honestly

The caller here frames his turn with an extensive construction of a number of relevant identity categories. He is a listener to the current programme and a member of a professional category (self employed/heavy goods vehicle driver), and, as such, someone with locally relevant expertise to talk on transport issues. He also speaks on behalf of the rest of his family: 'we all travel to work'.

As all the above extracts demonstrate, participants who are bidding for a turn with something to say, or who are making a call to a radio phone-in, display an orientation to their locally relevant identity both within the interactional context of the broadcast and in relation to the issue under debate. So, rather than speaking as just someone, they construct a situated identity from which to participate in relation to the topic, as someone who *is* X, or someone who *does* Y. The significance of this kind of discursive work is also relevant in the construction of a knowledgeable position from which to speak.

Identity and engagement

So far, I have used these short examples from TV talk shows and radio phone-ins to begin to build up some evidence for questioning the description of lay participants as 'ordinary', arguing that this is often not really congruent with the kind of identity work these speakers do when taking the floor. I now want to look in more detail at how questions of participant identity are tied in with relevant domains of expertise, by looking at some more examples from a range of broadcast contexts where members of the public get to challenge public figures and politicians by asking questions and putting their points of view. We find this kind of activity in such programmes as the long-established BBC television show *Question Time*, where members of the audience ask a panel of politicians or other public figures to respond to questions on topical issues without having any prior knowledge of what those questions are going to be. A similar format, but on radio, is the equally well-established *Any Questions* on BBC Radio 4, followed up the next day by *Any Answers*, where people can call in to air their views on the topics discussed and responses given with the host.[2] As well as these regular, weekly broadcast panel discussions, and one-off topical debates such as were broadcast during the BBC's 'Asylum Day' in 2003 (Macdonald 2007), there are many other dedicated local and national radio phone-in programmes that provide broadcast spaces for people to call in, ask questions and give their opinions on matters ranging from local issues to global politics (see, for example, Myers 2004). In this next section, I take more extended extracts from some of these broadcasts to show how issues of identity and expertise are made relevant by participants in these kinds of mediated, interactional environments, particularly when they are asking questions, making points and contributing to an ongoing debate.

Forms of engagement: Speaking 'on behalf of'

In any institutional context for interaction, it is likely that there will be some specialisation in the way talk is organised that enables the goals of the institutional encounter to be accomplished (Drew and Heritage 1992). This will typically involve a distribution of roles and types of turn between participants which results in discursive and interactional 'asymmetries' (Drew and Heritage 1992; Hutchby and Wooffitt 1998). In some institutional contexts involving interactions between professionals and members of the public – doctor–patient or lawyer–witness, for example – it is often the institutional representative or professional who is in the position of asking the questions while the non-professional participant is called upon to answer them (Freed and Ehrlich 2010). In public participation broadcasts such as radio phone-ins and TV audience discussion programmes, this asymmetrical relationship is partially disrupted. The caller or member of the audience asks the questions and the politicians, public figures or experts of one kind or another are called upon to provide answers. What we find in these interactions is that members of the public – whose identity is established simply by name and geographical location in a phone-in (e.g., 'let's go to Durham now and Jimmy Sturdy') and often not even that in a TV talk show or debate – do specific kinds of discursive work which (a) projects their upcoming discursive action as relevant (asking a question or making a point) and (b) provides some contextual frame for that action in which they routinely invoke some identity category and in which they frequently situate themselves as speaking on behalf of a wider public constituency. In other words, speakers build a specific, locally relevant identity into their initial turn at talk that provides a warrant for their institutional role as a participant in relation to the topic or issue under discussion. By claiming some form of contextualizing position from which to ask a question, and engage further in the debate by making a point, or expressing a concern, participants construct an identity that is not simply individual, but that enables them to speak as a representative member of a broader social group. To illustrate this, I turn next to some further examples from calls to the radio phone-in programme *Election Call*, and then to contributions to the television panel debate show *Question Time*.

Election Call 2010

Election Call is a phone-in programme broadcast on BBC Radio 4 in the run-up to general elections in the UK in which callers are invited to put their points and questions to the major political party leaders. The following data is taken from the 2010 general election. As previous research has shown, in most radio phone-in broadcasts, while the host models suggested topics for discussion in their introduction to the programme, all relating to the current policies or issues to be discussed on that day (Fitzgerald and Housley 2002; Myers 2004), it is up to the callers to initiate their specific, individual topics in their opening turns (Hutchby 1996). However, as well as providing a relevant topic, many callers also begin their first turn by invoking a particular identity category. This is the case in the next two extracts:

Extract 2.vi: 'Fuel prices', *Election Call*, 2010

1.	CALLER:	he- hello Mr Brown.
2.	GB:	[good to talk to you
3.	CALLER:	[u::m I'd just like to ask you uh I'm an owner driver
4.		I drive a truck for a living I own a truck (.) um (.)
5.		the fuel duty increases that we increasingly get every year
6.		we've got a three pence uh per litre

Extract 2.vii(a): 'In bed with David Cameron', *Election Call*, 2010

1.	MK:	let's go to Sheffield now and to John Lashmar
2.	CALLER:	hello Nick
3.	NC:	hello
4.	CALLER:	I'm a constituent of yours and uh (.) probably not
5.		a natural liberal democrat but I expect I'll be supporting
6.		you? (.) uh but my concern is exactly the
7.		opposite
8.		of the previous John (.) I'm concerned that you may (.)
9.		get into bed with David Cameron

In both these call openings, after the greeting exchange with the host and guest politician, each caller starts their main turn with a self-identification: 'I'm an owner driver I drive a truck for a living' and 'I'm a constituent of yours and uh probably not a natural liberal democrat'. The first caller gives his professional status before asking about the current government's fuel pricing policy, then he goes on to build his subsequent point not as an individual first person 'I', but as a plural first person 'we': 'the fuel duty increases that we increasingly get every year'. In so doing, he situates himself not just as an individual, but as a member of a broader category of 'owner drivers' who are being negatively affected by the policy. The second caller establishes his political location and affiliation before expressing concern about the potential relationship between Liberal Democrats and the Conservatives: 'you may get into bed with David Cameron'. In each case, the caller establishes a local, contextually relevant identity very early in their first turn, projecting a position from which they then deliver their questions to Gordon Brown and Nick Clegg. This identity emerges within the opening turn, and is thus made salient at the beginning of the call and can be developed into a more broadly representative category as the call progresses, as we see in the extract below:

Extract 2.vii(b): 'In bed with David Cameron', *Election Call*, 2010

1. CALLER:	and uh I'm wondering (.) how you would respond to
2.	somebody like me
3.	[who's who would vote for you to keep the Tories
4.	out=
5. NC:	[sure
6. CALLER:	=then find that in doing so might let the Tories in
7. NC:	well what I hope you'll do (.) uh John (.) is to is to vote
8.	for me ~not only as your local MP~ but but but because
9.	you agree with our values and our policies

Here, the caller uses the established identity to build his role as questioner on behalf of members of a wider constituency: 'somebody like me'. Shifting from first-person agency as questioner 'I'm wondering' into third-person reference 'somebody like me', his question is designed to display a concern that is not only his individually, but the concern of a category of tactical voters 'who would vote for you to keep the Tories out'. Clegg responds to the caller by addressing him singly, by his first name, as a potential Liberal Democrat supporter, and asking him to vote for their policies, rather than tactically against the Conservatives.

My last example in this section is a call where the caller does not produce a relevant identity in his first turn, but he does construct a particularly knowledgeable and articulate position from which to speak in his extended first turn, on behalf of 'an ageing population'. The topic is the provision of social services for older people:

Extract 2.viii(a): 'Social services', *Election Call*, 2010

1. MK:	well let's move on to another topic now and Keith
2.	Pollyblank is calling in from Brixham in Devon
3. CALLER:	Good afternoon Mr Clegg
4. NC:	hello,
5. CALLER:	uh social care reforms can bring about a fair and
6.	affordable care systems which provide older people with
7.	independence dignity and security when an incoming
8.	government will face a challenging economic climate
9.	requiring fiscal restraints with a projection that by
10.	twenty thirteen fourteen current spending plans

11.		will leave a twenty one billion gap between reliable
12.		<u>e</u>stimates of NHS funding needs and the money
13.		likely to be available (.) therefore (.) should there be
14.		a hung parliament and you are invited to join a new
15.		<u>go</u>vernment. uh how will you bring about
16.		these important societal reforms that will <u>stand</u>
17.		the test of time [and en<u>sure</u> that the demands=
18.	NC:	[mm
19.	CALLER:	=of an <u>age</u>ing population rightly receive <u>ex</u>cellent social
20.		care support as they grow <u>ol</u>der in this country.

This long first turn is unusual in the sense that the caller does not claim any relevant identity for himself. However, his elaborate series of statements produces an impression of someone who is knowledgeable about social care policies, who is well informed and who has carefully planned his question turn (something that is generally not encouraged or accepted in radio phone-ins where the spontaneity of live, fresh talk is the prized currency (Hutchby 1996)). Another unusual feature of this turn is that the question, when it comes at line 15, is not framed with the generally routine orientation to the caller's current institutional role of questioner, such as 'I'd just like to ask . . .' or 'I'm just wondering how . . .', as is the case in the previous two examples. Instead, it is placed at the close of the turn: 'how will you bring about these important societal reforms?' On the other hand, what this caller does very explicitly is to make it clear that he is speaking on behalf of people in society not just for himself.

We re-join this call towards its end, where the host offers the caller the chance to ask a follow-up question to Nick Clegg:

Extract 2.viii(b): 'Social services', *Election Call*, 2010

1.	MK:	Keith
2.	CALLER:	yes thank you uh Mr Clegg (.) I hear what you're saying
3.		if there is a hung parliament and say Brown <u>is</u> the prime
4.		minister and he invites you to join his administration (.)
5.		can you give an assurance to (.) uh all people of all
6.		generations cos it's not affecting just the <u>older</u>
7.		[generation=
8.	NC:	[no not at all
9.	CALLER:	=and I'm asking this question to you because it affects
10.		us <u>all</u> because in a in a society now with medical science
11.		and advances we are <u>all</u> living older (.)
12.		regarding dementia for example
13.		people are getting dementia
14.		at much younger age

15.		can you as<u>sure</u> that
16.		if you were <u>in</u> <u>a</u> government regardless
17.		of what people are saying about a hung parliament
18.		that it <u>could</u> be effective that you will see and you will
19.		fight to see that <u>this</u> important social care issue
20.		is head on addressed and we get >p<u>osi</u>tive results<
21.		for people in our society
22.	NC:	yes.
23.	CALLER:	thank you

In this final turn, Keith does a lot of work to construct a position, not as someone who is speaking as an individual, but, rather, as someone who is speaking on behalf of a much broader social category, which he refers to at several points: 'people of all generations' and not just 'older generations' but 'us all', 'people in our society'. He does this incrementally throughout this second turn: 'can you give an assurance to people of all generations' (line 5), 'we are all living older' (line 11) and, as the explicit reason for his call, 'and I'm asking this question to you because it affects us all' (line 9). Although this caller never does provide an individual, locally relevant identity from which to speak himself (although several features of this turn might lead one to infer one, particularly the assertion that 'it is not affecting just the older generations' (line 6)), in his display of knowledge and expertise regarding social care and economics in his first turn and in his expressions of concern on behalf of an ageing society in the second, this caller positions himself as both well informed and representative, not as 'ordinary' and not 'for himself'. The call also ends on an unusual note: a rare, unmitigated, direct answer from a politician ('yes').

Question Time 2007

Turning now to the more complex participation framework of a television panel debate, with multiple participants both on the panel and in the audience, we still find similar local identities being made relevant by contributors from the studio audience. Moving around the UK to a different location each week, *Question Time* involves five 'media professional' panel members (generally politicians, journalists or other public figures). The debate is chaired by broadcaster David Dimbleby and recorded live, with a participating studio audience drawn from the local population. It proceeds according to an established routine: a pre-selected member of the audience asks a question, then the chairperson offers the floor to panel members in turn to respond, after which the debate is opened up to the studio audience. When nominated by the chair, individual members of the audience can comment and give an opinion on what they have just heard. On this programme, when audience members invoke contextually relevant identities, this occurs in strikingly similar ways to the examples from radio phone-ins and TV talk shows just given above. We see this illustrated in the following three extracts:

Extract 2.ix: *Question Time* (Bath, England; 29 March 2007)

1. DD: the man at the back dead centre
2. AM: I'm a church leader of another church not an Anglican church
3.   and I'm very <u>happy</u> and I think it's <u>great</u> that we have (.) uh
4.   people who represent the faith community <u>express</u>ing issues
5.   of morality cos here we have an issue which is all about
6.   social good versus (.) commercial gain (.) an-and it just doesn't
7.   make any sense at all (.) so it's excellent that we've got
8.   people speaking out on what's good for society =

Extract 2.x: *Question Time* (Newcastle-upon-Tyne, England; 8 March 2007)

1. DD: = a number of people want to come in the man at the back on
2.   the right there
3. AM: yeah um I'm a-a-a mental health worker and I-I gotta tell uh
4.   (.) Margaret Hodge that our wards aren't full of uh
5.   people suffering from psychosis due to canna[bis]
6.   they are largely full of people
7. MH: [Yes]
8. AM: who are suffering from <u>social</u> problems and I have to tell you
9.   as well perhaps you don't understand but alcohol (.)
10.   and tobacco are both drugs

Extract 2.xi: *Question Time* (Colchester, England; 1 March 2007)

1.   ((continuing squabbling between the panel members))
2. DD: panel panel hold on
3.   I will come to you let's just hear some members of the audience
4.   because there was a lot of reaction to that the woman in red
5.   there yes what's your view
6. AM: my husband and I have been married for ten years
7.   my sister has been living with her boyfriend for ten years
8.   why should we get something and she doesn't

The first two contributors establish a relevant professional identity (church leader and mental health worker) before making their points about the political role of the church and criminalizing cannabis, respectively.

They both shift into a position of speaking for a wider group: the church community in the first ('we have an issue' and 'we've got people speaking out') and mental health workers in the second ('our wards aren't full of uh people suffering from psychosis due to cannabis'). The third invokes a relevant social identity (being married) in an argument for couples living together receiving the same tax and benefit status as married couples.

In these examples, using the term 'ordinary people' who are 'speaking for themselves' to distinguish lay participants in media discussion and debate from those who are institutionally positioned as experts does not capture the range and scope of situated identities that these speakers make relevant in their interactional encounters with those experts or public figures. In doing such identity work as a routine matter in their opening turns, speakers construct relevant, often representative and also sometimes specialised and knowledgeable positions from which to speak, such as the church leader in Extract 2.ix and the mental health worker in Extract 2.x above. This brings us now to the related issue of expertise, which is closely tied to identity categories, as the focus of the next section.

Situated expertise

In this analysis of the extracts above, I have been suggesting that the term 'ordinary' is not as straightforward as it might seem. In saying that television talk shows provide a forum where 'the ordinary person can communicate in an ordinary way to an ordinary audience', Livingstone and Lunt (1994: 97) were, as they acknowledged, making the word 'ordinary' do rather a lot of work. Having presented some evidence in support of the view that the category of 'ordinary people' tends to mask a whole range of contextualised participant identities that speakers make salient in their talk, in this section, I want to focus more closely on what it means to 'communicate in an ordinary way' in these broadcast contexts, in the sense of undermining discourses of expertise with everyday forms of understanding and experience. My question, then, is how do participants make their contributions, as Livingstone and Lunt have put it, 'real', 'meaningful' and 'grounded in experience' (1994: 102)? The answer is linked to aspects of participants' identity work I have been discussing above. In some of the examples given, we have seen how knowledge of particular facts, and experience of given situations, are mobilised in participant contributions to discussion and debate as they bring their own domains of expertise into play to support an argument or make a point. In this next extract, the truck driver talking to Gordon Brown has already invoked his professional identity as an 'owner driver' as a contextual frame for his upcoming question about the problems caused by fuel price rises. Here, he is responding to Brown's mention of the Labour government's 'time to pay' scheme[3] as a possible solution to this problem with a counter argument, supporting his point with a series of statements about credit, borrowing and profit margins:

Extract 2.xii: 'Fuel prices', *Election Call*, 2010

1.	CALLER:	right um so uh you mentioned obviously the idea of
2.		based on borrowing money (xx) you know
3.		for this recession period um-
4.	GB:	the time to pay
5.	CALLER:	yeah the problem is that that I don't want to extend
6.		credit um to get through this recession
7.		I need lower outgoings my outgoings are in<u>crea</u>sing (.)
8.		there isn't enough margin on top to pay back any kind
9.		of (.) <u>bor</u>rowing that I'm d- that we supposedly want
10.		the banks to do um just to get (.) through
11.		um you know through this recession it's in<u>crea</u>sing
12.		every year year on year and increasing duty
13.		on on uh all the transport industry and >as I said<
14.		to my own (.) cost fifteen hundred pounds a year
15.	GB:	(x x)
16.	CALLER:	a significant amount of money um just in one year um
17.	MK:	Gordon Brown

This caller takes issue with GB and his policy with a counterargument based not simply on his experience, but on his own professional expertise, or knowledge of the business, and balancing increasing costs against smaller profit margins. Similarly, as we saw earlier in Extract 2.x, the *Question Time* participant invokes his professional identity as a mental health worker to warrant his expert knowledge of patients' problems in hospital wards:

Question Time (Newcastle-upon-Tyne, England; 8 March 2007)

3.	AM:	yeah um I'm a-a-a mental health worker and I-I gotta tell uh
4.		(.) Margaret Hodge that our wards aren't full of uh
5.		people suffering from psychosis due to canna[bis]
6.		they are largely full of people
7.	MH:	[Yes]
8.	AM:	who are suffering from <u>social</u> problems and I have to tell you
9.		as well perhaps you don't understand but alcohol (.)
10.		and tobacco are both drugs

This situated expertise is similar in some respects to the phenomenon identified by Ian Hutchby in calls to a talk radio station as 'witnessing', whereby callers 'bolster their individual speakership and their viewpoints through "bearing witness" in the sense of "being there", of bringing first-hand knowledge in proof of a standpoint' (Hutchby 2001a: 495). In that context, where the host routinely expresses scepticism about callers' views to provoke an argument, witnessing is a way of strengthening their point against challenges from the host. In the two examples here, however, the caller to the *Election Call* phone-in and the member of the *Question Time* audience are not engaged in a two-party argument with a sceptical talk radio host. They are, however, drawing on their own firsthand knowledge, but in an interactional context where their expertise is used as a resource for a reasoned challenge to a position first established by a politician (Gordon Brown and Margaret Hodge, respectively).

We will return in more detail to the important connections between identity, expertise and opinion-giving in Chapter 5, and the kind of discursive resources that lay participants mobilise in order to take up positions and stances in an ongoing debate. But, to conclude the discussion of situated identities and expertise, we now turn to the issue of how web-based communication media have been incorporated within the more traditional frameworks of broadcast media participation that have been the main focus up to this point.

Identity, debate and the web-based audience

So far, in this chapter, I have been arguing that lay contributors to talk shows, debates and phone-in programmes routinely engage in actions through which they construct specific identities and domains of expertise from which to speak, as well as an orientation to being representative of others, not just speaking for themselves. In the final section of this chapter, I introduce a different kind of participant, located in the interactive web-based audience rather than a member of the interacting studio audience or a phone-in caller. The early years of the 21st century have seen a marked attempt by broadcasters to integrate some form of web-based or mobile technology into mainstream broadcasting. As well as the rise of interactive reality TV game shows like *Big Brother*, which streamed on the web, or *The Salon*, which could be seen live on E4, television and radio producers were experimenting with innovatory forms of interactive audience participation through the introduction of texting, emails and web-based forums into the production of existing genres such as TV debates and radio phone-in programmes. What impact has this introduction of online access to television debate and radio phone-ins had on public participation, and how does it affect participants in terms of what they say and how they say it? I focus on two specific events that have been the subject of media discourse research in order to address these questions.

Introducing 'new' media: Election Call *(2001)*
and Asylum Day (2003)

For the 2001 *Election Call* radio phone-in programmes covering the UK
general election in the spring of that year, BBC Radio 4 introduced the
opportunity for participants to email questions to the broadcast as well as
using the traditional telephone call. Each stand-alone programme, lasting
45 minutes, was simulcast on radio and TV, and also webcast, with the
webcast continuing for an extra 15 minutes with only email questions.
This was flagged up by the host Peter Sissons in his introductions to the
programme as innovatory and something that would widen access to and
participation in the broadcasts (Thornborrow and Fitzgerald 2002).

Extract 2.xiii: Introduction, *Election Call,* 2001

```
1. PS:    — you can still call us on 08700100 4(.)4(.)4(.)..h this year
2.        fuh the first time you can contact Election Call by email
3.        as well as vote two thousand and one? at bbc dot co dot uk,
4.        .hh and please remember on your email to say where you're
5.        calling from ..hh we're also being (.) webcast (.) live?
6.        on the bbc news online website at www dot bbc dot co dot
7.        (0.7) uk. (.) slash news (.) and the Internet programme will
8.        continue after the Radio 4 and BBC 2 programmes have
9.        finished. .hhh well (.) the first Election Caller is on
10.       the line. uh Jason R(oll) from Salisbury in Wilsh- in Wiltshire –
```

By 2010, the *Election Call* broadcasts had returned to a phone-in format
only, embedded into the BBC Radio 4 lunchtime news and current affairs
programme *The World at One*, with no television coverage, no webcasting
and no email questions. The host's introduction gave only phone numbers
to call, and suggested listeners 'grab a pen and paper' to write down
the numbers, with no mention of emailing or other forms of web-based
communication.

On 23 July 2003, the BBC dedicated their scheduled slots that day, as well
as special programmes, to the discussion of a single topic: immigration and
asylum in Britain. For Asylum Day interactivity – in the form of posts to the
website forum, emails, calls and text messages – was repeatedly invited. In
her study of the debates on that day, Myra Macdonald questioned whether
the integration of facilities for online participation into the broadcast
television studio discussions really did offer more possibilities for widening
access to public debate and engagement via the interactive media (Macdonald
2007). Commenting specifically on the participation framework and
organisation of two of the dedicated programmes, *Face the Nation* and *You
the Judge,* each of which included interactive participation, Macdonald
observed that 'distilled into voting statistics, or sound-bite extracts from
SMSs or emails selected by the programme makers, the voice of the viewer

punctuated rather than led discussion' (2007: 681). She also noted that, while interactivity was specifically encouraged, interaction between the studio audience and experts was discouraged, and that, when 'emotions ran high and interaction threatened to erupt, the presenter [. . .] diverted attention quickly onto a new topic' (Macdonald 2007: 681). She concludes that, 'while Asylum Day offered varied means of participating in the debate, it produced surprisingly little direct engagement between those holding different points of view' (2007: 683).

So what happens to discourses of public opinion and engagement when these are mediated interactively rather than through direct interaction via a telephone call? In a study of the 2001 *Election Call* (Thornborrow and Fitzgerald 2002), we found that, while the emails themselves were treated as co-present material objects in the studio by the host ('. . . we have an email here', '. . . got an email here'), who would proceed to read out the question, the senders of the emails were not. In fact, in the course of the whole series, only one emailer was ever addressed directly as a current listener by the guest politician. In effect, the introduction of emails resulted in a shift from a three-party framework for talk, comprising the host, the guest politician and the caller, to a two-party framework of host and guest. This had consequences both for the role of the host in relation to the interactional possibilities afforded to him, and for the guest, who is no longer dealing with a caller as well as with the host. So, whereas the introduction of new forms of participation, on the face of it, seemed to broaden participation and access, in practice, it did the opposite, restricting the talk to a two-party exchange that became much more like a news interview between two media professionals (the journalist and the politician) from which the lay participant emailer was largely excluded. It seems, then, that promoting direct interaction live on air in *Election Call* in 2010 was clearly designed to enhance debate and discussion between participants, much more than the introduction of interactively mediated questions had done in previous years (Thornborrow and Fitzgerald 2013).

In her study of Asylum Day, Macdonald also found some related changes in the forms of interaction taking place – this time, a shift from dialogue to monologue. Although, in theory, website postings enable 'freer forms of exchange' (2007: 681), in practice, the postings relating to Asylum Day were, in the great majority, monologic and not exchanges at all. Online contributors rarely referred to other postings or reacted to other posters' views; rather, they tended to engage in rhetorical forms of quasi-interaction and the expression of feelings, rather than in any direct interaction with one another in the debate. The integration of new forms of mediated interactivity thus, she argued, provided 'no greater guarantee of dialogic communication than occurs through traditional programming' (Macdonald 2007: 683).

These studies raise some important questions about the scope and value of interactive participation in broadcast media discourse. In the light of these findings, over the course of subsequent chapters of this book, I will address, whenever it becomes relevant, the integration of web-based and mobile technologies into existing, traditional media genres and their specific forms of broadcast talk. In particular, I will be paying attention to if and how participant identities are made relevant, and how the introduction of such interactive technologies affects interaction in terms of the participatory frameworks and the kind of discourse practices that emerge through the articulation of broadcast and digital environments of public and audience participation.

Summary: the ordinary person as 'someone who . . .'

In this discussion of the various identities taken up by lay participants while on air in the mediated contexts for discussion and debate of phone-ins and talk shows, I have started to chip away at the boundaries between the categories of 'expert' and 'lay'. In raising the question of what counts as ordinary, I have argued that, as participants in such interactional environments, members of the public engage with media professionals and/or named experts not as 'ordinary' people, but as people who have locally relevant identities and display forms of situated expertise. They are thus people who speak from positions of knowledge and experience in relation to whatever it is they are currently speaking about. However, we have also seen how the introduction of email and web-based questions and contributions to a traditional broadcast participation framework of direct interaction produces a different type of discussion and a different set of speaker roles and identities. In the context of television, this restricted the live, studio-based interactions and produced fragmented, monologic expressions of feeling rather than grounded, dialogic interaction and debate. In the context of radio, it removed the opportunity for direct interaction and shifted the talk into something that more resembled a two-party political interview than an engagement between a member of the public able to claim a relevant contextual warrant for their question and a political leader.

From this account of lay identities and forms of expertise, we turn next to another broadcast context for public participation: reality and lifestyle television. Here, too, questions relating to ordinary people and participant identities have been central to much research on tele-factual programming, and particularly in relation to notions of 'ordinary performance', which will be one of the main areas of theoretical discussion in Chapter 3. Once again, the role of ordinary people and the range of discursive environments in which their participation is produced and organised will be discussed, as well as how different types of participatory identities are made relevant in the mediated performances of reality television.

Notes

1 Broadcast on ITV from 1987 to 1998, *The Time, The Place* was hosted by John Stapleton from 1991 to 1998. It was a human-interest discussion show, competing with the BBC's morning talk show *Kilroy*, which broadcast from 1986 to 2004.
2 *Any Questions* is a topical debate programme on BBC Radio 4 in which guests from the worlds of politics, business, science, arts and the media answer questions posed by members of the public. Its follow-up programme *Any Answers* offers listeners the chance to phone in and contribute to the debate.
3 'Time to Pay' refers to a UK tax payment initiative that allows people to pay their tax when they can afford to, rather than according to official HMRC deadlines.

3 Performance and the mediated 'self'

Introduction: the real, the ordinary and the rise of tele-factuality

In this chapter, the focus of discussion moves away from the domain of audience participation (talk shows, panel debates and radio phone-ins) and into the realm of what John Corner (2002) calls 'tele-factuality': the phenomenon of reality show broadcasting that has emerged as one of the most productive and prolific media genres of the last decade. Although reality TV in the form of docu-soaps such as *Airport* or *The Cruise* and crime documentaries like *CSI* or *Crimewatch* has been around for some considerable time (Dovey 2000), it is nevertheless since the first British *Big Brother* series in the summer of 2000 that a host of generically related game show spin-offs have increasingly become the mainstay of what is known as reality programming across different networks, both public and private. Alongside this trend, there has been a proliferation of lifestyle programming and makeover shows that revolve around the participation of 'ordinary people' engaging with 'experts', mostly with the aim of achieving some kind of personal transformation. This is sometimes physical (e.g., *You Are What You Eat, Ten Years Younger*), sometimes socio-psychological (*Ladette to Lady* or *Brat Camp*) and sometimes material (*DIY SOS* or *Property Ladder*) – and, occasionally, can be a mixture of all three.[1]

The discussion in this chapter centres on the participation of 'ordinary' people in three reality TV series: *Big Brother, Wife Swap* and *Come Dine with Me*. These programmes all fall into the broad category of tele-factuality just described, albeit in rather different ways, but there are some discursive features that they share which can be found in the specific details of their frameworks of participation and rhetorical practices. In the first part of the chapter, some of the recent work relating to the concept of ordinariness in the context of reality television, and linguistic theories of performance more generally, is discussed by way of a backdrop to the subsequent analysis of extracts from these TV shows. Through this analysis, I will argue that the participation of members of the public in these broadcasts is organised and presented through their discursive performance of locally specific social identities, rather than through their being ordinary.

Participation and performance in reality TV

As we saw in the previous chapter, participants in radio phone-in discussions and television debate formats interact within a certain set of conventions and parameters, which form the institutional framework for that interaction. These are (a) that callers or studio contributors wait to be brought into and out of the interactional frame by programme hosts, and (b) that, once in that frame, it is incumbent on them to make relatively spontaneous contributions to the talk promptly, with little or no preparation or scripting and for a limited space of time – in some cases, only for a few seconds. In much tele-factual broadcasting, the participation of members of the public takes a different form altogether, and is produced within a different set of contextual parameters. However, in the formats and structures of reality television, and in the range of discursive activities between participants that these occasion, the pervading description of participants as 'ordinary' remains equally as problematic as it is in debate and discussion programmes. This notion of 'ordinary' will therefore again be addressed by drawing on work in two main theoretical areas: (1) current debates in media and cultural studies on the mediated construction of personal identity and the performance of self in reality television, and (2) sociolinguistic and discourse analytic theories of performance.

In his account of documentary film production at the turn of the 21st century, John Corner (2002) describes the changes that have taken place in the way television documentaries are made. He notes a shift from 'the naturalism of demeanor, speech and behaviour of classic observationalism' towards the emergence of a new 'ecology of the factual' which involves a more self-consciously reflexive and staged 'performance of self' (Corner 2002: 263). He relates this shift to reconfigurations of 'social knowledge and emotional experience' in late 20th-century Western culture which have brought about radical changes to the traditional boundaries between the public and the private spheres (Corner 2002). These changing boundaries are particularly evident in the rise of reality television programming, where, as Corner argues, in docu-soaps and other new factual TV genres, the shift from observationalism to reflexive self performance has produced a new kind of rhetoric, in which the principal discourses revolve around micro-social narratives, particular ways of seeing the world and what happens in it, presented through 'the self observed' and the 'self-in-performance' (Corner 2002: 265). It is these documentary practices that have now become central components of factual television and are generically constitutive of reality TV discourse.

Reality TV has, not unproblematically, come to be the generic label for programmes that, broadly speaking, observe the behaviours and relationships of participants who are non-actors, in situations which usually take them out of their everyday contexts and place them in constructed environments with others. So, of course, use of the term has begged the question of how real 'reality' TV can really be. As a result of these observations, some participants make the transition from their previously unknown, ordinary status to that of celebrity – another paradoxical quirk of the reality TV process. Arguably, though, what does remain 'real' in such programmes is the way in which participants deal with that constructed environment, relate to the other people in it and disclose their feelings about the experience. But is it ordinary?

Addressing this question in a discussion of reality TV formats, Jonathan Bignell comments that docu-soaps and other reality TV genres show us 'people who are represented as "like us", as ordinary as the television viewers watching them, yet being on television itself makes these people "not like us"' (Bignell 2005: 67). He suggests that participants in these shows occupy a form of mediated 'middle space', somewhere between ordinariness and celebrity, where they take on particular roles of the kind more often associated with fictional genres, as 'characters' in the unfolding docu-drama. The initial selection process of participants for reality TV shows thus becomes a form of 'casting', where people are selected not only because they are complex and interesting individuals, but also because they are representatives of some larger social group, whether this be a particular occupational group (e.g., hotel or airport employees), a set of celebrities (as in *I'm a Celebrity . . . Get Me Out of Here!*) or even 'the love-lorn' of *Would Like to Meet* (2005: 91). Bignell makes an interesting distinction between the 'ordinary' person and the 'real' person, where 'ordinary' tends to be used to represent members of social categories of people who are, in some ways, just like us ('familiar but individually distinctive') while 'real' tends to be used to describe the display of an authentic 'self' which occasionally is revealed beneath a façade of role and performance (2005: 66). The distinction is particularly useful in terms of understanding these middle-space performances: the revelation, or display, of an authentic self is one of the key hooks of reality TV, where celebrities can sometimes be seen to be 'real' people, and 'ordinary' people are valued most for being themselves. Andrew Tolson makes a similar point in his analysis of both 'ordinary' and 'celebrity' talk, where he argues that these forms of media discourse engage with a central preoccupation of modern everyday life, the concern about the presentation of self: 'however flexible they may be, lifestyles should ultimately cohere as morally defensible identities, demonstrated in authentic performances of "being oneself"' (Tolson 2006: 183).

These arguments relating to self presentation and authenticity raise some intriguing questions about the nature of public participation in reality TV programming and, in particular, about the construction of social identities in these media contexts. For example, what does the performance of an authentic 'self' look like and how do we recognise such a performance? What are the discourses of ordinariness and authenticity through which participants display these personal and social identities, and how are they woven into producing the 'middle space' performances that constitute much of reality TV? As I have already suggested in Chapter 2, examining what participants do and say more closely may well bring us towards a more critical view of the category of 'ordinary', and towards a more fine-grained understanding of the 'self in performance' that, as Corner claims, seems to be at the heart of these tele-factual genres. At the heart of this examination is the concept of participation frameworks (Goffman 1981) that structure and organise such events, and that set up environments for participants to interact in and positions for them to speak from, as well as theories of performance that help to underpin an account of what it is that they say and how they say it. I address each of these in turn below.

Participation frameworks

The formats of reality TV and makeover programmes are built around a specific range of participation frameworks and contextual patterns of inter-action that, as noted above, differ substantially from the interactional formats of talk shows and phone-in discussions which were the focus of Chapter 2. In a show like *Big Brother*, participants interact primarily amongst themselves, apart from during some of the routine, and often ritu-alised, events that involve the participation of media professionals, such as when the participants first arrive at the house, during nominations and eviction nights and in the diary room talk sequences. In programmes like *Wife Swap* or *Come Dine with Me*, as well as the filmed interaction between participants, there is also frequent direct to camera discourse during which participants express their views on some situation or event (e.g., when reading the household 'manual' in *Wife Swap*, or discussing the food they have eaten and giving the scores in *Come Dine with Me*). In makeover shows and competition formats, on the other hand, there are often extended interactions shown between the programme presenter(s) (e.g., Gok Wan in *How to Look Good Naked*) or other lifestyle 'experts' as well as with the other participants. These variations clearly depend on the remit and design of the individual show, but the kind of talk that is broadcast differs accord-ing to the participatory framework within which it is produced; either as interaction between participants, as talk directed at the audience or as interaction with a media professional.

Another key difference is that, unlike most radio phone-ins and audience debate programmes, and some (though not all) talk shows, reality TV genres are not broadcast live but are highly edited. Although some formats, such as *Big Brother*, have experimented with delayed live feed on the Internet and streaming (on the TV channel E4, in the case of *Big Brother*), and although the interaction between participants clearly does originate as spontaneous, non-scripted 'fresh' talk (Goffman 1981) as it is being recorded, what TV audiences are more likely to watch is the edited highlights version. This consists of using selected extracts from that talk, woven into a sequence as a coherent whole by the programme producers, and accompanied by an explanatory voice-over commentary. So, whereas contributors to phone-ins and talk show discussions construct their own locally relevant identities from which to speak in the short time that they are on air, participants in reality and makeover TV shows are more often the subjects of more manipulated identity work, positioned through selecting and editing choices into roles that function to produce a dramatic and narrative structure for the programme (Dovey 2000; Bignell 2005).

We will return to how these identities are constituted, and how they become established as routine and predictable discourses for a particular kind of self-in-performance, when we examine some examples of specific participatory frameworks in these programmes and take a closer look at the rhetoric of performance associated with them. But, before doing so, we need to introduce some of the key theories that have emerged from research into more sociolinguistic and interactional approaches to aspects of talk as performance.

Discourses of performance

While Bignell and Corner both invoke the notion of discourse as a key to understanding and theorising such performances in contemporary television genres involving the participation of ordinary people, the discourse they refer to tends to be the big sweeps – realist discourse, narrative discourse, naturalist discourse, consumerist, masculinist, feminised discourses and such like. As we will now see, using an interactional discourse analytic approach to talk and performance can help to provide a more nuanced understanding of how participants achieve these mediated performances of self, not as people who are 'just like us', the audience, but as people whose identity within the reality TV show is constructed as locally specific, socially representative and may well turn out to be not ordinary at all. Taking this approach, some of the theories of performance as a discursive phenomenon can be put to work as a basis for an empirical analysis of the self-in-performance that Corner and others have identified as one of the most important elements of tele-factuality.

'High' and 'mundane' performances

Performance is a many-faceted concept in the analysis of talk and social interaction, but inherent in most accounts is the necessary presence of an audience. In his discussion of the relationship between linguistic style and performance, Nik Coupland (2007) talks about 'mundane performance', referring to the way that speakers, in their everyday use of language, have a meta-linguistic awareness of contextualised variation. In other words, people are aware that the linguistic choices they (consciously) make will, to some degree, affect how a message will be perceived and received by its audience. He contrasts this kind of everyday performance with 'high performance events', which are normally clearly bounded, public and pre-planned; for example, various types of staged enactments, ranging from political speeches, storytelling or pantomime to semi-scripted radio banter (Coupland 2007: 156–171). In the type of speech events that are located towards the high-performance end of the scale, Coupland suggests that there is 'communicative focusing' across seven interlinked dimensions of form, meaning, situation, performer, relation, achievement and repertoire (2007: 147–148). This involves a set of features which can be glossed briefly here in terms of the array of structural relationships between what is said and how it is said, who it is said to, in what context and by whom, how it is evaluated and what kind of performance it is (i.e., its genre).

As an illustration of a high-performance event, Coupland takes an extract from a BBC Radio Wales show that contained a regular feature called *Today in History*. This involved two presenters 'gossiping' about history by engaging in a form of banter in which certain identities are made salient. As he explains, this produces a curious genre mix, where one presenter 'camps up the gossip-value of the historical moments' while the other 'plays the interested dupe' (2007: 152–153), and he goes on to argue that it is through these stylised performances that the *Today in History* feature became recognisable to its listeners as a bounded performance event, repeated daily and drawing on the stylised repertoires of camp, gossip and regional Welsh identity.

Today in History is performed by media professionals whose remit is essentially about being entertaining; to engage in this kind of banter, knowingly designed and produced to be funny. This is quite clearly and explicitly *not* a performance of self. The question then arises of whether it is possible to map any of these dimensions of high performance onto the forms of talk that occur in what Bignell calls the 'middle space' of reality television. Most reality TV programmes include a range of different types of performance contexts, or 'situations'. Many, like the talent competitions or game show challenges, incorporate some form of managed task or event, with some degree of pre-planning and possibly also a script. In terms of competition shows like *Pop Idol* or *X Factor*, there is a real performance on stage, in front of judges and an audience, but we also encounter the participants at particular critical moments backstage. On the other hand, many will also include more mundane social activities that are largely spontaneous and appear unplanned. In the constructed setting of the *Big Brother* house or the domestic contexts filmed for *Wife Swap* and *Come Dine With Me*, there is certainly a whole lot of unplanned, 'backstage' interaction taking place between participants. But certain activities and events are planned, structured and even semi-scripted, and it is often the discourses associated with these that form the rhetorical repertoire of a self-in-performance. It is also very often these routine activities that are selected and combined through editing processes to produce the dramatic, coherent narratives that reconfigure particular participant identities in the context of the broadcast. And, whether they are on a studio set or being filmed in more naturalistic settings of the home, the workplace or out in the street, there seem to be some identifiable patterns in the way non-professional participants who increasingly take centre stage in reality and makeover programming repro-duce these rhetorical repertoires as part of doing what Mark Andrejevic calls 'the work of being watched' (2004).

The paradox of the self observed

Finally, a note on the paradox of observation. As William Labov pointed out many years ago (Labov 1972), to successfully observe and record the mundane and the ordinary often requires those who are behaving in a mundane and ordinary way to be unaware of – or, more ethically these days, not attending to – the process of observation and recording. The presence of a camera or a recording device may result in a modification of behaviour such that the mundane and ordinary target (in Labov's case, the vernacular speech he was attempting to access) becomes inaccessible to the observer. Being observed is also central to Goffman's (1959) distinction between backstage and front-stage behaviours. Goffman characterises the 'back-stage' as any activity that is free from exterior scrutiny, while the 'front-stage' is essentially public, observed activity. Performance is thus integral to front-stage behaviours, while backstage behaviours are deemed to be private, personal and unobserved, but also, in some way, more 'real' and authentic. Since the process of observation and recording social interactions is a central dimension – indeed, the prime institutional goal – of reality television, based on the production of talk for a viewing audience, there is an inherent problem with the idea of the performance of an authentic self in such settings. The fact that any description of the performance of self in these mediated contexts will always be an account of a 'self observed', one might argue, makes the 'real', the 'ordinary' and indeed the 'self' in this context rather unreliable and illusive phenomena. However, by focusing on what participants actually do and say in the middle spaces of reality televi-sion, I want to examine what such observed performances entail and how local, contextually relevant identity categories emerge, and become salient, within those discursive interactions. We can then examine how these per-formances are handled and subsequently worked up in the construction of narrative character or dramatic plot through editing and production processes.

We now turn to the analysis of some data extracts taken from *Big Brother*, *Wife Swap* and *Come Dine With Me*, and examine some of the features of the kind of talk that has become increasingly pervasive and generically familiar in these and other reality TV genres. I will focus specifically on three ritualised contexts for that talk: (1) talking to Big Brother in the *Diary Room*, (2) discovering the new home and the wife's manual in *Wife Swap*, and (3) reading and commenting on the evening's menu in *Come Dine With Me*. These contexts involve specific discursive actions in each case: confessional self-disclosure, the construction of identity through processes of 'othering' (Hall 1997) and assessment and evaluation.

Performances of self in the *Big Brother* diary room

Over the past decade or so, *Big Brother* has continued to spark the interest of audiences, media scholars and discourse analysts alike (e.g., Corner 2002; Hill 2002; Scannell 2002; Jones 2004; Thornborrow and Morris 2004; Tolson 2006). Tolson summarises the appeal of *Big Brother* participants to viewers in the following terms: 'contestants appear to be successful in so far as they offer an effective performance of "being themselves" which is understood in terms of moral "worthiness" by the *Big Brother* audience' (2006: 169). As he points out, what is always at stake for *Big Brother* contestants is how to negotiate tensions between the interactional norms of the house, in terms of front-stage sociable engagement with others, and the risk of appearing two-faced, and therefore morally reprehensible, in more backstage moments like those afforded by the diary room. This kind of moral tension can also be observed in gossiping activity between participants in the house (Thornborrow and Morris 2004), where contestants display an orientation to two different contextual frames: on the one hand, to the sociability of the house in interactions with other contestants, and, on the other, to the competition, in terms of an awareness of the audience whose votes will determine the winner.

Talking in the diary room is a routine occasion for a particular performance of self in *Big Brother*. Participants are either called into the diary room by Big Brother, or they can choose to visit it of their own accord in order to discuss some issue or problem in the house. As Tolson (2006) notes, talking to Big Brother in the diary room constitutes a discursive event which involves forms of self-disclosure and is thus often compared to a confessional mode of discursive encounter. It is, on the one hand, a location for 'backstage' behaviour, in the sense that talking to Big Brother takes place away from the eyes and ears of the other contestants in the house, but, on the other, it is also a significant 'front-stage' discursive space, in which participants address an invisible interlocutor, while speaking straight to camera and thus directly to the viewing audience. Talk in the diary room thus constitutes an occasion for contestants to express their personal views and feelings, and, in so doing, to present a particular performance of self to the *Big Brother* audience: 'a privileged space for the performance of a persona styled for direct consumption by the viewer' (Tolson 2006: 170).

Below are two examples of diary room talk from the very first *Big Brother* (UK) series. These extracts are taken from the early weeks of the show, and are interesting on two counts. Firstly, since this was the first series of a new genre, described as a 'social experiment' by its producers at the time, these mediated social behaviours, along with the forms of talk through which they were accomplished, were not yet well established as routines – it was all new. Secondly, they enable comparisons to be made with instances of diary room talk from subsequent series, when the generic norms of the show had become more familiar to future contestants and the audience alike. In these next two extracts, both speakers express contradictory emotions regarding their situation. Anna had been considering leaving the house voluntarily, but had decided to stay, while Thomas ('Tom') had expected to be evicted that week, but, as it turned out, was not.

Extract 3.i: Anna in the diary room, *Big Brother*, 2000

VO:		Shortly afterwards Anna decides to talk to Big Brother
1.	ANNA:	I'm a lot better than I was yesterday
2.		.hhh and I had a big chat with the group which was
3.		lovely hhh. had a wee cry (.) which was embarrassing
4.		a::nd yea:h I've just decided that I'm not going to walk
5.		(.) I'll (.) go when I'm nominated and evicted but (.7)
6.		not before then
7.		(2.2)
8.	BB:	what has made you change your mind
9.	ANNA:	ts.hh the chocolate biscuits that Craig give me?
10.		no uuummm o::h it's just little things that (.)
11.		different people said (.) .hhh like Nichola and Mel
12.		saying hh. how it's only another few weeks (h)um
13.		(2.2)
14.		also (1.4) realising that there are bits of it here
15.		that I do enjoy (1.1) I do have a laugh

Extract 3.ii: Thomas in the diary room, *Big Brother*, 2000

VO:		Thomas comes to the diary room to talk to Big Brother
1.	TOM:	practically spent all day Friday preparing
2.		myself in my mind (1.0) to go out and see my
3.		family and friends (1.2) to step out into the
4.		real world again (1.3) ah (.7) there's a lot
5.		of disappointment that I haven't (.)
6.		stepped out (.) after seeing them through
7.		the doorway
8.		(1.6)
9.		ah (2.0) it's (1.3) I have to start tuning myself
10.		back into where I am again now (2.0)
11.		ahm (0.5) they're obviously very much on my mind at
12.		the moment (1.7) and (1.8) the other thing is that
13.		(1.2) being voted to stay in (1.1) by the public (.8)
14.		is obviously (.8) a great boost

The talk of both Anna and Tom contains a highly personalised discourse of self-disclosure. Their largely monologic talk is punctuated with quite long pauses, slowing down the delivery and producing a display of thoughtfulness and reflection. Both are also structured in a rhetorically similar way, moving from a series of first-person declarative statements about their feelings and ending on an upbeat note:

> Anna: there are bits of it here that I do enjoy, I do have a laugh
> Tom: being voted to stay in by the public is obviously a great boost

However, there are also differences between them. Anna tells a story about what has made her feel better: her talk is essentially a narrative, with two temporally ordered action clauses and a resolution:

> I had a big chat with the group
> I had a wee cry
> I've decided I'm not going to walk

She also uses a parallel evaluation structure for the narrative actions; chatting, 'which was lovely' and crying 'which was embarrassing'. In her response to Big Brother's question, she makes a joke and then ends with a strong display of affiliation to the group, of appreciation of the actions of other people and of her positive attitude towards them. On the other hand, Thomas's account of how he feels about staying in the house is much less narrative in its design. The pauses are slightly longer and he produces more introspective talk about his own feelings rather than about the actions of others:

> spent all day Friday preparing myself in my mind
> there's a lot of disappointment that I haven't stepped out
> I have to start tuning myself back
> they're obviously on my mind

In contrast to Anna, he expresses more ambivalent feelings about staying in the house ('there's a lot of disappointment that I haven't stepped out'), but also, in contrast to Anna, the positive turn ending ('being voted to stay in [. . .] is a great boost') expresses an appreciation of the audience and an orientation to the game. While Anna displays a strong affiliation to the group, and to the sociability frame of the house, Thomas orients primarily to the competition frame and the actions of the voting viewers, not to the group.

The difference between these two participants' performance of self in their acts of self-disclosure – and perhaps, thereafter, between their relative performances in the competition (Anna was the runner-up, while Thomas was voted out halfway through) – can be understood in terms of a particular form of identity work around sociability that has become relevant to the specific context of *Big Brother* (UK). Tolson argues that 'the successful display of sociability', of being 'a character' (i.e., game for a laugh and entertaining), is one of the three meanings of 'character' that are centrally at play in *Big Brother* (the other two meanings are of character as 'a function in a scripted narrative' and being of 'good character' in terms of moral worthiness) (2006: 171).

In his analysis of diary room talk from *Big Brother 5* (UK), Tolson describes how two contestants, Shell and Stuart, 'perform co-operativeness and sociability' in the diary room: they are literally shackled together (as part of one of the challenges in that series), but they also achieve a high level of co-operativeness and mutual affiliation in their talk through joint topic development, recycling of key phrases, completion of each others' turns and co-operative interruption. On another occasion, Stuart visits the diary room alone to talk about his emotional distress with regard to a developing relationship with one of the other participants, in which he displays a commitment to both the norms of sociability and those of moral decency. Comparing these discursive constructions of sociability and moral worth with those of another participant, Victor, who explicitly presents himself in the diary room as competitive rather than as sociable:

> you can't knock people for having a game plan if you're in a <u>game</u> you know
>
> let this be (.) the first time the bad guy wins

Tolson argues that, for the *Big Brother* (UK) audience, convincing (and thus vote-winning) diary room performances are by contestants who self-present as sociable members of the group, rather than as calculating game players, and not players of particularly 'good character' either.

In these examples, the performance of a contextually relevant participant identity in the *Big Brother* diary room appears to involve a choice between the presentation of a sociable self, in alignment with fellow housemates, or of a competitive self, in alignment with the frame of the game. In neither case, however, does talk in the diary room involve 'ordinariness'; rather, it involves a rhetorical packaging of a context-specific identity through self-disclosure and self-evaluation, designed for the invisible interlocutor Big Brother as addressee, as well as for the wider viewing audience. And this, it seems to me, is one example of what I am now going to call 'middle-space performance' that we find in a range of situations and forms of talk in reality television. This is the talk that is produced on specific occasions where participants are primarily engaged in 'the work of being watched', and that work is not about being ordinary, but about displaying particular kinds of relevant social identities.

This argument can now be taken a bit further in looking at more occasions for the rhetorical packaging of self-identity talk through middle-space performances in the highly successful TV format on the UK's Channel 4, *Wife Swap*.

Doing 'being not like': performances of difference in *Wife Swap*

In the next set of examples, I turn to the question of how identities are constructed through the routine rhetorical packaging of difference into a discursive performance. In *Wife Swap*, women from contrasting social categories and worlds change places for a fortnight to see how they cope with a different domestic situation and family lifestyle from their own, and 'what they can learn from each other' (as the programme voice-over begins). However, it is less the learning process and more the social and personal differences between them that are foregrounded and made into dramatic material in the hour-long edited programmes. For the first week, the new wife has to live according to the rules of the household; in the second, she gets to instigate her own rules and runs the house and family her way. So, what happens when you put a wealthy businesswoman and mother of three, driven by hard work and consumerist values, into a new-age hippy family who live on a houseboat, educate their children at home and are committed to values of sustainability and new-age eco-politics? Conflict ensues. It is the inevitable culture clash resulting from these domestic exchanges that provides the drama in the programme; selected moments where the differences in lifestyle and values are manifest through the interactions of family members. But, in order to arrive at this clash, a specific participant identity first has to be established, and this is primarily achieved through the discursive performance of difference on the part of the two women at key moments, which involves talk to camera.

Reacting to the new environment

The talk to camera that takes place in two of the routine opening sequences of *Wife Swap* – when the swapped wives first react to arrival at their new home, and then when they read the household manual left by the other one – are good examples of a-middle-space performance. These routines are regular generic features of the programme's structure, always occurring in the same order and always given the same kind of editing treatment. As I will show, they are also routine in their rhetorical structure, in the sense that there are recurring communicative patterns in the way the women display their reactions to their new homes. These sequences are key to two important kinds of identity work: first, through the wives' display of shock or surprise, both verbal and non-verbal, as they discover the domestic environment, and, second, their explicit evaluations of the manual, which are usually based around social and moral concerns.

The first extract – Extract 3.iii, below – is taken from the first series, and housewife Diane (who also works a few hours a week part-time outside the home) swaps with IKEA manager Anne. The second extract, Extract 3.iv, is taken from a later series and is a swap between Susan, a freegan Christian, and Debbie, the wife of a millionaire computer software designer, while in the third, Extract 3.v, the exchange is between two expatriate Brits in Spain, Cara and Anna. The programme works with a set of cultural codes that signify these contrasting lifestyles, dichotomised into clearly demarcated systems which can include ways of buying and cooking food, attitudes to clothes and shopping, choice of leisure activities, parenting styles, and so on. For example, participants Anne and her husband Rob are described as 'a modern family' (Rob helps Anne with household tasks), while Diane and Graham are described as 'traditional', and Graham leaves all the domestic work to his wife. The incompatibility of these different systems results in a clash of domestic cultures, and the conflicts that ensue become the driving theme of each episode. The presentation of the different values and lifestyles of each family is done primarily through showing the wives' initial reactions to their new environment. Discovery of the home and reading the manual are thus discursive activities that play an important part in establishing the women's social identity, both in terms of 'who I am' and 'who I am not', in the opening sequences of the show.

Extract 3.iii: Anne and Diane, *Wife Swap*

VO:	Anne and Diane get to explore their new homes before they meet the family
1. ANNE:	oooh look at the dog (.) he's gorgeous
2. (TC)	this feels really strange (.) going into somebody else's house
3. ANNE:	((pointing at mess)) that needs sorting out (.)
4.	I need to clear that w- clutter
5. DIANE:	looks like it'll be easy to keep clean
6. ANNE:	((pointing into fridge))
7. (TC)	you shouldn't put raw meat on that shelf in the
8.	fridge (.) it should go at the bottom
9. DIANE:	((looking in cupboard))
10.	I haven't got any of this in my house (.)
11.	she's gonna be upset

12.	ANNE (TC):	can I wash this up ((lifts up frying pan))
13.	DIANE:	I don't like walking around somebody else's house
14.		((goes into bedroom))
15.		two cats
16.	ANNE:	((pointing at mess)) that would really (.)
17.		I couldn't (.) couldn't cope with that
18.		((close-up shot of mess))

This sequence shows the swapped wives 'exploring' their new homes, commenting on what they see as they walk around. They have radio microphones and often directly address the camera (indicated by the letters 'TC' on the transcripts). These reactions are edited to produce sequences of utterances that are not temporally consecutive exchanges, or turns, but a selected set of contrasting statements spliced together which highlight the differences between the two women. Anne and Diane both comment on the strange experience of walking around someone else's home (lines 2 and 13) – but this does not happen so much in later series of the show as the format becomes better established. The high number of deictic references to what they see (that needs sorting out/I haven't got any of this in my house) in their comments is synchronised with visuals focusing on the things that draw their attention and comments (the animals, the fridge, the contents of the cupboard) and foreground the differences between the two women. Thus, Anne's statement 'I'll need to clear that clutter' (line 4) is followed by Diane's 'looks like it'll be easy to keep clean'(line 5), and their comments on food (lines 7–11) are also juxtaposed to highlight the contrasts in their households, but also to construct a different domestic identity for each participant. Note also that there are two comments addressed directly to camera by Anne: 'you shouldn't put raw meat on that shelf in the fridge it should go at the bottom' (lines 7–8) is a display of knowledge about food hygiene, while the second, 'can I wash this up?' (line 12), is a more light-hearted display of her own personal standards for household cleanliness. This short sequence thus not only builds a picture of each woman's different domestic practices, it also begins to construct their 'character' and subsequent role in the events of the fortnight's swap.

Anne's comments all relate to tidiness and hygiene:

> I'll need to clear that clutter
> You shouldn't put raw meat on that shelf in the fridge
> Can I wash this up?

but the repetition of these also builds a picture of her as rather obsessively clean: 'I couldn't cope with that', where 'that' is shown as just a pile of papers on a chair.

Diane, on the other hand, is presented as a more messy, easy-going but sensitive personality:

> Looks like it'll be easy to keep clean
> I haven't got any of this in my house
> She's gonna be upset

These observations are less judgmental than Anne's, and express her own concerns and unease rather than being negative about what she sees in her new environment. In each case, the selected utterances set up some key identity features for each participant that will contribute to the development of the ensuing drama.

There are two important points to make here. The first is that, while we may recognise or even identify with certain character traits, this programme hinges not on people being 'ordinary' or 'just like us', but as being markedly different from each other; the second is that the way this difference is established is through their talk to camera, a discursive performance during which they express their first impressions of their new home. These performances enable the construction of the women not just as individual characters and personality types, but as representatives of sociocultural categories that are then played off against each other precisely because of the differences between them. It is then through middle-space performance of a particular social self, rather than of ordinariness, that the programme achieves its dramatic clash of lifestyle values.

The same editing technique of juxtaposing the swapped wives' contrasting evaluations of their new environment can also be found in the next two extracts, both taken from a more recent series of *Wife Swap*. Here, we can see a more heightened level of performance in the wives' reactions than was the case in the examples from the first series, above. This is evident in the non-verbal as well as the verbalised display of surprise, shock or amazement in each case, and also in the amount of talk addressed to camera. In Extract 3.iv, Susan swaps life in a camper van for Debbie's Surrey mansion; in Extract 3.v, Anna lives in a mansion and Cara lives on a boat.

Extract 3.iv: Debbie and Susan, *Wife Swap*

VO:	Before they meet their new family, Susan and Debbie have a chance to explore their new homes
1. DEBBIE:	oh oh makes me feel sick just looking at it
2. SUSAN:	oh boy (.) and just one family lives here
3.	gee (.) oh my goodness this is the bathroom
4.	it's wa::y too big for (.) just a couple of people

5.	(TC)	you could probably have (.) you know probably thirty
6.		people living in a house this big
7.	DEBBIE:	eeow presume I'm sleeping up here which is a bit weird
8.		oh it's really damp it's really cold ugh
9.	SUSAN:	so who lives in here (.) the clothes (.) I see
10.		my wardrobe's probably smaller than that ((pointing at small shelf))
11.	DEBBIE:	they probably stuff their clothes in (.)
12.		that's all you <u>can</u> do in here
13.	SUSAN:	they've got ~an even bigger TV down here~
14.	TC:	Jesus said to sell everything you have and give your
15.		money to the poor it doesn't seem fair (.) that- that
16.		some people should have <u>so</u> much and other people
17.		should have so little.
18.	DEBBIE:	what's this then. is this school uniform.
19.	(TC)	starting to feel a bit upset really (.) that people live like
20.		this when they clearly um (3.0)
21.		((looks down away from camera))
22.		have high standards you know they still do school and
23.		you know ((crying)) I'm upse↑t by it

Extract 3.v: Anna and Cara, *Wife Swap*

1.	ANNA:	oh my god they live on a boat they live on a boat
2.		they live on a boat (.) so cool
3.	CARA:	((looking around))
4.		one two three four five six seven eight nine cars
5.	ANNA (TC):	my new home (.) wow
6.		((climbs on board))
7.	ANNA:	minimalistic is the word I think I would use for this
8.	(TC)	(.) at first it's a bit like (.) wuow
9.	CARA:	((looking in bathroom))
10.		oh my god it's like a swimming pool inside isn't it
11.	CARA:	((opens door)) ((lifts hand over open mouth))
12.	(TC)	it would be a bit like going shopping
13.		every time you went inside your wardrobe you know
14.		((on floor looking at shoes))
15.		o::h go::d she's gonna be in stillettos on the boat
16.		((doubles up laughing)) f- ((obscenity beep))
17.	ANNA:	((looking round lifting things up))
18.		but there's got to be a secret panel or something
19.		where she keeps her clothes
20.	(TC)	she must have clothes ((arms stretched down and
21.		open palms)) ~they can't just disappear~

22.	CARA:	((looking at boiler)) to heat up, (.)
23.		they have a fire in the ba↑throom?
24.		the money they must have spent on this place (.)
25.		they could have got themselves a- a <u>farm</u>
26.	ANNA:	she's got a white pot here saying ladies
27.		((chewing sun glasses))
28.	(TC)	which is <u>rea::</u>lly throwing me (.) it couldn't be that
29.		ladies have to pee in there that wouldn't be possible.

In both these extracts, reactions of surprise, whether in disgust or amazement, are articulated in a much more marked form than in Extract 3.iii. This is evident in the number of times 'oh', 'oh boy', 'oh my god' and 'oh my goodness' occur, and the use of physical gestures to express surprise and disbelief (e.g., Extract 3.v, lines 11 and 20), as well as amusement (line 16). The talk addressed to camera is also more prevalent, particularly the critical evaluations of lifestyle in Extract 3.iv (lines 5, 14–16 and 18–21) where the closing sequence of each woman's moral and emotional evaluation of the other's lifestyle is also addressed directly to camera, explicitly counterposing the different values of each household. In Extract 3.v, Anna's shock at seeing the interior of the boat is directed to the camera (line 8), as is her comment on the 'white pot [marked] ladies' (lines 26–29). The juxtaposition of Cara's counting out the number of cars in the driveway (line 4) and Anna's evaluation of the boat as 'minimalistic' (line 7), as well as Cara's astonishment that 'they have a fire in the bathroom?' (line 23) and Anna's puzzlement about the white pot (line 26), again highlights the contrast between the two domestic environments.

The development of these more heightened performances of difference, through reactions of surprise, shock or, sometimes, disgust, as the series progressed can also be seen in the next set of extracts, in which the activity of reading the manual left by the other wife becomes played out even more explicitly through discourses of surprise and evaluation.

Reading the manual

In Extract 3.vi, we see Diane and Anne from the first series reading each other's manual:

Extract 3.vi: Diane and Anne, *Wife Swap*

VO:	They also get a first look at the other wife's manual
1. ANNE:	it's been written quite quickly I would say
2. DIANE:	"gardening Rob cuts the grass Anne does the borders"
3. ANNE:	it's one word answers to a lot of questions
4. DIANE:	"what are your top three dinners (.) pasta fish and salad"

5.	ANNE:	maybe it's not somebody who's got (.) the attention to
6.		detail that I have I like to (.) be (.) well prepared
7.		and well organised
8.	DIANE:	I've put curry spaghetti bolognese and ((looks up))
9.		~anything ~and~chips~
10.	ANNE:	I don't normally cook chips
11.		((Graham's van pulls up outside))
12.	(TC)	I'm very nervous now

Once again, we see the utterances juxtaposed to produce a coherent sequence made up of the same two dichotomised personal and social identities, structured around Anne's judgmental evaluations and Diane's more down-to-earth attitude. Her smiley-voiced and to camera 'anything and chips' (line 9) cuts swiftly to Anne's negative 'I don't normally cook chips' (line 10), and the sequence ends with Anne's confession of nervousness in line 12. To eat, or not eat, chips thus signifies a potential area of conflict that contributes to the contrasting social identities of the two women. These contrasts become more marked and more discursively performed in the next two extracts. Here, we find Debbie and Susan reading each other's manuals, again focusing around the issue of food, but also the conflicting social values it signifies:

Extract 3.vii: Debbie and Susan, *Wife Swap*

VO:		Each wife has left a manual as a guide to the running of their home.
1.	DEBBIE:	"as <u>free</u>gans"
2.		((both arms up and out from elbow in surprise))
3.	(TC)	never heard that before (.) "we reject materialism
4.		capitalism and consumerism ((looks up)) oh Christ
5.		(.) OH:: CHRI::ST.
6.	SUSAN:	"our food is always fresh, and mostly organic (.) we don't
7.		eat any processed food as a healthy diet is a basis
8.		((smiling)) for a healthy life (.) I think it's irresponsible
9.		~to eat rubbish ~" huh huh huh huh huh huh
10.	DEBBIE:	o::h no please tell me what I'm not reading now
11.		"we get practically everything we need to survive
12.		from the bins (1.0) bin raiding (.) can be quite messy
13.		as you have s- to sometimes dig deep in the bin and s:ift
14.		through the spilt food items"
15.	(TC)	this is <u>shock</u>ing
16.	SUSAN:	last Christmas we spent" (3.0) ~wh:at~ "last Christmas
17.		we spent ten thousand pounds on the kids"
18.	(TC)	quite immoral (.) to be honest

19. DEBBIE:	"in our community we don't celebrate (.) birthdays"
20. (TC)	what has this child got to look forward to
21.	apart from rummaging through bins.

In this extract, we find the same marked verbal and non-verbal discourses of surprise; addressed direct to camera from Debbie, in her reaction to the term 'freegan' (line 1) and her evaluation of 'bin-raiding' (line 12). Susan also marks her disbelief (lines 16–17) with a laughing ~what~ followed by a long pause as she takes in the figure of £10,000. She, too, makes an evaluation of this information directly to camera: 'quite immoral' (line 18).

A similar pattern is found in this last extract from *Wife Swap*, in which Cara and Anna perform the same kind of evaluations. It is worth noting that the two sequences are edited to about the same length in terms of time, so there may be a generic norm being established for this activity, slightly extended from the earlier series where these activities took less time.

Extract 3.viii: Cara and Anne, *Wife Swap*

VO:	Each wife has written a manual as a guide to the running of their home.
1. ANNA:	this is going to be so:: interesting
2.	"my husband Dan and I have gone back to basics"
3.	yeah ((laughing)) telling me hah hah hah
4. CARA:	"I have a housekeeper" oohh
5.	((mouth open in amazement then covered with hands))
6. ANNA:	"we believe that men and women have different aptitudes
7.	and that as a wife ~my role is to take on the domestic
8.	and maternal duties~" ((puts both hands up to
9.	each side of face laughing)) aarghhh
10. CARA:	"the nanny looks after Hilton three (2.0) and I don't want
11.	to be running around after him all day every day"
12. (TC)	her nanny may know him better than (.) he- she does you
13.	know
14. ANNA:	"we also collect our (2.0) wee >in a big container
15.	to pour over vegetables for fertilizer"<
16.	((throws arms up behind head))
17. (TC)	I <u>knew</u> I shouldn't have opened that bucket
18.	and I was right
19. CARA:	"Chris is a workaholic and I believe that our marriage
20.	works precisely~because we see each other so little~"
21.	((puts one hand up to side of face laughing))
22. (TC)	oh this is so different hey?

In Extract 3.viii, Cara and Anna's heightened reactions of surprise, expressed through gesture and laughter (lines 3 and 5, 16 and 21)) are again accompanied by evaluations made directly to camera about parenting (line 12) and the fertilising process (line 17), which have been selected and juxtaposed in this sequence to build up the contrasting lifestyles of the two women that will potentially lead to conflict later on. Cara's final evaluative utterance to camera (line 22) selected to end the sequence articulates this explicitly: 'oh this is so different hey?'

These displays of emotional reaction, whether of shock, surprise or amusement, constitute rhetorical performances of a personal identity that demonstrate *difference* from the other: 'this is not me'. The explicit articulation of moral and social values, often to camera, also constitutes a performance of social identity through negative evaluations of that other, as in 'this is not what I do'. There are also a number of third-person references – 'they probably stuff their clothes in', 'they've got an even bigger TV in here', 'they have a fire in the bathroom', 'the money they must have spent on this', as well as 'she's gonna be in stilettos on the boat' and 'she must <u>have</u> clothes' – which also function to establish 'us' and 'them' dichotomies through the performance of a social identity that is different (i.e., 'not like that').

Through the analyses above we can start to define some of the discourses of middle-space performance by identifying the kinds of identities that are precisely and specifically tied to the context of the mediated event, as well as the rhetorics of 'othering' which are performed for and observed by the camera, and which become generically reified through repetition of similar routines across the range of tele-factual formats. At this point, we can usefully return to Coupland's seven dimensions of performance outlined earlier in the chapter, since there are some clearly identifiable features in the extracts from *Wife Swap* which situate these discursive performances towards the 'higher' end of the spectrum: the features of linguistic form (markers of surprise, reference to the other), of meaning (evaluations), of context and performer (the wife's encounter of the new domestic setting) and of relation (between wife and camera crew/audience). The construction of a specific identity in each case is partly a result of the wives' initial displays of surprise and their evaluations of the other, and partly the result of consecutively editing together these discourses of difference that distil each wife's performance of identity into a character role for the purposes of the programme. The middle space is thus articulated here not by ordinariness, but by a rhetoric of performance built around a highly specific set of personal and social identities, which can then be brought into dramatic collision and conflict in the production process.

From social identity to comic 'character'

On a lighter note, in the hugely popular Channel 4 series *Come Dine With Me*, each participant in turn cooks dinner for and entertains the others in their own home. The contestants then rate one another's cooking and hospitality on a scale of one to ten, with the winner being the one with the most points at the end of the week. Through the editing process and the voice-over commentary (often wickedly tongue in cheek and in a decidedly teasing key), each participant is built up as a particular type of 'character' which thus serves to dramatise the interaction of the contestants as well as the preparation of the meal. The camerawork and the edited sequences make very salient some of these particular personal characteristics, which then become part of the entertaining spectacle: the programme's knowing play-off between the performance of hospitality, cooking food and eating a meal with the particular set of characters brought together for that week, and the voice-over's mockingly ironic commentary.

As in *Wife Swap*, we find participant evaluations in the programme's recurring routine events being produced through talk direct to camera: one of these events is when participants are shown the menu for the upcoming evening and are filmed giving their reactions to it; another is when they get in a taxi to go home and give their scores for the evening. These evaluations are then reacted to by the voice-over commentary, as we will now see. The final example here is taken from an episode recorded in West Yorkshire, where the participants are reading and commenting on the menu for the third evening of that week, hosted by 'cash-strapped artist Jon', as he is described in the voice-over introduction. Jon is cooking Caribbean food for Ben, Jo and Linda. Ben has just made some disparaging comments about Jon's personality, and we join the sequence as the scene cuts to Linda's reactions to Jon and his menu. In the following transcript, the voice-over turns in italics signal a shift of tone and key into a faster-paced 'cooking' discourse that seems to be directed more at the audience and less as a response to the participants' talk.

Extract 3.ix: West Yorkshire, *Come Dine With Me*

VO:	and if that's not bad enough Linda's not looking forward to his night either
1. LINDA:	if I go on his personality (.) the cooking's <u>got</u> to be a little
2.	bit loopy
3. VO:	well Linda you're in for a bigger surprise because he's
4.	going <u>loopy</u> with your cuisine (.) cooking a Caribbean menu
5. JON:	I'm hoping that maybe (.) I'm gonna kick arse (in there)
6. VO:	good luck Jon
7. VO:	*kicking off his West Indian meal is a starter of jerk pork*
8.	*belly with rice and peas*
9. LINDA:	he int cookin this
10. BEN:	I would never order rice in a restaurant (.) ever. I don't like it.
11. JO:	yeah I'm not sure how Linda will feel about uh Caribbean
12.	food being on the menu tonight when <u>she</u> cooked
13.	Caribbean food last night

14. VO: well I can tell you (.) she's definitely not happy
15. LINDA: there's no way he's cookin this (.) he int cookin this
16. VO: he is (.) he's cookin it all right
17.   *starting by seasoning his meat with jerk and hot pepper sauce*
18.   *in a plastic bag*
19. JON: the bits (xxx) jerk (.) chicken
20. VO: er Jon it's pork
21. JON: there's loads an loads and loads and loads different
22.   versions of jerk yeah
23. VO: I can think of one
24. JON: right but this one in particular (.) is (.) grea::t yeah ((creaky
25.   voice))
26. VO: yea::h ma::n ((creaky voice)) let's hope Linda agree::s
27.   *if you want to jerk your pork like Jon*
28.   *check out the Channel 4 website for tonight's recipes*
29.   *he'll cook the meat later along with his rice and peas*
30.   *for now it's on with the main (.) Caribbean chowder*
31. JO: I <u>love</u> the sound of that
32. BEN: that's just a bowl of soup as far as I'm concerned
33. LINDA: he's not cookin this
34. VO: he is
35. LINDA: he's getting this brought in
36. VO: he's not
37. LINDA: if he cooks this an he pulls this outa t'bag
38.   I'll give him t'money mesself
39. VO: might hold you to that cos he's cookin it
40.   even the fish stock's from scratch
41. JON: it's a creative thing (.) I don't think there's very much
42.   difference between (.) the process of cookin and
43.   the process of makin art you can almost sort- use it as
44.   like a canvas you know
45. VO: what a load of jackson pollocks

This sequence is saturated with evaluations that do two things. First, they set up the forthcoming evening as problematic in various ways: Ben is very negative about the dishes on the menu; Linda is sceptical about Jon's ability to cook Caribbean food in the first place; Jo, although she says she likes the food, is worried about how Linda will react. As we will see in subsequent chapters, evaluations are a useful discursive resource, closely tied to the production of an opinion or stance, which, in turn, is closely tied to particular assumptions about social identities. Here, they are used to imply that Jon is a pretentious White man who thinks he knows how to cook jerk pork and peas, while Linda is a sceptical Black woman who *knows* she knows how to do it and Ben (White and male) is fussy and conservative in his tastes. The scene is set for the evening's drama.

The voice-over turns are also highly evaluative. They occur between the participant evaluations and are addressed directly to the prior speaker; as such, they are thus embedded in the edited interaction as responses to the content of the prior turn, so an adjacency relationship is set up between a participant turn and a voice-over receipt, as in the following utterance pairs:

11. JO: yeah I'm not sure how Linda will feel about uh Caribbean
12.   food being on the menu tonight when <u>she</u> cooked
13.   Caribbean food last night
14. VO: well I can tell you (.) she's definitely not happy

21. JON: there's loads an loads and loads and loads different
22.   versions of jerk yeah
23. VO: I can think of one
24. JON: right but this one in particular (.) is (.) grea::t yeah ((creaky
25.   voice))
26. VO: yea::h ma::n ((creaky voice)) let's hope Linda agree::s

33. LINDA: he's not cookin this
34. VO: he is
35. LINDA: he's gettin this brought in
36. VO: he's not

Unlike the voice-over commentary in programmes like *Big Brother* and *Wife Swap*, which provides an orientation frame for the talk and activity on screen – that is, information about who is doing what, where and when, such as 'Before they meet their new family, Susan and Debbie have a chance to explore their new homes' – in addition to information about what is being cooked and how, the voice-over in *Come Dine With Me* provides a highly evaluative framing of the talk itself.[2] We start with Linda's evaluation of Jon as 'loopy' in line 2, which is taken up by the commentator in line 4. In line 23 of Extract 3.ix, following Jon's comment about different versions of jerk, the comment 'I can think of one' uses the pun on 'jerk' to imply that Jon is one, too. In the next voice-over response turn (line 26), he imitates Jon's stretched, creaky voice quality 'yea::h ma::n' styling of a Caribbean accent in order to poke fun at Jon's pretensions to be able to produce this kind of food. After Linda's two declarative expressions ('he's not cookin this', 'he's getting this brought in'), the two counter-declarative turns constitute a knowing evaluation of her statements as wrong. And the final turn in the sequence (line 44) provides a dismissive send-up of Jon's views on the relationship between cooking and art.

In these spliced sequences of talk to camera made up of participants' reactions to the proposed menu and the commentator's responses to those reactions, the middle-space performances of the participants in their talk to camera are worked up into specific identity categories and then knocked sideways into comic character roles by the voice-over for the development of the show's narrative 'plot'. As already mentioned above, Bignell (2005) has made the point that the people taking part in reality television shows are often selected for their potential to be interesting characters, akin to fictional characters, in the overarching narrative of the docu-drama. However, he also notes that these are often also people who are recognisably representative of particular social groups, and therefore 'ordinary' in the sense that they are perceived by the audience as 'just like us' (Bignell 2005: 66). I would push this point in a different direction and argue that it is through these middle-space performances that participants can be seen to be doing not 'ordinary' but to be doing specifically noticeable as 'someone who is X or who does Y', maybe 'just like me' or possibly 'not like me at all', as a member of the audience. Below are some comments taken from the *Come Dine With Me* Twitter site that clearly articulate audience members' recognition of some of these various social categories and identities:

> I would definitely be that person on "come dine with me" that, on the second day, had forgotten everyone's name

> I am so much better at being a snob than these commoners on Come Dine With Me.

> Haha this woman on come dine with me is such a prick, 'yeh I just go out n flirt with guys to get them 2 buy me drinks all night.' Trollope

It is participants' specific identities and behaviours that are being noticed and commented on here: 'that person who' forgets names, 'being a snob', 'those commoners' and 'trollop' are social categories that are recognised in third-space performance and provide material to be worked up through programme editing into watchable character roles.

Summary: middle-space performance and participant identity

This chapter began with a discussion of some of the current theories relating to genres of reality television and the increasing presence of lay participants on our TV screens, and the notion of 'ordinary' that is often at the centre of debates around what Turner (2010) refers to as 'the demotic turn' in contemporary broadcasting, and is, in Bignell's (2005) terms, the 'middle space' of reality TV. Through the analysis of examples taken from this selection of reality television shows, I have argued that, just as in the talk shows and broadcast debates discussed in the previous chapter, while 'ordinary' can be used as a way of distinguishing the people participating in these programmes, and who are drawn from the general population, from those who are media professionals or known celebrities, it is not a sufficiently accurate description of what those people are actually represented as doing and (perhaps most crucially) saying in this context. To be ordinary is not to be noticeable or watchable, and thus being ordinary is not usually appropriate behaviour for those who are engaged in 'the work of being watched'.

By linking the concept of self in performance to a more discursively based account of the features of talk and interaction produced in the context of reality television, I have developed the notion of middle-space performance as a way of describing the routine ways that participants can construct very specific identities, which are then brought into dramatic conflict in the edited sequences of the broadcast. Through the analysis of some of the key discursive routines from these three programmes that involve talk that is both 'backstage' (in terms of not being produced in interaction with other participants in the programme) and also 'front-stage' (in terms of being specifically designed for the camera and the viewing audience), we have seen how these sequences function to establish specific participant identities. For instance, the participants' talk in *Wife Swap* sets up identities based on difference and 'the other', as the women visit their new home and read the other wife's manual, whereas, in reading and reacting to the menu in *Come Dine With Me*, the participants' talk contributes to the construction of comic identities through the intervention of a highly judgmental, ironic voice-over. In the latter programme, the commentary text is less a voice *over* the on-screen actions than a voice *within* them, through the use of adjacency structures and evaluation to produce humour. In all three cases, I have argued that what is centrally at stake is the performance of an identity that serves the local purpose, be it of competition, of conflict, or of entertaining, characterful eccentricity.

Discursive evaluation has emerged in these sequences as a crucial component of identity construction, functioning to establish 'who I am' and 'who I am not' in relation to certain social groups, norms and moral values, and we will return to discourses of evaluation and judgement in more detail in Chapters 6 and 7. The particular significance of identity work in relation to opinion-giving, expertise and the construction of stance will also be central to the discussion in Chapter 5. We move on now to the first of four chapters dealing with specific aspects of the discourse of public participation, which focuses on one of the primary discourses of lay participation in talk on television: narrative and stories of personal experience.

Notes

1 One reason for the rise in popularity of such programmes is that they are cheap to make, but they are also constructed around themes of personal appearance, self-development and material lifestyle choices, which are intricately connected to consumerist discourses and the marketplace of contemporary culture and leisure industries (Lorenzo-Dus 2009: 180), and thus continue to contribute to 'the flow of consumption' that John Hartley sees as the role of much network television: 'the purveyor of what was needed to sustain domestic life' (Hartley 2009: 22).

2 The voice-over is, in fact, often seen as one of the major reasons for the success of this series, generating comments on Twitter such as 'If Come Dine With Me ever changed its narrator I wouldn't watch it ever again'. Indeed, the identity of the commentator clearly matters, too, since, on one programme, he changed his voice-over style and voice completely, and, on Twitter feeds, viewers were asking where he had gone!

4 Discourses of participation
Telling stories

Introduction: mediating narrative discourse

This chapter deals with the one of the most significant aspects of public participation in broadcast talk: telling stories of personal experience. Storytelling is a fundamental human activity, and, according to Jerome Bruner, 'an organizing principle by which people organize their experience in, knowledge about, and transactions with the social world' (1990: 35). Narrative is therefore a discursive resource that we draw on in many different communicative contexts, and the broadcast media are no exception. Many programmes that are organised around some form of public participation include narrative activity, and this is particularly so in the case of television talk shows, where the telling of personal stories has been well documented as one of the primary discursive activities engaged in by lay participants (Livingstone and Lunt 1994; Thornborrow 1997; Tolson 2001). Narratives also occur in other broadcast contexts; for example, in 'experiential' news interviews (Montgomery 2007), as anecdotes in chat show interviews (Tolson 1991, 2006), as well as in designated storytelling spaces embedded in popular radio shows (Montgomery 1991).

Here, I will focus on three specific contexts for the production of broadcast narrative discourse by lay participants: (1) stories that are told by participants in TV talk shows; (2) stories that are told by participants in a TV court; and, finally, (3) the stories that radio listeners send in to a popular radio show and which are read out on-air by a host narrator. In each case, I describe the participation frameworks that structure this narrative activity, and the ways that the mediation of narrative functions to produce a different type of performance in each context.

Narrative as a discursive activity

This is not the place for an in-depth introduction to oral and conversational narrative theory – such accounts can be found elsewhere (e.g., Rimmon-Keenan 1983; Toolan 2001; Thornborrow and Coates 2005) – so the main features of spoken narrative discourse will be sketched out just very briefly in the following paragraphs. Most important for the analyses in this chapter is the fact that a story can be told many times, in different ways, by different tellers on different occasions. The formalist division of narrative into two components – 'fabula' (the basic story materials and events, the 'stuff' of the narrative) and 'sjuzet' (the story as it is told, or the representation of those events) (Propp 1968) – partly captures this variation, providing a sense of stability of content on the one hand, but variety in structure and delivery on the other. More useful still for an analysis of spoken narrative is Shoshana Blum-Kulka's model of narrative events, in which she distinguishes three important analytical components of narrative discourse: tales, tellers and tellings (Blum-Kulka 1993, 1997). Adopting Goffman's concept of 'footing', which describes a speaker's potentially possible relationships to their utterance as 'author', animator' and 'principal' (Goffman 1981), she notes that storytellers 'first of all enact the role of speaker as "animator", while if they are also accountable for the tale, then they are also the "principal"' (Blum-Kulka 1997: 103). In personal, first-person narratives, we find all three of the speaker roles (author, animator, principal) merged into one, whereas, in third-person narratives, the narrator may be the 'animator', but not necessarily the 'author' of the tale, and may take up a range of evaluative stances regarding the 'principal'. Finally, the 'telling' is 'the act of narrating in real time, the actual performing of a story before an audience' (Blum-Kulka 1997: 102).

The 'telling' of a story on radio or television is a situated narrative event that is distinctively shaped by its mediated setting. In broadcast narratives, various aspects of the particular occasion for telling as well as the role of those involved in that telling – for example, as story elicitor, as storyteller(s) or as story recipient(s) – are contextually specific. First, many of the stories told are elicited narratives, which means that they do not emerge out of the ongoing talk, as conversational narratives generally do (Jefferson 1978). Instead, a participant is invited to tell their particular story – which may be the reason why they are participating in the broadcast in the first place – by a host, at a relevant moment. Secondly, the story is produced for a non co-present audience listening to or watching the broadcast, as well as for co-present recipients, the host and studio audience. How that story is produced and performed for its various recipients therefore becomes a salient issue, and this will be different from other conversational, or, indeed, other institutional, contexts for narrative discourse.

As Blum-Kulka suggests, Goffman's concepts of footing and participation frameworks are useful in any analysis of narrative events that requires some examination of who does what in the situated production of a story. In mediated narrative discourse, there may be more than one storyteller. Talk show hosts often participate in narrative production, having prior knowledge of what the story is about, and why it is relevant for the show, while other participants may offer competing versions of the story (i.e., slightly different 'tales'). In their account of narratives produced during family dinner talk, Ochs and Taylor (1992) analysed the various roles taken up by participants in the talk, which include story elicitor, protagonist(s), storyteller(s), recipients and story problematiser (the participant who takes a particularly evaluative role in relation to the narrated events). Many of these roles, as we will see, also become relevant in the configuration of participants in media narratives. In TV talk shows, for example, the host, who is in the position of already knowing the story and why it is significant for that particular broadcast, generally takes up the roles of story elicitor and primary recipient, sometimes acts as problematiser and may also, on occasions, contribute to its telling to make it more dramatic for the audience (Thornborrow 2001a). The studio audience, as secondary recipients, may sometimes contribute evaluations of the story. And, as we will see, on radio particularly, the increasing use of texts and emails expands possibilities for wider audience participation in evaluating and problematising activity. The array of participant roles therefore becomes locally specialised in terms of the mediated environment for storytelling.

Finally, stories have to be tellable, which is to say they must have a point (Labov 1972; Polanyi 1979). As a discursive activity, telling a story involves according the teller more conversational space over an extended sequence of turns than is usually given to a single speaker in conversational interaction. Other participants become the story recipients, withholding their next turns until an appropriate moment in the telling (Jefferson 1978). The rules of turn-taking are thus temporarily modified for the duration of the narrative, since other participants wait for the story to come to a recognisable end point before starting to speak. An important part of the interactional work that story recipients do is to demonstrate their understanding of the point of the story, and to react appropriately to it. If a story appears to have no relevant point, recipients may challenge the narrator for taking up so much conversational space to tell it, and the 'so what' factor (Labov 1972) emerges as a likely response. To tell a story with no recognisable point is essentially to fail as a storyteller. In mediated narratives, 'point' is almost always determined by the context of the broadcast. There may be a theme, or a topical issue, that will provide a relevant link between the points of various stories told, for example, in a talk show discussion or argument. In such programmes, narrative discourse plays an important role in the development of an array of arguments and positions that are built up as the show progresses. In other types of programmes, such as celebrity chat shows, narratives are more likely to emerge as one-off anecdotes, embedded into the talk as humorous repartee (Tolson 1991), or accounts of a particular known-about state of affairs, elicited by the host and explicitly designed by tellers to be funny.

'You should find this interesting . . .'

To illustrate the relevance of point and its relationship to a mediated context, let's now look at a story, taken from a UK chat show, that has no point whatsoever. The 'tale' is utterly ordinary in the sense that nothing interesting happens at all. The absence of narrative point, however, becomes another kind of 'point' in terms of this particular show. *The Kumars at No. 42* was an award-winning BBC spoof 'chat' show series, which ran from 2001 to 2006, featuring three generations of a fictional Asian family (grandmother, parents and son) who take turns to interview real-life celebrity guests, and it plays with many of the established conventions of the chat show genre. Although this show often came across as improvised and spontaneous, it was largely scripted, apart from the guests' contributions. The extract below is taken from an episode in which the celebrity guests are six members of the 1980s' pop group Madness. Host Sanjeev has just offered the floor to his father as his turn to ask one of them a question:

Extract 4.i: 'Crossing the Channel', *The Kumars at No. 42*

1.	SANJEEV:	Dad
2.	DAD:	Mr Parson you::: should find this interesting
3.		a friend of mine sailed from Amsterdam in a barge to
4.		London in the summer of 1977
5.		(2.0)
6.	PARSON:	yea:::h.
7.	SANJEEV:	did anything happen on the way
8.	DAD:	no no it was a very smooth crossing
9.	SANJEEV:	fantastic uh= ((turns to group))
10.	DAD:	=actually something interesting did happen
11.		once they alighted at Pickets Lock
12.	PARSON:	huh huh
13.	DAD:	do you know the Lee Valley Market
14.	PARSON:	yeah
15.	DAD:	he went there
16.		((laughter))
17.	SANJEEV:	good good good

There are many parodic elements bound up in this short stretch of talk: first of all, it is conventionally chat show guests who tell stories, not the hosts; second, it sets up expectations of tellability that are then not met; and, third, it maintains an already contextually inappropriate topic that had been initiated several turns earlier. In a previous question turn, Dad had been asking Parson technical questions about electric power generators (Parson happened to live on a barge in Holland at the time), a topic of potentially little interest in a celebrity chat show! As we see above, in his allocated next question turn, Dad pursues this incongruous line of talk, again selecting Parson as his primary addressee and recipient of the story in line 2:

> Mr Parson you should find this interesting

This is a story 'preface' (Jefferson 1978), which, here, sets up a designated recipient, and also projects an appropriate reaction to the upcoming story. Story prefaces are a conversational signal that the teller will require enough interactional space to tell their story, but also an indication of how the recipient should respond to it (i.e., in this case, that it will be worth waiting for and 'interesting'). Dad then proceeds with the orientation elements of the story – the *who*, *where*, *what* and *when* –then stops. We can note the two-second pause in line 5, during which Parson waits for a complicating action, and then, as primary recipient, offers a continuer prompt ('yeah') when none is forthcoming. It is Sanjeev who remarks on the absence of any such action in line 7:

> Did anything happen on the way

What is being played out for comic effect in this short sequence is the expectation that something 'tellable' *should* happen in a story; in Bruner's (1990) terms, there should be a breach of the canonical script. When it turns out that there is no such breach and no exceptional event ('it was a very smooth crossing'), it is the absence of tellability that becomes the joke, which is continued in the next turns (lines 10–15):

> Actually something interesting did happen—
> Do you know the Lee Valley Market
> Yeah
> He went there

What makes this sequence funny is precisely the continued absence of point. Not only is this a parody of story, as we see in the reactions of Parson and Sanjeev, it is also wholly incongruous as a piece of chat show interaction. Its contextual relevance here is to maintain an inappropriate topic for a chat show within an inappropriate narrative activity, and it gets a laugh. This is a storytelling performance that is deliberately designed to be point-less, and that, of course, is the joke.

Stories produced by members of the public – whether they are listeners writing in to a radio show with a personal experience narrative, or talk show participants using narrative as a resource to make an argument, or to justify a particular stance – always have some kind of contextually and locally relevant narrative point. In the next section, I turn to data from a TV talk show in which the participants are using narrative discourse as a resource for evaluating, justifying or accounting for particular problematic behaviours. As we will see, the contextual environment changes both the participatory framework and the function of the narrative event quite considerably.

Personal experience as performance

Television talk shows abound with talk about lay participants' life stories and life crises. This narrativisation of lay experience has become one of the most pervasive discourse genres in public participation broadcasting, and has been extensively researched over the past two decades or so (Livingstone and Lunt 1994; Thornborrow 1997; Lorenzo-Dus 2001; Tolson 2006). Programmes such as *Kilroy*, *Trisha* and *The Jeremy Kyle Show* in the UK, as well as *The Oprah Winfrey Show*, *The Sally Jessy Raphael Show* and *The Montel Williams Show* in the USA, deal with thematic and topical issues such as relationship breakdown, abuse, divorce and other forms of social and family troubles: the protagonists are there in person, on stage, to tell their own tales, even to enact them. At the more extreme, 'trash TV' end of the talk show market, programmes such as *The Jerry Springer Show* or *The Jeremy Kyle Show* pushed these crisis narratives into domains of dramatic, and sometimes physical, embodied confrontation and conflict. To appear in this kind of show is therefore much less about being ordinary than it is about being in crisis: someone whose life is troubled, whose problems and social relationships are made spectacular in various ways for the audience (Hutchby 2001b; Myers 2001). The narrative events in this type of talk show are rather different from the stories of personal experience that occur in the issue-based shows, and I will return to a discussion of these in Chapter 5. For now, the focus will be on how participants tell their stories in examples taken from issue-based talk shows such as *Kilroy* and *Esther* (UK) and *Montel* (USA) as a particular form of mediated narrative discourse.

One might reasonably say that all narrative events are performed events to the extent that every story needs an audience. Storytellers design narratives for recipients, from the initial story preface to the resolution, or coda. As we know, an abstract signalling appropriate reactions to and alignments with the story events, a recognisable point and an indication of what it will take to bring the story to an end are all important components of successful narrative performance. Talk show narratives are no exception. Many of the stories in talk shows are rhetorically designed by their tellers to elicit a response, or a reaction – of laughter, of disapproval or of sympathy – from the audience as recipients. However, not all tellers share the same narrative competence, and on a stage, in front of a studio audience, hosts frequently participate in the narrative activity in order to get a story told for its intended audience. In other words, when lay participants are asked to tell their stories, the narrativisation of lay experience is often a collaborative event involving more than one teller.

'Has it ever happened to you?'

In order to examine how participation frameworks can vary between narrative tellings, we can compare the differences between a story that is told by a speaker who has quite extensive experience of media participation and one told by a lay participant who does not. The first is a highly performed narrative by a competent storyteller, ex-member of the UK government-turned-author, Edwina Currie. This story is elicited by host Esther Rantzen, in an episode of her show that dealt with publicity, the press and unwanted attention from the paparazzi.[1] Currie is a practised public speaker, and her story about how she escaped from the press at the time of her resignation from the government in 1988[2] is told with great aplomb:

Extract 4.ii: 'Paparazzi', *Esther*

```
 1. ER:   has (.) it ever happened to you
 2.        have you ever had that sort of attention from the paparazzi
 3. EC:   oh I beat them once (.) I had a wonderful time actually
 4.        (.) sort of (.) I don't know whether it was you
 5.        but after I left the government
 6.         it was Christmas time=
 7. ER:   = when [the salmonella=
 8. EC:          [and I-        =1988 over the salmonella thing
 9.        and we wanted to get home for Christmas=
10. ER:   =you put me off boiled eggs for life
11. AUD:  ((laughter))
12. EC:   no boiled eggs are all right it's the raw ones you shouldn't
13.        touch .h erm and I contacted my local police and they said
14.        well actually there's about thirty (.) of these cars sitting on
           your lawn if you come home now (.) they're just gonna
15.        be taking lots
16.        of pictures an' they'll be there (.) right through the holiday
17.        an' they'll make your life a misery=
18. ER:                                     =but couldn't you have
                                            done
19.        what you suggested Princess Diana did n'just go there
20.        smile=
21. EC:       =well
22.        what we did was we hid in a friend's flat for a little while (.)
22.        until we hel- we felt that the (.) story should have moved on
23.        .hh an' then I contacted the police again they said they're
```

24.	still here (.) so I said (.) hang on (.) now let's see what
25.	we can do .h I phoned our local pub .h
26.	in the pub was er an ex police officer
27.	who's a good friend (.) I told him the problem an' he said (.)
28.	leave it to me Edwina uh an' very ostentatiously 'cos by
29.	then these guys were all in the pub having a drink
30.	'cos they got a bit bored waiting .hh um he said
31.	um I'm going to fetch them from the station (.) got in his car
32.	and drove off an' of course the pub emptied all the paparazzi
33.	got into the cars an' they drove off into rural Derbyshire
34.	.h he drove them until (.) he had almost run out of petrol
35.	an' then abandoned them in a field.
36. AUD:	((laughter))
37. EC:	by which point we had got home an' we were in (.)
38.	the gates were shut the doors were locked the curtains were
39.	drawn (.) and they didn't get any pictures=
40. ER:	=(he hey)
41. AUD:	((applause))
42. ER:	but if you'd been the Princess of Wales (.)
43.	i- there would have been a second lot—

This narrative is tightly structured, which adds to our sense of its heightened performance. There is a clear indication in the abstract (line 3) of what the story is about (beating the paparazzi) and a possible alignment to it (she had 'a wonderful time'). The orientation details are swiftly given between lines 5 and 10, and, after the host's interruption with a joke about boiled eggs, Currie gets into the complicating events of the story. It is quite long, but she is not interrupted; the audience withhold their first response until the point where the paparazzi are abandoned in a field (line 35), when they laugh. The resolution in lines 37–39 provides a clearly structured ending to the story: there is a three-part list (gates shut/doors locked/curtains drawn) followed by a neat coda that brings the story to a close: 'they didn't get any pictures'.

Here, we have a story of personal experience, delivered in response to the host's question in a neat and complete narrative package. The teller is not contributing to any particular argument, but her story has a high level of tellability, illustrating how she was able to outwit the press. The host has little work to do in terms of co-telling, other than specify an additional orientation detail in line 7 (clarifying for the audience why and when exactly the events in the story occurred) and making the joke about eggs in line 10. Her role is more one of 'problematiser' (Ochs and Taylor 1992), in so far as, in both her turns (lines 18 and 42), she takes issue with a particular aspect of the story. These problematising turns start with a turn-initial 'but' and have a disjunctive function, producing a critical evaluation of the story, rather than a strong alignment with the narrated events.

On other occasions, with less practised storytellers, hosts may have to do much more work not just to elicit a narrative, but to keep it focused and relevant for the current telling. In contrast to 'Paparazzi', the second example illustrates how the host intervenes in the telling in order to produce a narrative that is maximally performed for its audience. This extract is taken from an episode of *The Montel Williams Show*, where the topic is troublesome relationships between teenage girls and their parents. After the host's narrative-eliciting turn in line 1, Angel tells the story of how she has been thrown out of her parents' home:

Extract 4.iii: 'The break-in', *The Montel Williams Show*

```
 1. MW:    What did your mother do to you
 2. ANG:   .hhh well (.) she kicked me outa the house
 3.        because she took away my keys (.) n'so I had
 4.        to break in to get clothes out of my house (.)
 5.        while they were out of town .hhh=
 6. MW:                                  =while your Mum
 7.        and Dad were outa town (.) you broke in to their
 8.        house
 9. ANG:   [huh - wu- (x x x x x)]
10. MW:    [and to get some things and you said well]
11.        so now I (already) broke up may as well have a
12.        coupla friends over
13. AUD:   ((laughter))
14. MW:    so the friends came over had a little party (s)
15. ANG:   (w)ell no (.) three friends I wou[ldn't call that=
16. MW:    [three friends]
17. ANG:   =a party but
18. MW:    little beer=
19. ANG:             =they they acted like it was a party
20.        y[eah]
21. MW:    [little beer]
22. ANG:   a little beer [yeah]
23. MW:    [little] pizza
24. ANG:   little pizza [yeah]
25. MW:    [what] else did you do
26. ANG:   erm nothin' we just watched movies (.) stayed there
27.        for a little while (.) pizza man came an' (.)
28.        went n' (.) snitched on us for not paying him
29.        (.) a dollar that we owed him .hhhh [and-]
30. MW:                                        [then] they called
31.        back up and told your mother that
```

32. ANG: yeah (.) and she fr<u>ea</u>ked <u>out</u> about it like always
33.   (.)'cos (.) s'just how she is I guess she's a little
34.   church lady
35. AUD: ((x x x x))
36. MW: and she pitched y<u>ou</u> outa the house
37. ANG: yeah

Montel's role here is not simply that of story elicitor; he intervenes as a co-teller, using his position as host and primary recipient of Angel's story to shape the way the story gets told. He repeats elements of the narrative action 'you broke into their house' (lines 7–8); animates her words, 'I might as well have a coupla friends over' (lines 11–12); and supplies a further complicating action in the story when the pizza company called her mother to complain (lines 30–31), as well as the final complicating action (for Angel) and resolution (for the parents): 'and she pitched you out of the house' (line 36). The audience laughter at line 13 follows Montel's shift of footing into animating Angel's words, and their murmurs of disapproval follow immediately her evaluation of her mother as 'a little church lady' (lines 33–34). Comparing the audience's receipt of this narrative event with that for the 'Paparazzi' story above (where the audience laugh after the teller's resolution in line 35 and applaud after the coda in line 40), we can see how these moments of heightened performance are produced in different ways. As the sole storyteller in 'Paparazzi', it is Currie who designs her narrative to produce responses from the audience, while, in 'The break-in', as well as having a marked evaluative function, it is the repeated intervention of the host as co-teller that transforms the telling of Angel's story into a narrative performance for the audience. Indeed, Montel here, to a certain extent, takes over the story as tale; it is his version that becomes dominant while Angel is put in the position of having to contest that version of events; for example, 'three friends I wouldn't call that a party' (line 15).

In both of these examples of talk show stories as narrative events, there are two points to be made. The first is that the role of the storyteller as narrator of the events plays a significant part in how the story is produced for the local occasion – its telling. The second is that each narrative telling involves a different kind of performance. The difference between the two tellers, as protagonists of their stories, is not simply one of competent media professional (Edwina Currie) and ordinary lay participant (Angel). In a different context, for a different audience, both of them might well have told their story differently. The relevant identities of each narrator here are those that emerge in the telling through distinct structural footings. Currie is author, animator and principal; as sole teller, she is in control of her narrative – while Angel is not. Angel's footings of author, animator and principal are constantly under threat: she has to deal with an intrusive co-narrator whose problematising and dramatising actions also render the control of her own narrative practically impossible. Currie does her own dramatising work; the orientation, the succession of complicating actions, the resolution and the coda are all characteristic of a well-structured narrative rhetorically designed and performed by the teller for the audience. The dramatising of Angel's story is not her own, and its production as a performance is almost entirely in the hands of someone else: the host Montel.

Conflicting stories as performance

I now turn to another media context for the production of narrative events, one that involves a different kind of performance by the storytellers: the American television courtroom series *Judge Judy*. In this televised small claims court, the plaintiff and the defendants tell different 'tales' (i.e., conflicting versions of a set of events) in order to plead their case in front of the judge and a courtroom studio audience. Central to this narrative event, therefore, is the issue of credibility: the defendant, going second, has to put across another version of events as convincingly as possible, in order to persuade an audience that has already heard the first version of the story from the plaintiff. Consequently, the design of a narrative 'telling' in this context takes on particular significance if there are conflicting versions at stake. As I have shown in a previous analysis of these data (Thornborrow 2000), one of the ways in which participants do this is by using the conversational historic present tense (CHP). The CHP is a grammatical resource on which narrators routinely draw to accomplish specific actions in storytelling. In performed narratives, such as folktales, a switch into the CHP frequently marks the onset of a complicating action, and also often occurs where dialogue is being recounted (Leith 1995). It has also been found to be a stylistic device used by narrators to signal vividness and drama (Schiffrin 1981), as well as a speaker's level of commitment to what is being said.

In this next example, the case involves a dispute over repairs to a car that led to a fight between two men, Nathan and Dave. In the extracts below, all three storytellers have an experience of the event; they were present when the fight occurred, so they are in a position to tell the story as it happened to them. Again drawing on Goffman's (1981) concept of footing, they take up the positions of 'author', 'animator' and 'principal', and they also 'figure' centrally in the story they tell. The three stories are produced in succession here; the first by the plaintiff, Nathan, the second by an unnamed witness in support of Nathan and the third by the defendant, Dave.

Extract 4.iv: 'The fight' (1), *Judge Judy*

1.	JUDY:	let's hear it now let's hear about the violence (2.0)
2.		'cos that's what your suing [for right]
3.	NAT:	[the first] violence
4.		occurred like I say was on Wednesday in his drive where
5.		he grabbed me by the throat and threatened that I could
6.		not back out of this deal that we're too far <u>in</u> to it

```
 7.              and would cause me traumatic injury if I (.) insisted
 8.              (.) he had me by the throat and ripped my shirt off
 9.              n'punched me in the guts three times=
10. JUDY:                                          =did you do that sir
11.             (1.0)
12. NAT:        his father [was]
13. JUDY:                  [ju–] u– did you do that
14. DAVE:       oh no Ma'am
```

In Nathan's account, there is no use of the CHP. The main event narrative clauses are all in the past tense:

> he grabbed me
> threatened that I could not back out
> he had me by the throat
> ripped my shirt off
> punched me in the guts

Next in the sequence is an account given by an eyewitness to the fight. Although this is told from a different perspective, his version of events is similar to the first one, and it is produced in support of the first teller's version:

Extract 4.v: 'The fight' (2), *Judge Judy*

```
 1. JUDY:   ok could you just take your hands out of your
 2.         pockets [you're not] afraid of that right=
 3. WIT:            [yes ma'am]                  =no ma'am
 4. JUDY:   alright (.) did you witness anything physical on that
 5.           date between these two [people]
 6. WIT:                            [yes I] did
 7. JUDY:   tell me exactly what you [saw]
 8. WIT:                            [well] I was sitting
 9.         in the car as they were doing their conversation
10.         (.) Dave ended up taking a swing at Richard (1.0)
11.         and hit him in the side
12. JUDY:   Richard is this (.) person who (.) who was al– who I
13.         call Nathan 'cos that's [what's] in it=
14. WIT:                            [yes]        =yes [Nathan]
15. JUDY:                                             [ok]
16. WIT:    Richard didn't do nothing (.) Dave got irritable (.)
17.         grabbed him by the neck (.) threw him up against a
18.         door in a wall (1.0) then threw him to the ground (.)
```

19.		and then started hittin' to him (.hh) I jump over (1.0)
20.		opened up the door (.) said Nancy please call the
21.		police (.) I jumped on Dave's neck (1.0) and as I did
22.		that (.) he got off Richard (.) Nathan (.) and then we
23.		both rushed into the house
24.		(1.0)
25.	JUDY:	ok (.) would you have a seat thank you

The narrative action clauses through which the witness recounts the key moments in the development of the fight as he saw it – from the opening orientation in lines 8–9 ('well I was sitting in the car') through the complicating action clauses of the fight until the moment when he became involved, and up to the resolution in lines 22–23 ('then we both rushed into the house') – are all in the past tense. The account does, however, contain one occurrence of the CHP: in line 19: ('I jump over'). This tense switch corresponds to Deborah Schiffrin's observation that the CHP occurs when a new episode in the story is being introduced. In effect, here, the clause 'I jump over' also marks the moment in the story when the current speaker himself becomes involved in the action, a dramatic moment for him. After that, he switches back to using past tense forms to finish his story.

However, when the defendant, Dave, is called to give his account of the fight, he uses the CHP from the very beginning of his story, and continues to use it throughout. This is the third time the story has been told, and, in this account, the only occurrence of a past tense form is when Dave uses the reporting verb 'said':

Extract 4.vi: 'The fight' (3), *Judge Judy*

1.	JUDY:	OK
2.	DAVE:	I walk out (1.0) I'm very aggressive (.) I'm yelling
3.		(.) I'm cussin' at him (.) everything (1.0)
4.		I'm saying I want my car back (.) I'm saying I don't
5.		wanna deal with you any more (1.0) I'm not fixing the car
6.		you're not keeping my car you gotta get outa my life
7.		(.) all deals are off (.hh) he then looks at me
8.		(.) an he says well (.) that ain't gonna happen (.)
9.		I say (.) a little while ago you told me you're gonna
10.		bring my car back I'm at my house waiting for two
11.		hours I call you four times (.) you're hanging up on me
12.		(.) what's the deal you change your mind again
13.		I want my car back (.hh) I physically get in front of him
14.		before he go– goes in his house (1.0) I'm like this
15.		both hands up (.) Nathan (.) stop this (.) you don't wanna
16.		do this (.) so (.) next you know he physically grabs me
17.		(.) goes to push me out of the way

18.   (1.0) Nathan (1.0) he's pushin' [me]
19. JUDY: [ssh] he's pushin' you
20. DAVE: yeah (.) yeah he's not fighting with me (.) he's not striking
21.   me (.) he's pushin' me outa the way (.)
22.   he's just trying to get in his door
23. ??   (cool?)
24. DAVE: I grab onto him problem is is his porch is slippery
25.   (1.0) I'm falling down he's pushin' me outa the way
26.   (.) I pull him around (.) spin him around (.) put him
27.   on the ground I got my arm on his neck (1.0)
28   an' I'm holding him
29. JUDY: somebody said to me (.) somebody that I was
30.   having a verbal dispute with
31. DAVE: alright —

In Dave's version of the fight with Nathan, the pervasive use of the CHP contributes to the highly performed character of this telling, in contrast to the two tellings that have just preceded it. In the prior accounts, it was Dave who allegedly started the fight, but, in Dave's account, he claims (lines 16 and 17) that it was Nathan who 'physically grabs' him, thus putting him in the position of having to defend himself.

Dave's use of the CHP in this sequence functions on various levels. First, it is a stylistic device that dramatises the performance of his story; second, it is what Schiffrin calls an 'internal evaluation device' (1981: 46), reproducing the fight as he experienced it from his perspective; and, third, it is an indicator of his level of commitment to this version of events, strongly foregrounding the 'principal' of his story. The design of this telling – and its heightened level of performance – is thus an outcome of the local, sequential context in which it is delivered, and the teller's use of the CHP marks his commitment to this account of events not just as different, but as believably different from the previous tellers' versions.

In this context, then, the narrative events have a different framework of participation in terms of their narrative participant roles to those we saw in the extracts above taken from TV talk shows. In the TV court, the primary recipient of the story, Judge Judy, intervenes at points in the narrative to clarify matters of orientation and question the facts. The tellers, as the key protagonists in the story, each provide their own version of events, and, after the first version of the tale, the telling becomes increasingly dramatic – particularly with the third teller Dave's predominant use of the CHP. The narrative performance on this occasion is thus produced by the speakers in their courtroom identities of witness and defendant, and in their narrative roles as tellers/protagonists of conflicting versions of the disputed events.

We will return to the topic of conflicting narratives, with particular attention to their specific relationship to the discourse activities of opinion-giving and argument, in the next chapter. In the last part of this chapter on mediating narrative and performance, there will be a shift of medium as well as of participant framework and footing as we turn now to the radio as an environment for narrative discourse, and at a form of storytelling where the narrator is animator, but not author or necessary principal, of a listener's story.

Telling someone else's story

As we have already seen in relation to both the TV talk show and the courtroom narratives analysed so far, one of the most significant features of mediated storytelling is the production of experiences from the private domain as public, performed, broadcast narrative discourse. The way this is accomplished varies, depending on the contextual location of the narrative and the particular media genre in which it occurs, but the transformation of the story materials, the 'tale', into a mediated 'telling' for television audiences will usually involve a specialised distribution of narrative participant roles and specific forms of narrative design. When a radio DJ host narrates personal experience stories sent in by listeners, the narrative event has an equally specialised, generic set of organisational features, participatory framework and roles. First adopted by BBC Radio 1 DJ Simon Bates, and, until 2009, still part of Jo Whiley's morning show on the same station, the format has undergone some interesting shifts in its design and participation framework, particularly in relation to the availability of online and mobile phone technologies.

In the 1980s, Simon Bates developed a storytelling slot that gained a great deal of popularity with his morning show listeners: *Our Tune*. His narration of stories sent in by members of the public – mainly dealing with personal issues such as relationships, illness, loss, divorce and family break-up – had a distinctive, elaborate narrative style, constructed upon the footings of animator and principal, as narrator, evaluator and problematiser in these tellings, but not as author of the tale (Montgomery 1991). In his study of the *Our Tune* narratives, Martin Montgomery argues that they contained predictable generic elements, reproduced on a daily basis by a narrative 'machinery' the function of which was to organise these stories of private domestic crisis into public discourses for the Radio 1 audience (1991: 172).

'I've got a letter from a young lady, let's call her Julie . . .'

Montgomery shows how many of the *Our Tune* narratives typically began with Simon Bates framing the story as coming from outside the broadcasting institution, a real-life story from a real person, although the identity of that person is kept secret. Then came the narrative 'focusing', which established the narrative point from the outset of the story. Point in *Our Tune* narratives tended to be consistently recycled as recurrent themes in the programme, such as survival through difficult times or challenging personal circumstances. For example:

> **Extract 4.vii: *Our Tune*, Simon Bates, BBC Radio 1**
>
> I guess it's also a story about the way people survive things because you have preconceptions about divorce and you have preconceptions also about the way it affects kids and sometimes you forget about how it affects the adults as well in a family.
>
> (Extract from Montgomery 1991: 146)

This focusing work was very generalised, with little to give away the content of the upcoming story, and was often mitigated, leaving open the possibility for other interpretations of the events in the narrative. It also projected the moment when listeners would get the point of the story, once it had been heard:

> you'll understand why when we get through it

After the initial framing and focusing, Bates moved to 'situating' characters and their relationships, often re-situating them at significant moments in the developing story:

> **Extract 4.viii: *Our Tune*, Simon Bates, BBC Radio 1**
>
> by this time really her daughter had become her mother's daughter if you understand what I mean the mother was looking after her constantly and the daughter looked to her grandmother not to her real Mum for everything
>
> (Extract from Montgomery 1991: 148)

Montgomery argues that this situating and re-situating work on the part of the broadcast narrator foregrounds one of the major concerns in *Our Tune* narratives: the quality of personal relationships between protagonists in the story, and particularly those of the 'epistolary narrator' who is the central protagonist (1991: 148). This concern with relational aspects of the story is contrasted with the orientation of the narrator, on behalf of the audience, to both the events of the story and the position of the audience. Montgomery calls the first type 'empathetic orientation', which projects assessments about what a particular experience would be like, as in the following examples:

> and you know how an atmosphere can go out of a room and up the
> stairs and right around a house
> and you know there's something dreadfully wrong

He calls the second 'orientation to the audience', which projects possible reactions to that experience from the position of the listener:

> and you're looking straight at the radio now and saying
> ah she met somebody
> no
> one evening at the end of May last year she was in the bath
> and she found a lump

In both cases, the narrator appealed to the audience through forms of direct address in order to 're-align the discourse with the process of reception' (Montgomery 1991: 150).

The presence of 'generic maxims' or 'segments of commonsense wisdom' (Montgomery 1991: 151) also contributed to the orientation to the audience, providing an evaluatory component constructed as shared and available to narrator and audience alike:

> and you can't make any . accusations . about whose fault it was
> because these things do happen in relationships
> they just provided shoulders
> and that's something that you usually need at those times

These maxims are the typically taken-for-granted forms of cultural knowledge that are mobilised by the narrator, generally, as Montgomery notes, at points in the narration when the evaluative structure of first-person narration (i.e., the epistolary narrator) clashes with the third-person broadcast narration. Evaluation is always tricky to manage without risk of a perceived threat to positive face, as other assessments are generally more weighty in terms of threat than self-assessments (Pomerantz 1975). Through the strategic resource of such generic maxims, Bates was thus able to provide evaluations of the story while maintaining it discursively at arm's length. *Our Tune* was a narrative event the generic specificity of which emerged in a clash between the private confessional letter and the public media narrative, and Montgomery argues that its appeal lay precisely in this clash between two different genres and discursive domains: 'crossing the boundary from private to public in *Our Tune* is given an extra frisson by representing – in a generic form more often associated with fiction – the everyday crises of real lives' (1991: 175).

'Now don't get me wrong . . . .'

In the 1990s, a similar format called *Love Letters* was taken up by the radio station Heart FM and DJ Nigel Williams in *Late Night Love Songs*. However, the complex narrative organisation of the *Our Tune* stories is notably absent in *Love Letters*, and Williams' narration of listeners' letters was given a very different treatment from the style of narration identified by Montgomery in Bates' *Our Tune*. We can see some of the differences illustrated in the next extract, which is taken from the opening sequence of one of these *Love Letters* stories:

Extract 4.ix: 'Maureen's story' (1), *Love Letters*, Heart FM

1. tonight it's Maureen's story
2. she says when I was seventeen I was (.) so desperate
3. to get away from home
4. now don't get me wrong 'cos I had a very happy childhood
5. and I do love my mum and dad
6. but I had two sisters (.) and a brother and we were just
7. always on top of one another
8. and I couldn't wait (.) to get my own space
9. so when Mark came along (.) I was determined (.)
10. to get him to show me the way out
11. hh. we'd only been going out for four months
12. when Mark (.) asked me to marry him
13. I said yes straight away
14. now says Maureen my family didn't take the engagement terribly
15. seriously saying >>you're too young<< ((funny voice))
16. and you should see a bit of the world before settling down
17. but I was headstrong says Maureen and (.) all the more determined
18. nothing was going to stop me

One of the most striking differences between the two narrative events is that Williams tells the story entirely in the first person, taking up Maureen's voice as protagonist and literally 'animating' her words. (Neither are we told if this is her real name or a pseudonym.) Another marked contrast between this narration and the *Our Tune* stories is the absence of any framing, focusing or situating work on the part of the narrator. The audience is told nothing about what the projected point of this tale might be. Instead, the narrative is delivered to the audience directly as the voice of the epistolary narrator, punctuated at various moments by the reporting verb phrase

'Maureen says', or 'says Maureen'. These phrases tend to be inserted at points of evaluation in the telling, such as the reaction of the family in lines 14–16 and the self-evaluation in line 17 ('I was headstrong'), and distinguish the narrative voice of the DJ from that of the epistolary narrator. Furthermore, in this first-person narration, Williams does not intrude into the telling of the story by taking up any problematising or evaluating role via the footings of author or principal, as Bates did through the use of empathetic orientations to the audience and his use of generic maxims. There is one orientation to the audience in line 4, projecting a negative evaluation ('now don't get me wrong'), but this is articulated as Maureen's voice directly addressing the audience, not Williams'. The only point at which the narrator takes up a position in relation to the story is his stylised voicing of the words of the parents in line 15, 'you're too young' – one example, perhaps, in this narration of a generic maxim, a commonsense, clichéd reaction to the daughter's announcement of her engagement.

To continue with the tale: after her first marriage ended and following a series of other disasters, Maureen meets someone else, who then has a terrible accident falling off a ladder and can't continue to work as a result. With poverty again imminent, she finds out she is pregnant and has to tell her new partner. We rejoin the narrative at the final complicating event and its resolution:

Extract 4.x: 'Maureen's story' (2), *Love Letters*, Heart FM

43. and on top of that
44. I was beginning to feel a bit weird (.) in myself
45. and I knew what that probably meant
46. I did one of those home pregnancy tests
47. and my heart leapt into my throat as I saw the little blue line
48. showing up in the tester I was dreading telling Lee (.) so much
49. but eventually I mustered up all my strength (.)
50. and told him he was going to be a dad
51. at first (.) he was silent (.) I was shaking (.)
52. he grabbed my hands and said (.)
53. that's the most wonderful thing in the world
54. Lee (.) you're world's most wonderful man
55. I love you says Maureen

The thematic similarity of the tale content in *Our Tune* and *Love Letters* is clearly visible; the arrival of a child, even in straitened circumstances, represents a powerful ideological notion of families winning the day together, as it were, against adversity. But, in terms of its style of telling, the narration of *Love Letters* constitutes a much simpler treatment of the story materials than *Our Tune*. The transformation of those materials into a public narrative is achieved by the DJ simply taking up the role of 'animator', and thus the role of 'Maureen' as 'author' and 'principal' is foregrounded in this first-person narration. Neither is this narrative loaded with the kind of culturally and ideologically motivated evaluations of family values and survival that underpin Bates' third-person narration of *Our Tune*. That is not to say that the story has no ideological evaluation or point; Maureen's tale is still firmly grounded in problematic relationships, clashing family values and the resolution of personal trouble through the arrival of a child and the couple sticking together. It is just that the point is not worked up in the same way, and the telling is much less elaborate than *Our Tune* in terms of its participant roles. The absence of third-person narrator framing and focusing work, and the presence of the voice of the epistolary narrator through the use of first-person narration, results in a mediated telling that is arguably less explicitly oriented to its audience than *Our Tune*. However, although it might not quite warrant the status gained by *Our Tune*, which allegedly became the chosen listening and focal point for a morning break in a factory or office, *Love Letters* nevertheless proved very popular and successfully boosted Heart FM's ratings at the time.[3]

'Tons of people getting in touch . . .'

In a more recent realisation, we find another reshaping of the original *Our Tune* format in DJ Jo Whiley's morning show broadcast on BBC Radio 1 from 2001 to 2009. Like Williams, Whiley takes on the role of first-person narrator, but she addresses the story protagonist as a ratified listener directly, by their first name, and, as we will see, the listening audience is accorded a much more active participant role through Whiley's integration of text messages and web-based media. Here, following, is the opening sequence to one of the *Changing Tracks* stories narrated by Whiley: with music playing in the background, and long pauses that break up the narrative into discrete 'idea units' (Chafe 1980), the story develops as a tale of rehab, recovery and relapse. Kev meets 'the love of his life', gets married, but then returns to the drugs and everything falls apart until he hears his life-changing track and pulls himself together.

Extract 4.xi: 'Kev in Taunton' (1), *Changing Tracks*, Jo Whiley

1. >Let's do this?<
2. it's Changing Tracks and today's story (.)
3. is from Kev in Taunton (.) morning to you Kev (1.0)
4. when I was fourteen I::: (.) got into drugs (1.0)
5. I thought I was fine living my life to the extreme (.)
6. but when I was twenty-one my lifestyle caught up with me (1.0)
7. I couldn't think clearly a:nd my work and my home life suffered
8. (1.0)
9. by the age of twenty-two I'd lost my job (.) and I was homeless::

10. (1.0)
11. after six months. of living on the streets I was admitted <u>to</u> hospital
12. and I was diagnosed with psychosis.
13. my family tried to help (.) <u>but</u> I just kept going back to drugs (1.0)
14. over the next three years I went in and out of rehab and from job
15. to job (1.0) my friends and close family helped a lot
16. but drugs were my <u>own</u> worst enemy

After her greeting (line 3) to 'Kev in Taunton', which works to position him as a real person as she addresses him directly by name and thus bypasses any question of anonymity, Whiley shifts immediately into the animating role of narrator. Like Williams, she adopts the role of first-person storyteller. However, she does nothing to distance her voice as narrator from that of the epistolary narrator. There is no explicit reference to the voice of the protagonist as 'author' through the use of reporting verb 'says X', as we hear in *Love Letters*, and the evaluations are delivered as unattributed, unmitigated self-evaluations:

> when I was twenty-one my lifestyle caught up with me (line 6)
> drugs were my own worst enemy (line 16)

In the extract below, we see the narrative resolution in line 34 – being forgiven and taken back – and the coda in line 35, followed by an explicit moral point, which, like *Our Tune* narratives, is expressed through a set of clichés or generic maxims, but as part of the first-person narration:

Extract 4.xii: 'Kev in Taunton' (2), *Changing Tracks*, Jo Whiley

29. weeks later I was in a coffee shop (1.0)
30. and my changing track was playing (1.0)
31. immediately .hh I realised how stupid I'd been (.)
32. and I hoped that if I begged for forgiveness
33. I might be able to save the best thing I ever had (2.0)
34. fortunately my partner took me back (.) and two years on (.)
35. I've got a >beautiful baby boy< and we're <u>rea:</u>lly happy (.)
36. I learnt the hard way (.) but I'm just thankful to have two people
37. in my life that I love more than drugs (.) and myself
38. and I would give up <u>anything</u> for them (2.0)
39. this is Kev's changing track

After the coda in line 35, 'I've got a beautiful baby boy and we're really happy', the story is rounded off with a series of generic statements: 'I learnt the hard way', 'I'm just thankful' and 'I would give up anything for them'.

These, like Bates' use of generic maxims, reinforce the point of the story as a lesson in getting through addiction and dereliction to a place of socially valued family life, and, of course, the power of love to achieve that state. Echoes of *Our Tune* again abound – the telling may have changed, but the tale remains the same.

On the other hand, where we do find a significant difference between the previous two narrative frameworks and *Changing Tracks* is the opening up of active recipiency to listeners once the story is over and the special track has been played. First of all, Whiley herself provides an assessment of the song in line 40 (see Extract 4.xiii, below), then shifts into an empathetic orientation to the audience in lines 44–46 ('you're . . . thinking . . . please turn out alright'), and then she again directly addresses Kev as a listener himself in line 47. She then, from line 49, starts to read out listener responses:

Extract 4.xiii: 'Kev in Taunton' (3), *Changing Tracks*, Jo Whiley

40.   wonderful wonderful song (.) it's Snow Patrol .hh and Set the Fire
41.   to the Third Bar and that is Kev's changing track
42.   it's one of those stories (.)
43.   where you're reading it or you're listening to it (.)
44.   and you're just thinking all the way through (.)
45.   please be good please
46.   >please turn out alright please turn out alright< and it has
47.   and Kev hopefully from here on in .hh um
48.   you'll just keep going in a straight line
49.   uh Pat in Islington (.) instant goo (.) instant goosebumps
50.   great song .hh I've been in the same situation myself
51.   Gary in Essex (.) life just gets better as you know keep smiling and
52.   good luck
53.   .hh Chris in Bolton just shows that love conquers everyone
54.   and everything great story Kev
55.   oh boy great song (.) good on you man that's from Richard in
56.   Stoke (.) now that is a changing track .hh glad you came through
57.   and all the best Michael Jennings from (Despera)
58.   ahh and from Stuart on the A14 near Kettering
59.   great changing track and well done pal all the best
60.   hh just tons of people getting in touch Kev (1.0)
61.   good luck to ya (1.0)
62.   hh thanks for choosing Snow Patrol as well
63.   I've loved that song

We can see here a series of story receipts in the form of appreciative assessments and encouragement from listeners across the nation. The specific medium for these story receipts – whether from calls, texts or posts to the Radio 1 website chat room – is not given, just the volume of response: 'tons of people getting in touch' (line 60). The familiar radio phone-in format of host introductions of callers by name and geographical location (Hutchby 1996) is reproduced here, followed by Whiley reading the incoming message as animator:

> Pat in Islington – instant goosebumps - great song
> Gary in Essex – life just gets better – keep on smiling
> Chris in Bolton – just shows that love conquers everyone and everything
> Stuart on the A14 near Kettering – great changing track – well done pal – all the best

What we find in *Changing Tracks* is that the integration of listener receipts produces a directional shift in empathetic orientation, which now flows back from the listening audience towards the protagonist, rather than from the host towards the listening audience. The integration of messages expressing encouragement and solidarity as well as appreciation of the chosen song opens up a new mediated participation framework in which the audience members become active story recipients rather than simply occupying the role of ratified hearers. It is interesting to note the presence of generic maxims contained in these listener responses, too, such as 'love conquers everything' (line 53) or 'life just gets better' (line 51).

To sum up, in contrast to the participation framework of *Our Tune* or *Love Songs*, the use of web-based and mobile technology in the storytellings of *Changing Tracks* opens up new interactive roles for listeners as participants in the narrative event. In these responses, we do find some of the same kind of empathetic discursive work that was previously done by Bates in his story evaluations, but organised through a very different kind of telling that foregrounds the voice of the epistolary narrator and minimises the evaluating role of the host narrator. The receipt of the story by its audience then becomes a process of empathetic alignment with the epistolary narrator and positive assessment of the story and the chosen track.

Another kind of response to the storytelling in *Changing Tracks* (as with *Our Tune* and *Love Letters* before it) is the question of whether or not these narratives are authentic, and the responses to them 'real'. These questions are discussed in web-based locations where a certain degree of listener scepticism is expressed regarding this new, interactive, participatory format, which, as I noted above, addresses, positions and constructs the 'author' and the responses to the story as 'real' people. The following comment is taken from a web-forum discussion of media content:[4]

I love Jo Whiley, but I've still never been convinced the texting and e-mailing part after the seven song shuffle or the changing tracks feature is that truthful.

If the programme producers can be suspected of 'faking it', then interactivity becomes more a matter of production style and performance than an actual shift in participant framework and recipiency. And, as Theo van Leeuwen notes, in an age where authenticity is constantly being called into question, it becomes more appropriate to ask not 'how authentic is this?' but 'who takes this as authentic and who does not?' (Van Leeuwen 2001: 396). This is clearly at stake for some Radio 1 listeners who take up a different kind of recipient role outside the mediated participatory space. Web-forum postings produce far more resistant and critical evaluations of these tellings as a performance, rather than the institutionally framed listener assessments of the tale, and I will return to a discussion of this relationship between authenticity, interactivity and the shifts in participant frameworks and roles for audiences as participants in subsequent chapters.

Summary: narrative, participation and performance

This chapter has provided an account of various contexts for the telling of personal experience stories in the broadcast media, with examples taken from a range of contextual environments for narrative discourse. From television talk shows to television courtrooms, I have examined how stories are designed and identified some of the features through which these narrative events are constituted as public performances. In particular, I have shown how these performances are achieved through context-specific participation frameworks for narrative activity, with specialised roles for hosts, tellers and recipients, both in the studio and in the listening or viewing audience. Finally, I examined a specific context for personal narrative discourse on radio: the mediated narration of someone else's personal experience story. Building on Montgomery's (1991) work on the generic discourse structure of *Our Tune*, we have seen how a similar narrative event was handled subsequently by other radio DJs, and the effect of their different narrative 'tellings' on the production of personal stories as public discourse. Whether these stories are elicited, semi-scripted or invoked by speakers who are engaged in another activity such as argument and debate, as we will see in the following chapter, narrative discourse is clearly centrally implicated in many forms of broadcast talk and interaction. The design of stories as performed narrative events is a result of their local, situated context of production: in other words, the footings and participation frameworks of the storytellings. In all three media contexts discussed here, I have argued that mediating narrative is a contextually sensitive discursive activity and that narratives are performed in structurally different ways, depending on the particular activity at hand. Furthermore, how that activity is accomplished has much less to do with participants being 'ordinary', and much more to do with their contextually relevant roles and identities as constituted in the narrative event. As we will see next, narrative also has a significant role to play as a discursive resource for the construction of arguments and participant stances in the context of media debates.

Notes

1 This programme was recorded just before the death of Princess Diana in Paris at the end of August 1997.
2 Edwina Currie was a member of the Thatcher government in the 1980s and a former health minister. She famously resigned her ministerial post over the salmonella in British eggs scandal in 1988, and, since then, has developed a career as a media personality and author.
3 Nigel Williams subsequently published a collection of the stories entitled *Love Letters Straight from the Heart: True Stories of Passion and Heartbreak* (Robson Books, 2003).
4 Jono (2007) 'Jo Whiley fakes seven-song shuffle', forum message to *Unofficial Mills*. Available at http://www.unofficialmills.co.uk/communities/showthread. php?7753-Jo-Whiley-fakes-seven-song-shuffle (accessed 9 March 2011).

5   Discourses of participation
Opinion and argument

Introduction: opinion-giving in the mediated public sphere

The main focus of this chapter will be the activities of opinion-giving and argument in two contexts for public participation – radio phone-in programmes and TV talk shows – both of which, in their different ways, invite opinions, comment and discussion from members of the public. In addition, I will also examine how digitally mediated participation is being integrated into these traditional genres of broadcasting that are built around opinion-giving and debate, taking a look at how web-based media were used by broadcasters in the course of the first prime ministerial debates on UK television in order to broaden public access and engagement, and the kind of impact this had on the ways that opinion-giving and arguing get done in that environment.

The broadcast media have long functioned as a site for the expression of both political and public opinions from many different quarters, and, as such, constitute an important arena of the contemporary 'public sphere' (Habermas 1989). There is a whole raft of programmes on both radio and television where an engagement with current issues – social and political – on local, national and international levels is the primary activity. News and current affairs programmes feature interviews in which politicians and public figures are invited to express their views on topical issues where contrasting (and often directly conflicting) stances are regularly elicited and presented as alternative perspectives on the same issue. Radio phone-ins and panel interviews with representatives of different political parties and organisational bodies frequently generate debate and arguments. At the height of talk show broadcasting in the late 1990s, programmes like *The Frost Programme* and *Kilroy* in the UK or *The Oprah Winfrey Show* and *The Sally Jessy Raphael Show* in the USA were considered, by some scholars, to form part of a contemporary public sphere where members of minority political and social groups were given access to the media and a voice that was not generally available to them in mainstream news and current affairs broadcasting (Carpignano et al. 1990; Livingstone and Lunt 1994; Tolson

2001). Nowadays, many of these audience discussion programmes have been superseded by the proliferation of reality, lifestyle and makeover programming, while, at the same time, the web now provides another arena of the public sphere in which opinions and arguments are being generated by 'netizens' in an unprecedented range of contexts, through blogs, web forum comments and posts and the use of social media such as Twitter.

The discursive activities of opinion-giving and argument are so closely intertwined in many media settings that it sometimes becomes difficult to separate the two. Greg Myers observes that many media interactions are indeed 'built around disagreements' (2004: 112); panel debates, talk shows and radio phone-ins, for example, are all contexts where the production of disagreement between participants, or between host and callers, is the main point of the programme. And, in order to disagree, there must be a difference of opinion. These are then programmes where the design and organisation of the interaction function precisely to enable space for the expression of differences of opinion and views. Furthermore, these views are not presented as separate, discrete objects, but are situated contextually and discursively; they are woven together to project alternative perspectives, to be for or against a position and, often, to be linked with social attributes, categories, or other relevant participant identities (see Fitzgerald and Housley 2002).

On radio phone-in programmes, this work of eliciting opinions in order to produce a discussion or argument is normally accomplished through the institutional role of the host, whose task it is to introduce topics and callers, invite callers to speak and manage transitions between them. It is also the task of the host to ensure relevance of callers' opinions and establish meaningful contrasts between the different views expressed. The business of the caller is to produce something that recognisably counts as an opinion on whatever issue happens to be the focus of debate. Similarly, in talk shows, it is the role of the host to elicit opinions and stances in order to generate discussion and oppositional points of view, and the role of the invited participants and audience members to establish such stances. There exists, then, a range of media contexts where the expression of opinions, and the ensuing debates and arguments that arise out of the expression of those opinions, are the staple business of the broadcast. In order to explore how this talk built around opinion-giving and argument is locally designed and organised in mediated settings, for the purpose of comparison, it will be useful to introduce some aspects of elicited opinion-giving and argument in two other, non-mediated interactional contexts: a research interview (analysed by Billig 1991) and a focus group discussion (analysed by Myers 2004).

Opinions, views and 'sociable' arguments

Opinions differ, and expressing strong views is likely to generate opposition and argument in many discursive contexts. Michael Billig makes two important points when he notes that 'what can be assumed is that, the more unpopular a view, the more argumentative possibilities exist whenever that view is aired, and the more unpopular it is, the stronger the opposition it is likely to encounter whenever it is publicly aired', and that 'the holding of views cannot take place outside of a general rhetorical context' (Billig 1991: 188). Whether this context is conversational or institutional, opinion-giving is a situated action that is collaboratively accomplished by participants in the talk event. In many conversational contexts, it has generally been assumed by discourse analysts that speakers tend to avoid argument and disagreement, and that, when disagreement does occur, it will be hedged or mitigated in some way. For example, in some contexts, differences of opinion can be seen as constituting a threat to face (Brown and Levinson 1987), and there is thus a tendency for a preference for agreement between speakers. Conversational disagreement is often marked as dispreferred through the use of mitigating strategies in turns that, in one way or another, display a different perspective to the prior turn (Pomerantz 1984). But, as Deborah Schiffrin has observed (1984, 1990), what she calls 'sociable argument' can take place among friends and family members without necessarily constituting a threat to solidarity or intimacy between them. Harvey Sacks also noted that one way to get people involved in talk is to have an argument, and that sometimes, contingent on who the participants are, argument can be used 'as a technique for generating happy conversations' (Sacks 1995: 707). This technique depends on the readiness of speakers to engage in the expression of different views and opinions, rather than to avoid doing so.

Similarly, through his analysis of a discussion about the British monarchy, recorded in an interview with a family in which the father was known as holding 'strong views' on the topic, Billig argues that disagreement is maintained as an activity by the participants rather than curtailed. In the following extract, he illustrates how the discussion develops between different participants' views, with the mother moving from a position of agreement with the father to a different, opposing view in the space of a few turns at talk:

Extract 5.i: 'Royals coming to Derby'

1.	MOTHER:	if, if they just had Buckingham Palace
2.		and they didn't have Windsor Castle
3.	DAUGHTER:	yes
4.	MOTHER:	and Balmoral
5.	DAUGHTER:	yes
6.	MOTHER:	and all those, and all the servants that have to be
7.		looking after those big places=
8.	DAUGHTER:	=that they don't really need=

9.	MOTHER:	=that are only lived in for a certain amount of time
10.		of year to me the money that they need would be
11.		cut by a third, I think=
12.	FATHER:	=it is it's only a tip of the iceberg, this is,
13.		you know when you're talking about just the royals,
14.		because every time they go somewhere, it's the count,
15.		every time, you say=
16.	MOTHER:	=yeah, well fair enough if=
17.	FATHER:	=every time, say they come into Derby
18.	MOTHER:	yes
19.	FATHER:	to see or something like that, the whole of the place
20.		it'll be cleaned from top to bottom, it'll cost thousands
21.		and thousands and they'll deck the whole place and=
22.	SON:	=security and things
23.	MOTHER:	yes, yes but don't you think that probably those
24.	FATHER:	not . . . paying wages=
25.	MOTHER:	=don't you think those probably need doing anyway
26.		and then it just puts the ideas of the people
27.		that are going to be there=
28.	FATHER:	=ha ha, I'd rather put a few more beds in the hospital,
29.		than sweep the streets for two days
30.	MOTHER:	yes, I would, yeah, but I still maintain that if they got
31.		rid of all the different places that they do live=
32.	DAUGHTER:	=yeah
33.	MOTHER:	I mean, they could go to some big house and take it
34.		over, for a hotel or whatever for a weekend
35.		or whatever, at a lot less cost than keeping
36.		all those other houses going

(Transcript from Billig 1991: 180)

Having expressed her own views at the start of this sequence (lines 1–11), the mother produces agreement tokens in lines 16 and 18, seeming to align with the father. Then she produces a different view in line 23 with her turn starting 'yes, yes but don't you think . . .' and pursues her own point after another turn initial agreement followed by a return to her initial opinion in line 30 'yes, I would, yeah, but I still maintain . . .' Without this maintenance of different points of view, the discussion as an activity could not take place.

Since this stretch of talk was generated as part of an interview in which the family had been asked to give their views on a specific topic, it is not naturally occurring conversational data in so far as it was produced in a particular context for a particular research purpose. In fact, some of the features of this interaction are very similar to those identified by Myers (2004) in his analysis of focus group discussions, another discourse context where disagreement, or, at least, the expression of differences in opinion, is deliberately encouraged by the moderator. Myers points out that:

> [T]he observation of preferred (agreement) and dispreferred (disagreement) second turns does not imply that people will always agree, but that, when there is disagreement, it will typically be delayed, or will be presented in the form of weak agreement followed by disagreement, or will have markers of dispreferred turns, hedges, questions, concessions, attributions, and devices of repair.
>
> (2004: 119)

The next extract, taken from Myers' analysis of a focus group discussion about the nuclear power industry, contains an example of the way speakers use concessions (e.g., 'no . . . but', 'yes . . . but', 'I know . . . but') to preface their disagreement, which is similar to the mother's turn design in Extract 5.i above:

Extract 5.ii: 'Nuclear power'

1.	F:	I think they don't ad<u>mit</u> that the when /
2.	M:	/they
3.		they
4.	F:	they've <u>had</u> problems . they seem to / . they
5.		do cover them <u>up</u>
6.	M:	/no they
7.		don't like to admit <u>little</u> problems when they
8.		know they'll be blown up into <u>big</u> ones/
9.	F:	/you
10.		know like the the
11.	M:	but on the <u>other</u> hand I'm not saying that
12.		/ (xxx)
13.	F:	/like the houses where the dust was very <u>high</u>
14.		in radioactivity . . .

(Transcript from Myers 2004: 121)

In this extract, in line 6, participant M first seems to align with participant F, and, as Myers shows, he expresses his understanding of the prior turn by expanding on what F has just said. But, in line 11, M comes back in with a concession, 'but on the other hand', indicating that he is about to express a different view from that held by F. So, the pattern of a weak agreement followed by a disagreement works as an interactional means of maintaining argument, in the sense of expressing different opinions, in both the contexts of the research interview as well as in the focus group discussion.

Opinions and identities

The relationship between the context for the talk event, on the one hand, and the identity and participant role of those people involved in the event, on the other, is another fundamental aspect of how the expression of opinions and views is framed, designed and received as an activity. For example, regarding the family discussion about the monarchy, Billig argues that the father was already seen as 'a holder of strong views' by other family members, and the mother's mitigated disagreement turns seem designed as an interactional resource to avoid agreeing with 'a holder of strong views', rather than as a reluctance to disagree (Billig 1991: 179). On the other hand, in the focus group discussions, the participants are constructed as 'bearers of representative views': 'that is how they are addressed in the moderator's introduction and that is how they treat each other's contributions' (Myers 2004: 130). The way that opinions are constructed and responded to is therefore inextricably tied to the social and discursive context in which they are produced, and the participants' collaborative understandings of the kind of activity that is going on and their role within that activity. The rhetorical context of opinion-giving, and its relationship to the talk event, is thus absolutely fundamental to the kind of responses that are made to the expression of controversial views.[1]

Opinions on-air

Opinions and arguments that occur in the broadcast media are similarly shaped by that contextual setting. The identity of the participants, as well as their institutional role, plays a significant part in how opinions are elicited and situated within any given mediated framework. But having an identity is by no means a straightforward, taken-for-granted matter for lay speakers who participate in mediated interaction, as we will see. For example, in *vox pop* interviews in television news reports, Myers has noted that members of the public are often treated by the interviewer not as holders of individual opinions, but as representatives of the opinions of a given social category. So, he suggests, the real question is not '"what do you say" but what does "someone like you say" – and it is the interviewee's job to figure out what "someone like you" means in this case' (2004: 209). In the following extract, taken from BBC news coverage of the US election in 2000, Myers argues that the 'voter' interviewed is not questioned as a voter per se, but as an observer and expert on Black voters:

Extract 5.iii: 'Have you voted today?'

1. MC: tell me sir have you voted today
2. IE1: yes I have
3. MC: who for (1)

    4. IE1:   Gore and . Clinton? Ms . Hillary Clinton?
    5. MC: and is is Al Gore as popular among . <u>black</u> voters around
    6.   here as Bill Clinton was?
    7.   (3)
    8. IE1:   I would think so . yeah
    9. MC: you think as many of them will come out
  10. IE1:   yeah they'll come out .
  11.   they'll show a little later on=
  12. MC: =d'you
  13. IE1:   =before the polls <u>close</u>
  14.   tonight
  15. MC: do you think perhaps um . Al Gore should have made
  16.   a little bit <u>more</u> of Bill Clinton . . .

                    (Transcript adapted from Myers 2004: 214)

The role attributed to the interviewee by the interviewer is not one that is immediately oriented to by the interviewee. As Myers shows in his analysis, the response to the interviewer's question in line 5 is strongly marked by the delay of three seconds, but also by the facial expression of the interviewee, described as 'a kind of wry wince' (2004: 214), and by the mitigated design of his response turn, 'I would think so . yeah'. Here, the agreement 'yeah' is in post position, but, in line 10, he shifts the 'yeah' into a declarative turn-initial position, 'yeah they'll come out', thereby effecting a transition in his role from individual opinion-giver to the expression of a more certain stance in his contextually constructed role as 'expert on Black voters'. In fact, in all of the BBC news reports of the US election he analysed, Myers found that the interviewees were routinely categorised by the fact of where they were located, as in the example above where the interview took place in Harlem.

Furthermore, in *vox pop* interviews, opinions are often presented and categorised as dichotomous oppositions. Asking members of the public for their opinion can provide for the voicing and expression of opposing views, while both the neutralism of the broadcaster and institutional balance (in public service broadcasting in particular) are seen to be maintained. For example, in the following BBC news report dealing with climate change and the use of low-energy light bulbs in Britain, the reporter claims he cannot tell the difference between the old and the new bulbs, while *vox pops* are used to represent two conflicting views – either they are just as good as old high-energy bulbs, or they are not:

Extract 5.iv: 'Climate change', BBC News, 7 March 2009

    1. REP: So very soon we could all be made to change our light
    2.   bulbs but there is a bit of a problem with that
    3.   The German leader Angela Merkel says she has got the
    4.   new star lights in her home as I am putting in here

5.		But when she drops something on the floor, she can not
6		always find it because it is so dim
7.		So ((inserting light bulb)) let us just get that in.
8.		And see the difference.
9.		New light. Old light.
10.		Well, I can not spot the difference. But what do people
11.		in this market in Leeds think about the switch?
12.	VOX 1:	I find them a lot better, they last a lot longer.
13.		They are a lot brighter as well.
14.	VOX 2:	We have used them for ten years.
15.		And I think we have changed one in ten years.
16.	VOX 3:	I find that they are very, very weak.
17.		You know they take some time to light up.
18.		So they are not instant. So it takes some getting
19.		used to them.

The reporter 'tests' the lights (line 7), takes a neutral stance claiming 'I can not spot the difference' (line 10), then the report switches to the views of people in the 'Leeds market' who can. The *vox pop* is thus used to represent the conflicting opinions of British consumers as they are doing their shopping, and provides a way of what John Hartley (1982) termed 'realising' the story, which is that there is 'a bit of a problem' (line 2) in taking the old bulbs off the market if the new ones don't give enough light.

To return to the point that particular opinions seem to be routinely associated with corresponding identity categories, Myers concludes that 'the category of the public is constructed not by enumerating the opinions of individual members of the population, but by packaging a series of interactions that can be seen as suggesting different categories' (2004: 220). As we will now see, this kind of packaging can also be observed at work in radio phone-in interactions where the relationship between social identities and recognisable categories of opinions is routinely attended to in the talk between hosts and callers.

In their work on calls to radio phone-in programmes, Richard Fitzgerald and William Housley (2002) specifically address this relationship between categories of speaker identity and categories of opinion, using Sacks' concept of membership categorisation analysis (1995 1: 244–245) to explore the sequential relevance of opinion-giving and identity in calls, and the different role relationships at stake for participants. As well as occupying the institutionally relevant categories of host and caller, callers to radio phone-in programmes also occupy the role of 'opinion giver'; which is to say, using Billig's (1991) term, callers are 'holders of views' who will have something to say on the topic under discussion. Hosts assume that 'within any particular call, the opinion advanced within that call will indicate implicitly, or more often explicitly, the position of the caller on the topic at hand' (Fitzgerald and Housley 2002: 592). What is more, the absence of an identifiable opinion in relation to the topic constitutes a problem for hosts, who will attempt to place callers on one side of the debate or the other. We can see this in the following example, taken from a phone-in discussion on lowering the age of consent for homosexuals:

Extract 5.v: 'The word gay'

1. CALLER: yes but the word gay gives a wrong colour altogether for
2.   the life I'm talking about () that's the unfortunate part
3. HOST: you you..don't. you don't like homosexuality?
4. CALLER: I didn't say that
5. HOST: arh:: () well then why do you object to the use of this
6.   this=

(Extract from Fitzgerald and Housley 2002: 595)

In this extract, the host has some trouble situating the caller in relation to the debate, and his question in line 3 is an attempt to establish explicitly whether the caller is anti-homosexual (and therefore will be against the lowering of the age of consent) based on his stated dislike of the word 'gay'. As Fitzgerald and Housley (2002) show in their analysis of this call, there are two significant points to note: first, that the caller has not made their position explicit in relation to the debate, which poses a problem for the host, and, second, that, in order to resolve this problem, the host attempts to attribute an opinion category to this caller, based on an assumption that someone who dislikes the use of the word 'gay' to refer to homosexuals will be against homosexuality. Thus, 'displaying and utilising an opinion category on a particular topic' (Fitzgerald and Housley 2002: 596) is a crucial action for callers to phone-in programmes, since it is the production of an opinion that enables the host to maintain the flow of the calls and the ongoing construction of the debate. Fitzgerald and Housley argue that, within these overarching identity categories of 'caller' and 'opinion-giver', the opinions that callers produce, as with the *vox pop* interviews above, will locate them on one side of the debate or the other. Furthermore, the opinion given by the caller 'is heard as a predicate of their personal identity' (2002: 592) in so far as categories of social or personal identity will generate a particular stance on the issue under discussion, as assumed by the host in relation to the word 'gay' in the above extract.

It also seems to be the case that a similar set of categorical assumptions is at work in public opinion-giving in focus groups, in so far as 'opinions are taken to go with social interests . . . and individual experience . . . that they are imagined in opposing pairs . . . or they are on a continuum' (Myers 2004: 133). Participants in focus groups tend to be attributed opinions that are for or against an issue according to their social identities. But, as Myers points out, this is an assumption that the participants themselves resist because they resent the idea that their own opinions can be taken for granted, '"read off", as it were, from their identity' (Myers 2004: 133). So, although there is a general tendency by phone-in hosts and focus group moderators to assume that certain categories of people will hold particular kinds of opinions, like the caller in Extract 5.v above, focus group participants see their opinions as much more fluidly negotiated and mitigated within the talk: 'Other people may have fixed opinions because of where they live or what they do for a living or how old they are, but *we* talking right now, are open to see what happens in the next turn' (Myers 2004: 133). However, in calls to radio phone-in programmes, there is much less space for this kind of negotiated opinion-giving between host and caller. Instead, what seems to be required is the production of a clear and identifiable stance, for callers to be explicitly either for or against a particular issue, in order for the host to construct an argument that has demonstrably two sides to it, and to develop the debate around these dichotomies of 'for' and 'against'. Let's now look at the resources that callers use in order to produce such stances.

Opinion warrants: 'grounding' and 'witnessing'

As already discussed in Chapter 2, one very significant aspect of the relationship between opinion-giving and social identity in radio phone-ins and TV talk show debates is the contextual identity that callers and speakers claim for themselves in relation to the topic at hand. While expert guests on these broadcasts are identified by name and professional status by the host, which warrants their contribution as one of 'expertise' on a given matter, lay participants are not. However, opinions do not just appear out of nowhere, and lay opinions are generally not randomly offered. Participants do a considerable amount of work – what I have called the discursive grounding of their identity as a participant in the debate – to establish a relevant identity category in relation to what it is that they have to say (Thornborrow 2001b). This difference between expert and lay identity attribution is illustrated in the next two short extracts, both taken from *The Frost Programme* (1997) where the topic is begging on the streets of London:

Extract 5.vi: 'Begging in London' (1), *The Frost Programme*

1. HOST: John Bird who's the- you're the editor of The Big Issue (.)
2.   you've been hearing these two points of view (.)
3.   which stri-what strikes you (.) so far

Extract 5.vii: 'Begging in London' (2), *The Frost Programme*

1. HOST: man over there (.) yes sir you wanted to speak
2. MAN: well I'm on benefits (.) an' I live in a shed (.)

3.   I'd like to see him live on- on what <u>we</u> live on

As we can see here, the host, in Extract 5.vi, both names John Bird and identifies his professional status as 'editor of *The Big Issue*'.[2] As such, he is asked for his professional opinion as an 'expert' on the problems of homelessness and begging. The lay participant in Extract 5.vii addressed by the host as 'man over there' quickly establishes a relevant participatory status for himself as soon as he is brought into the interactional frame. This involves a shift in footing from member of the audience to current speaker with an opinion to give, and he does this by referencing first his own status as a 'beggar' before he proceeds to offer his opinion on the topic at hand (that people should be able to live on state welfare benefits). In so doing, he establishes his relevant public identity on this occasion, speaking not just as a 'holder of views' about begging, but as someone who has firsthand experience of the matter being discussed and therefore legitimately speaks from that identity category.

In the next two examples, one from a TV talk show and the other from a radio phone-in, we can see further evidence of how callers routinely ground their opinion-giving by providing a topic-relevant identity as a warrant for holding that opinion:

Extract 5.viii: 'Should women box?', *Esther*, 1997

1. HOST: the lady back here (.) what do you say
2. WOMAN: um I'm a (Thai) boxer I've been Thai boxing
3.   and kick boxing for ten years (.)
4.   believe me I'm a hundred per cent woman

Extract 5.ix: Gordon Brown, *Election Call*, BBC Radio 4, 2010

1. GB: Gordon Brown here nice to talk to you
2. CALLER: he- hello Mr Brown.
3. GB: [good to talk to you
4. CALLER: [u::m I'd just like to ask you uh I'm an owner driver
5.   I drive a truck for a living I own a truck (.) um (.)
6.   the fuel duty increases that we increasingly get every year
7.   we've got a three pence uh per litre increase this year
8.   um that's a real cost to me of thirty pounds a week
9.   >fifteen hundred pounds< a yea:r uh
10.   we're never told (.) why these increases are necessary
11.   uh we're never told <u>where</u> the extra revenue <u>goes</u>
12.   I don't know how many trucks are on the road um but
13.   if it's costing me I average about a thousand litres a week

14.	in fuel <u>used</u> (.) so if it's costing me (.) one and a half
15.	thousand pounds a year u::m that's an awful lot of money
16.	uh we don't ever get to find out the general public
17.	uh where this money goes

Here, again, in turn-initial position, the participants in each extract produce a contextually relevant identity *before* they go on to give their opinion. Thus, the speaker in Extract 5.viii implies that, as a woman boxer, she is *for* women boxing. The point of view of the caller in Extract 5.ix is given after he has established his own identity category as an owner/truck driver, and after he has provided a highly detailed account of his experience as a member of that category. His point, reframed as relevant to himself and the general public with a shift from 'I' to 'we'(lines 10–11), about paying so much tax without knowing what the money is used for, is thus strongly grounded through his own personal identity and experience.

I have already suggested that callers do this identity work right at the beginning of their turns in order to legitimise, or authenticate, their identity as someone who speaks from their experience of the particular problem, or who has knowledge of the issue under discussion. That identity and knowledge provide a warrant for the opinion that they hold. In other words, whereas the host warrants the participation of experts, lay speakers do their own warranting, and, as I argued in Chapter 2, these callers are not simply participating as ordinary members of the public, they are members of the public who display their particular situated expertise in relation to the issue being discussed.

A similar resource used by lay participants to construct a warrant for the views they hold is through the discursive device of 'witnessing' (Hutchby 2001a). In an analysis of calls to radio phone-in programmes, Hutchby found that lay speakers 'offer grounds for their remarks, observations and opinions to be considered legitimate, true or authentic' (2001a: 484). Examples of such witnessing devices include the following declarative statements made by callers to a radio phone-in:

I was actually at the student demonstration yesterday
We've got a real problem here with dogs fouling our footway
I have got three appeals letters here this week, all asking for donations
I'm a pensioner myself of seventy-two

These devices all function to justify the caller's contribution and to claim 'authentic speakership in a public discursive arena' (Hutchby 2001a: 484). Through these devices, callers can display firsthand knowledge of the topic they are calling about, either through perceptual access to events (e.g., 'I actually saw X') or through claiming membership of a social category on behalf of which they are speaking (e.g., 'I'm a pensioner myself'). This orientation to witnessing as a routine feature of the production of lay opinions in public participation broadcasts is also displayed by hosts, who sometimes ask callers for evidence of their firsthand experience or knowledge if it has not been provided, as in the following example:

Extract 5.x: 'Food hygiene practices'

```
 1. HOST:    I mean have you had personal experience [of the wa: ]y=
 2. CALLER:  [yes I have]
 3. HOST:    =some of this food is now served up [becuz] uh .h I=
 4. CALLER:  [ I:- ]
 5. HOST:    = think in fact it's w- it's one o'the most
 6.          importa[nt] issue:es, .hh that we currently, don't,=
 7. CALLER:  [yes]
 8. HOST:    =take enough, notice o:f.=
 9. CALLER:  =yes.=.h now this in in- actually in: the borough of
10.          Southwark loads of places an' I have been to numerous
11.          ones an' once I've seen it happening I don't go back.
12.          .hh now I've seen people picking up chopped meat, (.)
                                    (Transcript from Hutchby 2001a: 490)
```

In this extract, the host explicitly asks the caller for their 'witness status', which the caller readily supplies with an affirmative 'yes' in line 2 (before the host has finished his question turn) and then in their next extended turn (lines 9–12), where they provide evidence for that status: 'I have seen it happening'. A similar request from the host for witness status can also be seen in the next example, where the caller is invited to give their own personal experience of the problem under discussion:

Extract 5.xi: 'Pensions'

```
 1. HOST:    Have you found this?
 2.          (0.5)
 3. HOST:    have- has y[our pen-[has your pension allowance bin cut?]
 4. CALLER:  [ye:s, [ye:s, uh they've taken]
 5.          two pound- uh two pound sixty out of my money.
                                    (Transcript from Hutchby 2001a: 491)
```

Here, again, we can see the caller supplying affirmative answers to the host's question in line 4, then providing personal experience as evidence, in line 5, that £2.60 has been taken from their pension. Both callers and hosts then display an orientation to the relevance of witnessing as a key aspect of caller identity in relation to public opinion-giving, not just as an individual, but as someone who is knowledgeable, through firsthand experience, about a particular topic or issue.

From this overview of data taken from a range of studies of opinion-giving as an interactional activity in radio phone-ins and TV talk shows, it emerges quite clearly that lay participants are not particularly concerned with establishing ordinariness; rather, they are concerned to establish relevant, authentic and knowledgeable identities for themselves through such discursive devices as grounding and witnessing when they are giving their opinions on air. While experts are attributed relevant identities in relation to the topic by hosts, lay speakers work discursively to establish their own relevant participant identities, and to construct a position of situated expertise from which to produce a point of view and give an opinion. However, this is only part of the story, as the production of an opinion in and of itself does not make an argument. The way that opinion-giving contributes to making arguments is the focus of the next section, where we turn to the kind of discursive work involved in generating arguments on-air, and the interface between opinions and arguments within the context of public participation broadcasting.

Arguments on-air

In conversation, arguments rarely just 'happen'. When they do, the people involved in them often remark afterwards on how unexpected the argument was, with comments like 'I don't know where that came from' or 'I don't know what started it'. But something usually does. There has been a considerable amount of work undertaken within the field of conversation analysis and interactional sociolinguistics on argument and interaction in various social contexts that focuses on the way that arguments start, proceed and end. 'Arguable actions' (Maynard 1985) can either be explicitly oriented to as triggering a dispute – as in Schiffrin's analysis of family arguments, 'Oh you: want to start a fight here' (1990: 253) – or treated as arguable matters through opposition by another party. As interactions, arguments are typically built around 'assertion/counter' pairs (Coulter 1990), or, more broadly, 'action/opposition' sequences (Hutchby 1996).

Furthermore, although people often talk about having 'won' or 'lost' an argument, one significant finding in studies of conflict talk and conversational argument is that often disputes do not get resolved, but can end in various ways depending on the context in which they occur. Some arguments are built to last, as Marjorie Goodwin found in her study of a community of schoolchildren in Philadelphia: 'Maple Street children, as well as other children observed in multiparty settings [. . .] display an orientation toward sustaining and promoting rather than dissipating dispute' (1990: 143). On the other hand, in the context of family disputes and arguments, various strategies, such as withdrawal, can be used to terminate a conflict (Vuchinich

1990), or with one of the parties physically walking out on the other (Dersley and Wootton 2001).

To return to the context of the media, we find that the end of an argument rarely entails winning or losing. For example, in his study of confrontational interaction on talk radio, Hutchby (1996) has shown that arguments between hosts and callers can be ended in different ways by the host, but that endings do not necessarily constitute agreement or alignment between participants. In TV and radio news interviews, conflicts between speakers are usually ended by the interviewer without a resolution or consensus ever being reached (Clayman and Heritage 2002). Arguments on talk shows similarly do not get resolved, but they do have to be made to progress over the course of the programme, and, as we will see, hosts have various strategies available to them in order to accomplish this argumentative progression.

As noted earlier, the activities of opinion-giving and argument are very closely entwined in media contexts that are built around generating discussion and debate. The notion of argument as a form of entertainment, as in the context of social occasions for the kind of 'happy conversations' described by Sacks (1995), can also be related to media genres where the objective is to produce lively talk between participants expressing a variety of opinions and contrasting views, talk that is mediated by a host and designed for a listening or viewing audience. An example of this kind of 'liveliness', as Andrew Tolson (2006: 11) defines it, can be seen in the following extract, which is the opening exchange from a call to the radio phone-in series, BBC Radio 4's *Election Call*, broadcast in 2010.[3] In this programme, callers were invited to put their points and questions to Gordon Brown, the outgoing prime minister at the time. The host is Martha Kearney, and this call occurs about half an hour into the broadcast. The caller's topic is the proposed regulation of MPs' expenses, an issue that had caused considerable public outrage the previous year, when leaked MPs' expenses claims were published by the *Daily Telegraph* newspaper:

Extract 5.xii(a): Gordon Brown, 'MPs' expenses', *Election Call*, BBC Radio 4, 2010

```
 1. MK:      Robert Hanna now who's calling from (.) Glasgow
 2. CALLER:  good afternoon
 3. GB:      good afternoon Robert
 4. CALLER:  my point is um that we've all just lived through
 5.          the MPs' expenses scandal (.) um the two reports
 6.          to look into this and recover the one point two
 7.          million involved it cost about one million pounds
 8.          to do so I believe but (.) what I'm staggered by is that
 9.          your government has now moved on from this
10.          to create yet another quango which costs (.)
11.          six and a half billion pounds a year and eighty
```

12.		people (.) to monitor (.) MPs' expenses (.) I don't know
13.		how you can <u>jus</u>tify that
14.	GB:	what we had to do Robert was end a system of
15.		self regulation what used to happen for centuries
16.		basically was that MPs used to agree amongst themselves
17.		what to do it wasn't even a matter for the government
18.		it was a matter for the MPs in the [house of commons
19.	CALLER:	[yeah but I'm sorry
20.		for cutting across you but why do you need
21.		six and a half
22.		million [pounds and eighty people. [that's one person =
23.	GB:	[because- [bu-
24.	CALLER:	=for each eight MPs' expenses [that is utterly] ludicrous
25.	GB:	[but hold on]
26.	GB:	but hold on I- what we've had to do is move from self regulation
27.		so that is unacceptable you agree with me [quite wrong
28.	CALLER:	[well (xxx) if it works
29.	GB:	well you would agree with me it's quite wrong for MPs
30.		to abuse the system because there's no proper way of
31.		regulating them [and self regulat-
32.	CALLER:	[well I agree with you that MPs shouldn't
33.		do that [but I don't anybody was] tremendously surprised
34.	GB:	[well self regulat-]
35.	CALLER:	quite frankly
36.	GB:	look I was [shocked]
37.	Caller:	[I wasn't specially shocked but –

In many ways, this call exhibits exactly the kind of lively debate that programme editors aim for: a well-informed caller who takes issue with the guest politician without host intervention. It is also unusual, in so far as the caller here is one of the few who does not establish a relevant individual identity in his opening turn (line 4). However, he does frame this initial turn with 'my point is', and then invokes the category of people who have 'all just lived through the MPs' expenses scandal', which locates his contribution as speaking on behalf of the general voting public as a context for his upcoming point, a strong challenging statement: 'I don't know how you can justify that' (lines 12–13). The talk that follows is notably free of host mediation as the caller and GB engage directly with each other.

How does this occur? First, the caller's extended opening turn is designed to make a clear and well-structured point. He initially provides background information on the topic, which he then follows with an emphatically marked opinion-framing device, the syntactically 'wh'-cleft structure in line 8: 'what I'm staggered by is. . .'. This explicitly positions him as someone with strong views on the subject and as critical of the action taken by Gordon Brown's government – 'yet another quango' (lines 9–12) – and, as I just noted, the final component of this turn is a direct challenge addressed to GB: 'I don't know how you can justify that'. Further, the framing of this final turn construction unit as a marked challenge rather than as a question (i.e., 'can you?' or 'how can you?') carries the inference that such an action cannot, in fact, be justified. GB begins his response to that challenge in line 14, 'what we had to do Robert was . . .', using first-name address and another syntactically marked cleft structure to frame the justification he is about to give. I will return to the significance of these forms shortly.

If we compare the design of this opening turn to those given in Extracts 5.viii and 5.ix above, we can see some clear differences. Whereas the caller in Extract 5.viii framed their question *as* a question, and the caller in Extract 5.ix never really arrived at a well-formulated question at all, but made a series of statements about their views on the level of tax being paid by lorry drivers, here we have a clear turn-final challenge. This strongly critical position is maintained by the caller in Extract 5.xii(a) as he interrupts GB in line 19, with another question and strong opinion statement: 'why do you need six and a half million pounds and eighty people that's one person for each eight MPs' expenses that is utterly ludicrous'. What happens from there onwards is a series of assertion/counter pairs, with GB and the caller each taking much shorter turns as they interrupt each other, talk in overlap and disagree. From line 19 onwards, after the caller's interruption, they also both start to preface their turns with dispreferred next-turn markers such as 'well', 'but' and 'look'. As Billig notes, 'in arguments, one does not merely state a position, but typically one argues for the superiority of one's own position over that of the rival position' (1991: 171–172), and that is precisely what we see happening here: argumentative talk with both parties defending their views.

So, how does this argument end? We re-join the call at the point where GB is responding to the caller's prior turn, which ends with another challenging question (line 54):

Extract 5.xii(b): *Election Call* 2010, Gordon Brown, 'MPs' expenses'

```
54. CALLER:   [–] so what what are you checking=
55. GB:                                    =Robert I don't
56.           want to have to spend money monitoring MPs
57.           but the system of self regulation failed
58.           and a lot of MPs did things that they should never
59.           have done and it was completely unacceptable
60.           you cannot then allow MPs to regulate themselves
61.           so you've got to bring in a statutory regulation
62.           authority=[and that's what we're now doing monitoring=
63. MK:                [yeah
```

64.	GB:	=MPs' expenses getting transparency throughout
65.		preventing anything like what happened happening again
66.		and I think you would agree with me we do not want
67.		to see what we saw with MPs [making mistakes and=
68.	MK:	[mm-
69.	GB:	=and abusing the system.
70.	MK:	Robert. thank you very much indeed

For the second time in this call, GB addresses the caller by his first name, 'Robert'. In his study of the use of first-name address terms in news interviews, Steven Clayman (2010) found that one of the functions of addressing another participant by their first name is to signal some form of upcoming disalignment with the content of that speaker's prior turn. It is therefore not surprising that, at this point in the call, GB begins his turn with 'Robert' (line 55), then strongly restates his own view (lines 60–61). He marks his continued disalignment with the caller's position by addressing him by his first name and by using emphatic deontic modal forms:

you cannot then allow MPs to regulate themselves
so you've got to bring in a statutory regulation authority.

It is also here that the host intervenes for the first time since the beginning of this call, with what looks like an agreement token in line 63 ('yeah'), but is, in fact, her first call-closing move (Schegloff and Sacks 1973), which she follows up, in line 68, with 'mm' in overlap with GB. This is not a minimal response but a time-to-close signal, and, in line 70, she intervenes again with a turn directly addressed to the caller: 'Robert thank you very much indeed', thereby ending the call at a point that, in this case, leaves GB with the last word, but without either of them having won this argument.

In this analysis, we have seen how an argument between guest and caller in a three-party radio phone-in framework can constitute successful, lively talk. It gets underway and is left to run by the host, who withdraws from the interaction and only intervenes to close the call and move on to the next caller. Stepping now into a different media context for lively talk as a form of 'sociable argument', the next section will focus on the work of talk show hosts who use narrative discourse (one of the most pervasive forms of lay participant discourse, as discussed in Chapter 4) as a resource to build up conflicting points of view in issue-based TV talk shows. These shows are concerned with the discussion of social concerns, and involve an array of speakers giving their opinion, from invited 'experts' to representatives of particular social constituencies and contributing members of the audience, in order to build up arguments in a debate.

The debate: opinions, arguments and narratives

Within the broad spectrum of programmes labelled 'issue-based' talk shows, there are many types of show, with differences in the individual detail of organisation and presentational style. But most share at least one common institutional goal, which is, broadly, the public expression by a studio audience of points of view and opinions on topical issues of concern. The scope of topics can be vast, ranging from the political and the social to the intensely personal. TV talk shows are thus, by nature, argument-saturated events; conflicting opinions are staples of the talk show diet, whether in the spectacle of confrontation offered on *Ricki Lake* and *Jerry Springer* or in the discussions of the more issue-oriented shows such as *Oprah* and *Kilroy*. But, essentially, what we see and hear on most public participation talk shows are forms of argument that are embedded in lay experience, and this experience is often *narrativised* in one way or another as the argument proceeds. Louann Haarman points out, however, that there is an inherent difficulty in identifying a structure of argumentation in the lay narratives of talk shows, given 'the haphazard, often chaotic way in which they are offered (some are repetitious, some not quite to the point, some interrupted, some at cross purposes)' (1997: 79). Traditional models of argumentation theory, based on reason, logic and persuasion (see van Eemeren, Grootendorst and Kruiger, 1987), are therefore not really appropriate to an analysis of the forms of argument in talk shows, which emerge in the dynamics of situated interaction and lie beyond the theoretical scope of logic and persuasion. A different approach is needed in order to understand the shape and organisation of argument in these shows, and we can find this in the work of discourse analysts who have studied the actual talk produced in a range of talk show environments.

For example, in his study of argument in *Jerry Springer*, Myers comments that the 'trash' TV talk shows 'present a genre in which topics that might end conversation, with other participants and in other settings, instead open it up' (2001: 174–175). He shows how such topics are made into 'issues' through three progressive stages: the development of opposing stances through question-and-answer sequences between the host and participant, followed by the development of controversy by bringing the opposing views of the participants into conflict, and then the dramatisation of that conflict as an on-stage fight between them, sometimes literally on the physical level. The mediation of argument in this context hinges precisely on the host working up topics of conflict and confrontation between participants as a spectacle for audiences. On the other hand, in discussion-based shows like *Kilroy*, topics are turned into issues in a different way: first, through the host eliciting more explicitly narrative sequences in which invited participants tell stories of personal experience, and, secondly, through the various evaluations of these stories by both the host and the participating audience

(Thornborrow 2001a). In both contexts, however, the reactions of the audience to the production of a particular stance or opinion are crucial to the way the arguments are developed. Turning now to some data from issue-based talk shows, we can see how opinion-giving and narrative function as discursive resources for the production of opposition and argument.

'Positional' narratives

While some researchers have pointed to the function of narrative discourse in talk shows as a way of foregrounding the voice of the individual, privileging lay experience within the public, institutional domain of the media (Livingstone and Lunt 1994; Fairclough 1995; Scannell 1996), others have shown how narrative is widely used as an interactional resource through which participants establish points of view within a debate (Thornborrow 1997; Haarman 2001; Lorenzo-Dus 2001). In her analysis of an episode of *Kilroy* dealing with children and poverty, Louann Haarman notes that 'stories occur in a remarkable 36% of turns [. . .] where they actually underlie and give form to lay argumentation' (2001: 40). Stories and accounts are therefore not simply the principal discursive forms through which lay participants express and validate their personal experiences, they also serve a range of other functions within the framework of talk show discourse and structure the interactional dynamic between host, experts, lay participants and audience.

When we examine talk show interaction in close detail, one of the most frequently recurring phrases used by all participants as a meta-discursive gloss on what they are doing is 'having their say'. This is realised by expressions such as 'I'm just saying that. . .' or 'this is what I'm saying . . .', 'could I just say . . .', 'I would say . . .', 'I'm just coming to what I'm saying . . .' and the confrontational 'you've had plenty to say already'. Both hosts and participants use the inclusive 'we', as in 'what *we*'re talking about here is . . .', often as a means of taking issue with a previous speaker's contribution, or of refocusing on what they consider to be the central point for debate. Hosts elicit a next turn from a participant using the phrase, 'Well, what are you saying?'. Having one's say, then, is the overarching discursive activity that participants explicitly orient to and are publicly engaged in; it is this 'saying' that becomes the main business of discussion-based talk shows. But, having one's say is a complex activity that does not just involve lay participants telling stories of personal experience. Indeed, the framing of a speaker turn with 'could I just say' often tends to preface an opinion given in response to a previous speaker, rather than a narrative. So, if the expression of views and opinions is the raw material of talk shows, how is it that such a substantial amount of the talk that is produced seems to consist of narrative discourse? In the following extracts, we will see how speakers produce various kinds of stories, accounts, anecdotes and reports, which may or may not be based on personal experience, but which all play a central role in the discursive construction of a stance in relation to the argument.

The next extract is taken from an episode of *The Frost Programme* that was concerned with the problem of homelessness, and, particularly, with the growing numbers of beggars on the streets of London in the mid 1990s. This became newsworthy when the then-Conservative prime minister of the United Kingdom, John Major, suggested that many beggars were actually deriving more than a subsistence-level income from begging, combined with stories of aggression and intimidation by beggars on the streets of big cities. It is one of these stories that Tim Montgomery,[4] at that time representing the Young Christian Conservative Movement, tells in the following sequence:

Extract 5.xiii: 'Begging in London', *The Frost Programme*

```
 1. TM:    – there's a lot of frightened people (.) who are faced with
 2.        beggars (.) often in dimly lit passages or (.) little (.) doorsteps
 3.        who do frighten people and I think the contrast between
 4.        those (.) who are living basic lives on benefit (.)
 5.        and the intimidatory sort of behaviour of some beggars
 6.        is what the prime minister was drawing attention to (.)
 7.        unfortunately (.) there are some situations where (.)
 8.        like as er (.) the story of er (.) some (.) beggar (.)
 9.        being discovered by erm (.) the Manchester police
10.        and as they passed him his mobile phone rang (.)
11.        [the thing is (.)
12. AUD:   [(laughter_____)
13. TM:    sometimes (.) begging is earning people (.) a lot of money
14. AUD:   (laughter _____ audience noise _____)
```

The anecdote about the beggar is referred to explicitly by speaker TM as a 'known-about' story, one that is already out there in the public domain:

> like as er (.) in the Sunday papers this weekend there was a story of er

The narrative structure here is prototypically Labovian, with an abstract (some beggars being discovered by the Manchester police), two narrative clauses in temporal sequence ('as they passed him his mobile phone rang'), followed by an evaluation, which makes the story relevant for its present telling: 'the thing is sometimes begging is earning people a lot of money'. It is not TM's story – he specifically attributes it to another source (the Sunday papers) – but telling it enables him to move from his own personal views about begging to making a more generalised claim in relation to the issue under debate. This positional function of narrative is a recurring feature of many of the stories told in TV talk shows, produced to justify a particular stance relating to the issue at hand, and to situate the speaker within that debate. In other words, participants draw on narratives of various types as a resource for constructing a position from which to argue.

A further illustration of how this works can be seen in the next extract taken from an episode of *Oprah*, where a lay member of the audience tells a story in answer to the host's opinion-eliciting question, 'What do you think?'. The topic for discussion on this programme is racism in the Chicago police department:

Extract 5.xiv: 'A racist incident', *Oprah*

1.	OPRAH:	and what do you think
2.	WOMAN:	my son and two other white guys, and a black friend
3.		were driving along the cops stopped them,
4.		.h pulled the black guy out, .hh pushed 'im against the
5.		hood threw 'im on the floor, .hh roughed 'im up (.)
6.		a::nd, didn't do anything to my so::n and his friends but
7.		pat them down so it was clearly a racist incident

This narrative is produced as a relevant next turn to a question, which, on the face of it, is designed to elicit an opinion rather than a story. But, in this interactional environment, the story functions to establish the grounds for what the speaker thinks (line 7) – that is, as evidence for the view that there is racism in the Chicago police department. The evaluatory statement that closes this extended narrative turn ('it was clearly a racist incident') serves the same purpose as that in Extract 5.xiii ('sometimes begging is earning people a lot of money') in so far as they are both used to position the teller in relation to the tale, and in relation to the issue under debate.

One final example of how narrative discourse is used to construct a speaker's position in relation to the ongoing argument can be seen in the following extract from *Kilroy*. This particular series had been recorded in New South Wales, Australia, where adoption laws had just been changed to allow gay and lesbian couples to apply to adopt a child. Here, a lay participant in the audience uses habitual and hypothetical narratives to strategically build her argument about adoption policy and to disagree with another member of the audience:

Extract 5.xv: 'The best home for the child', *Kilroy*

1.	KILROY:	—well what are you saying up at the top
2.	A1:	well I'm infertile I'm infertile and my husband
3.		we have an adopted child (.) and I see so many families
4.		the supposed wonderful family even executives
5.		the father isn't home until ten eleven every night (.)
6.		he's gone by seven in the morning (.)

7.	you are lucky you have ten children I mean snap (.)
8.	drive up the driveway (.) drop a sperm up and you're pregnant
9. AUD:	((laughter))
10.	and I mean that isn't the way for everybody
11.	and to me I would much rather see a child-
12. A2:	no
13. KILROY:	[listen
14. A2:	[(x x x x x) my husband driving up the driveway and
15.	dropping a sperm I think there's a lot to it as that
16.	and I'm not talking about a lifestyle that is potentially fertile
17.	as a married couple I am talking about a lifestyle
18.	where you have two of the same sex coming together
19.	that is of itself a contradiction to having a child [so why-
20. A1:	[but on the
21.	other side hubby tomorrow might run off with the
22.	secretary you may be a single mother (.) and what
23.	it's gotta be is the best (.) home (.) for the child

Speaker A1 here first uses two present-tense clauses in lines 4–5 to give a generalised description of what happens in 'the supposed wonderful family', and then produces a further present-tense narrative-event sequence in lines 5–6 to give a rather facetious account of how people like participant A2 (who has already disclosed that she has ten children) manage to conceive so easily:

> I mean snap
> drive up the driveway drop a sperm up and you're pregnant

This gets a response of laughter from the audience. Neither of these sequences are descriptions or accounts of her own experience; they are versions of what happens to other people. The final mini-narrative (lines 20–21) is another hypothetical event sequence, a possible future story, which, again, functions to continue the argument speaker A1 is having with speaker A2:

> hubby tomorrow might run off with the secretary
> you might be a single mother

This participant then mobilises stories about generalised states of affairs, both present and future, in order to establish her own position in the debate. Most importantly, the two mini-narratives are both followed by evaluations:

> and I mean that isn't the way for everybody
> and what it's gotta be is the best (.) home (.) for the child

It is these evaluations that mark out A1's own position in contrast to the previous speaker's. Just as for Tim Montgomery in Extract 5.xiii and the woman in Extract 5.xiv, it is the presence of an evaluation that provides the situated relevance for her using these narrative sequences at this point in the debate.

We have seen here how three different narrative types – stories of personal experience (the woman telling the story of what happened to her son and his friends), 'known-about' stories from a third-party source (the story about begging in London) and generalised or hypothetical stories about getting pregnant and what happens in families (A1's story in Extract 5.xv) – are used to construct a speaker's position in relation to the issues under discussion. In each case, a crucial component is the production of narrative evaluation, which has an important function in that it provides the link between the story that is being told and its situated 'point' in this particular telling. Evaluations are also key elements for hosts, who use them to structure and develop arguments, as we will now see.

Hosts' use of narrative evaluations

In order to show how hosts use narrative evaluation as a resource for building up debate, I turn to an episode of *Kilroy* where the issue under discussion is how to deal with con men, and where the studio audience included some people who had stories to tell about being conned and losing a lot of money. This particular sequence comes after one participant, Pat, had told a story about how she had lost £500 in a scam. We join the talk at the point where a series of contrasting evaluations and problematising actions are being made by other members of the audience, which the host then uses to develop the debate:

Extract 5.xvi: 'Can you spot a con man?', *Kilroy*, 2002

1. WIN: [it's it's just] very sad (.) very sad
2. KIL: is that the problem though that people (.) [are greedy
3. WIN: [are very- (.)
4. no I think she was just very very gullible and she wanted to

5.		help somebody (.) she thought she was helping somebody
6.	PAT:	yeah
7.	WIN:	is that right
8.	KIL:	why is she going to make two hundred pound profit
9.	AUD:	yeah
10.	PAT:	I thought that was fun
11.	KIL:	[what
12.	WIN:	[I think she was just very very gullible huh huh huh huh
13.		ve:ry gullible huh huh huh
14.	KIL:	Derek
15.	PAT:	and [he knew I was on my own too]
16.	KIL:	Derek [is it greed] is it greed
17.	DER:	no (.) it's not greed
18.	PAT:	no
19.	WIN:	no I don't
20.	DER:	I got conned

The first evaluation of Pat's story about getting conned is in Win's turn: 'it's just very sad'. The host then offers an alternative view in his question turn in line 2: 'is that the problem though that people are greedy.' Win disagrees (line 4) and offers a further evaluation of the story: that Pat was very gullible and well meaning rather than greedy. We can note here the pivotal relationship between evaluation and opinion – Win frames her evaluation of Pat's story as an opinion with 'I think'. This has now become a clear stance that can be argued with, and it is countered by the host's problematising turn in line 8: 'why is she going to make two hundred pound profit?', and we hear a member of the audience aligning with this point of view (line 9). Pat herself then provides a further evaluation of her own story, 'I thought that was fun', again to counter this view that people are greedy, and Win restates her opinion that Pat had been 'very very gullible' (lines 12–13).

In this short sequence, we see how opposing stances are produced through the process of narrative evaluation. These are used by the host to build up a series of alignments between participants who take up a stance either for or against the view that people who get conned are motivated by greed. Once he has established these stances, the host selects the next speaker with a story to tell with the question, 'Derek is it greed?' (line 16). Although this is a story-eliciting turn rather than a request for an opinion, Derek treats it initially as the latter, and his response, 'no it's not greed', enables two further alignments with him (lines 18 and 19) before he goes on to provide an abstract for his own story: 'I got conned' (line 20). Derek's narrative will, in turn, be subject to participant evaluations that produce a set of stances in relation to the issue under debate.

We have seen in the extracts above how opinion-giving, argument and narrative are interactionally woven together as discursive practices in the context of television talk shows, where participants are actively engaged in producing opinions that, in a variety of ways, are built up through the stories that they tell. Most crucially, I have argued that it is in the evaluation component of narrative discourse that opinion-giving is generated, and that evaluations are central to the development of debate as they produce specific stances that can then be argued with, opposed or countered in some way by other participants. In the final section of this chapter, I focus on another context for debate where the participation framework and role for the audience shifts considerably: the UK prime ministerial debates of 2010, in which broadcasters introduced web-based participation but strictly limited that of the audience. Given this shift, how are the resources for opinion-giving and argument mobilised in this new interactive context, and how similar or different are they from what we have seen so far?

Opinions, arguments and the web-based audience

In the three programmes devoted to the prime ministerial debates, broadcast in the run-up to the 2010 UK general election on BBC, ITV and Sky networks, viewers were invited to submit questions to the party leaders prior to the broadcasts on email via the website, which were then read out by the host in front of the live studio audience. However, during the debates, the live studio audience was not allowed to respond or show any form of reaction such as applause or laughter, but viewers were invited to post their reactions on the BBC News 'Have Your Say' web forum. These constraints radically changed the participant status of the studio audience members, whose role became one of awkwardly silent spectators to the debate taking place between the three candidates, rather than of active participants in that debate. Audience reactions were taking place elsewhere: on-line.

The examples that follow are taken from the BBC's Have Your Say interactive blog for the final debate. These responses were posted to a question on the website forum shortly after the debate had started, which was:

> **At 20:34 on 29 Apr 2010, BBC News wrote:**
>
> The party leaders have finished their opening remarks. Who did you think was the most impressive?

Looking at the contributor postings that follow, three questions can be asked. First, is the monologism identified by Myra Macdonald in her 2007 study of the BBC's 'Asylum Day' (see Chapter 2) still in evidence here? Second, are any of the discursive constructions of situated identity and expertise, routine in broadcast contexts for public participation, part of the discourse of online participation? And, third, do these contributors display any orientation to speaking – or, rather, 'posting' – on behalf of a wider constituency or social group? Given the question prompt 'who is the most impressive?', it is perhaps no surprise that, in more than 2,000 posts that evening, many comments were evaluations of the performance and appearance of each leader; as one poster put it, 'how they did and what they looked like' as much as evaluations of their policies.[5]

The posts[6] below appeared in sequence, between 20:43 and 20:46 on 29 April 2010. Out of the 14 posts, one was removed by the moderator, five were comments evaluating the candidates' appearance and performance (27, 30, 35, 37 and 38), while five expressed an opinion (25, 26, 29, 31, 36) and three asked a question (32, 33, 34).

25. At 20:43 on 29 Apr 2010, J_____7 wrote:

That's it. . . . . I've had enough, is DC sponsored by Mothercare? Every week, M&S this, Mothercare that! Hmph!
With Respect.

26. At 20:43 on 29 Apr 2010, C_____s wrote:

Greedy businessmen say the tories are right – no suprise. A bit like bankers saying they deserve their bonuses. Same old Tory values!

27. At 20:43 on 29 Apr 2010, b_____e wrote:

some stabbing now going on! Fight!!!

28. At 20:43 on 29 Apr 2010, A_____e wrote:

This comment was removed because the moderators found it broke the house rules.

29. At 20:44 on 29 Apr 2010, D--e wrote:

I love it when cameron says marks and spencer, mothercare, sainsburys do not support "tax on jobs" but lets face it if the bosses from these places took alittle off there fat bonuses maybe it wouldnt be so bad. it just seems like all the big spenders dont wanna help they want to keep there money so the smaller working classes get footed with the bill.

30. At 20:44 on 29 Apr 2010, J_____7 wrote:

15. At 20:40 on 29 Apr 2010, E_____m wrote:
I'm going to focus on the real issues. They are wearing far too much foundation.
[E_____m]..fair point, well made.
With Respect.

31. At 20:44 on 29 Apr 2010, K_____e wrote:

Brown going back to good old-fashioned Keynesian economics – like it!

32. At 20:45 on 29 Apr 2010, S_____e wrote:

Where are the millions of jobs for those out of work Mr Cameron?

33. At 20:45 on 29 Apr 2010, E_____b wrote:

getting the scroungers and wasters back into work is a great aspiration . . . how will the conservatives do it?

34. At 20:45 on 29 Apr 2010, B_____n wrote:

Cameron is like a record stuck in a grove; has he got nothing new to say?

35. At 20:45 on 29 Apr 2010, b_____e wrote:

Confused government and taxes?/
It will be a fight now even more

36. At 20:45 on 29 Apr 2010, C_____s wrote:

cameron is kidding hiself if he thinks you can get an extra 12bn efficiency savings in 9 months - and yes it will take cash out of the economy

37. At 20:45 on 29 Apr 2010, A_____y wrote:

Why does Gordon continually shake his head, it just makes him look even more like he doesn't want to be on camera and he is shying away from the real questions . . .

38. At 20:46 on 29 Apr 2010, W_____l wrote:

Q1 : The Deficit
Cameron: 5/10
Clegg: 5/10
Brown: 5/10
dull and predictable

Here, within the space of three to four minutes, although several opinions are expressed, the only post that responds to a previous contribution is number 30 (in agreement with the ironic comment 'I am going to focus on the real issues: they are all wearing too much foundation' posted four minutes earlier). One poster (32) addresses a question to Cameron: 'Where are the millions of jobs for those out of work Mr Cameron?', but this rhetorical, 'quasi-interactional' question gets no response from other participants online. In post number 27, we also find a rhetorical, direct address to the 'combatants' in the debate: 'Fight!!!' It appears that, although the possibility for exchange and discussion between posters is clearly available, the majority of these posts were indeed monologic and serial, rather than dialogic and intersubjective. In the question posts, although these are formally marked as questions, and, as such, might be expected to elicit some form of response from other online posters, none are forthcoming (at least in the immediate response environment shown here).

Secondly, they are discursively entirely different from the kind of audience questions, opinions and responses delivered in live exchanges that occur in the kind of media contexts presented in the earlier parts of this chapter. Identity attribution is minimal, partly due to the technology format (in which individual poster identity is only given in their screen names), but, in this particular sequence of posts, none of the posters provide any further relevant identity or expertise to discursively ground their comment or question. The online activity consists of the delivery of questions and opinions that are largely disconnected from any form of relevant speaker identity or situated expertise.

On the one hand, while this web-based forum certainly enabled a much greater number and variety of participant contributions in a relatively short space of time than would have the traditional studio audience, the posters were mainly commenting on the televised event rather than engaging with any ongoing political debate. The views and opinions they express are fragmented and disconnected from one another, appearing as individual comments on what is occurring on screen, rather than an exchange of views and argument in an ongoing debate. Furthermore, and, again, in contrast to the television and radio interactions, the posts show little evidence of any contributor speaking as a representative of any wider social group. This is perhaps unsurprising in the sense that the primary activity they are engaged in on this occasion is individual commentary, as spectators reacting to what they see on screen, rather than as representatives of any particular social category.

On the other hand, posts to the BBC forum had, in fact, been very interactional on previous days, with people commenting on the two debates that had already been held on the other broadcast networks – ITV and Sky – and it is worth a brief examination of the differences. So, when, on 22 April, the BBC Forum question prompts[7] were in the past tense after the event, as follows:

18:37 UK time, Thursday, 22 April 2010

The leaders of the UK's three main political parties have locked horns over foreign affairs in the second prime ministerial debate. What did you think of the programme?

Gordon Brown, David Cameron and Nick Clegg discussed a wide range of issues including the European Union, the Catholic Church, overseas military action and immigration.

What's your reaction to the debate? Who do you think came out on top? Were your questions on foreign policy being answered?

---

this generated a very different type of response: the posts were frequently much longer, more elaborate, detailed and informative, as well as more argumentative. They were also often creative, playful and humorous. Some were, again, monologic expressions of opinion or questions, but many were extended exchanges between online contributors. Below is a selection of some of these posts, taken from the sequence numbered 1504 to 1516 and posted between 16:54 and 17:12 on 23 April 2010:

1504. At 16:54 on 23 Apr 2010, P_____1 wrote:

///// Make no mistake,13 years of LABOUR has messed up Britian big style and they will continue to mess thing up.//////

Obviously you dont know politics.
The screwing up of this country began in the 80's under Thatcher, New Labour have merely continued it.

This contributor quotes a previous post, directly addresses the poster ('obviously you don't know politics') and proceeds to present a different view in their last declarative sentence. In the next extract, we see a complex embedding of texts from previous posts, where the three participants are responding to one another's views. In post 1506, h_____s evaluates a prior comment from E_____r, who was responding to a comment from M_____n, who then posts a further evaluative response in post 1507:

1506. At 16:57 on 23 Apr 2010, h_____s wrote:

1474. At 16:11 on 23 Apr 2010, E_____r wrote:
Re: comments posted earlier. . . . . Schrodinger's name was Erwin, not Edwin, and frankly, if you were "going to vote Labour" then switched

to Tory on the strength of a lack of apology from Brown, I would rather hear an opinion from your cat!

Meeow. I am Mr Schrodinger's cat. I can tell you that I am going vote Liberal Democrat because it will keep Gordon Brown in power. Although Mr Brown has ruined the country, he has promised me I won't have to chase mice any more and can just sit around supping cream, which he has borrowed from the milkman without any intention of paying for it. Purrrrr.

Good one

1507. At 16:58 on 23 Apr 2010, M_____n wrote:

Mr Schrodinger said, in riposte to me: "Meeow. I am Mr Schrodinger's cat. I can tell you that I am going vote Liberal Democrat because it will keep Gordon Brown in power. Although Mr Brown has ruined the country, he has promised me I won't have to chase mice any more and can just sit around supping cream, which he has borrowed from the milkman without any intention of paying for it. Purrrrr."

And all I can say is "excellent"! Fantastic reply! I may not agree with you, but great shot! Well done! Lets see if we can keep a bit of humour in this!

In these examples, there is a lively mix of point scoring and banter as well as the expression of political opinions, where the comment from M_____n at the end acknowledges the postings meta-discursively, 'fantastic reply!', evaluating the interaction and responses received. In a similar vein, if rather less self-reflexively playful, the next extract is an interaction between two posters that refers back to an exchange between them earlier that afternoon:

1511. At 17:05 on 23 Apr 2010, h_____s wrote:

1476. At 16:13 on 23 Apr 2010, E_____t wrote:
1431. At 15:23 on 23 Apr 2010, h_____s wrote:

You cannot say that the Tories are a party of untried youngsters . . .

I'm afraid you tripped at the third hurdle, and missed my real point at the end of the note.

There needs to be just one job-stopper policy from each party and suddenly NOTA is the most important option on the ballot paper. If it's offered as a standard option you don't have to use it. A party standing under the None of the Above ticket is campaigning for your vote.

Big difference.

But unless we start demanding it, we'll never get it.

I got your point, I was just having a bit of fun, I understand your views but I cannot see it working in practise.

The potential for missing the point is also evident in the next embedded set of posts. This time, M_____n comments on a previous exchange with h_____s, but the reply is less mitigated: 'LIGHTEN UP!'

1515. At 17:12 on 23 Apr 2010, M_____n wrote:

1487. At 16:26 on 23 Apr 2010, h_____s wrote:
1453. At 3:48 on 23 Apr 2010, M_____n wrote:

PS Well done for the first "Hard Working Families" comment of the day! Personally I think there are more votes in appealing to lazy families!

If the British electorate wanted any better proof of Labour Party policy, then here you have it.

IT WAS A JOKE!!!!! LIGHTEN UP!

In this online environment, exchange sequences are occurring in posts where participants are engaged in political discussion and argument. Contributors give their opinions, and they take issue with the views of others. In addition, they frequently offer these views in creative ways, through stylised responses that are knowingly funny and designed to provoke a reaction from readers not just of agreement/disagreement, but of appreciation. One poster even developed his evaluation of the debates in an extended analogy based on the conceit that the political party leaders were in a motor race:

1510. At 17:03 on 23 Apr 2010, s_____t wrote:

1st (by a whisker) Dave in his Aston (still British built , room for a family in the back [just],smooth ,fast and graceful but may be too conservative in its design for some , also lacks real crackle and oomph. [. . .]

2nd. Nick in his Ferrari (brand new , only driven twice, revs well, engine may lack torque. Beautiful Italian design , and turns heads in the street, however rather sharp and flashy , built in Europe [. . .]

3rd. Gordo in his Austin Healy 2000 (1977 model, the company went bust years ago [under Labour] but you can still get the parts [probably from China or India. [. . .]

The participatory framework of the online environment for opinion-giving and argument, compared to that of the traditional studio-based shows, offers very different sets of affordances. The interaction of hosts, guests and members of a live studio audience produces different forms of discursive actions to those that are found in online interactivity, even when they are dialogic rather than monologic. As Macdonald has pointed out, interactivity does not challenge existing structures when treated simply as 'a technical, if highly marketable, innovation' by the broadcast media (2007: 687). I would suggest that one important reason for this is that participants in a live, television studio discussion and participants in an online discussion display an orientation to entirely different kinds of recipients, through actions that are situated in different parameters of space and time. Questions and opinions that are delivered in direct inter-action with other participants – the guests, hosts or other audience members who are either co-present in a studio or taking part in a live phone-call – for a listening/viewing audience are routinely produced in turns that exhibit speaker orientation to relevant social identities, exper-tise and representativeness. Questions and opinions delivered online – for a non-co-present, post-event, interactive reading audience – are not. Indeed, online opinion-giving is rarely framed by any relevant identity work, and online discussion is contingent on possible uptake by any other similarly non-specified recipient; that is to say, if and when it occurs, it is often between individual posters, in non-sequential exchanges over an extended period of time.

As we have seen, many of the posts on the BBC website consisted of a great deal of direct, unmitigated opinion-giving and comment, and, in some cases, creative displays of textual inventiveness. The way these posts are framed thus often involves a shift of key, recontextualising serious political points through banter and playfulness that is designed as a display for the wider recipiency of an online reading audience as much as it is for the target recipient of the post. Finally, in the BBC forum, comments by viewers who were simultaneously watching the debate as they posted are short, evaluative and of the moment – the web-based audience are spectators to the event, not contributors to it. As such, their online reactions are bound up with a different kind of situated activity altogether: the assessment and evaluation of the debate and the candidates' performance in real time. The participation framework for this activity requires no other locally relevant participant identity than that of current spectator to the live broadcast event as it unfolds on screen.

Summary: discourses of debate

The focus of this chapter has been the place and design of opinion-giving and argument as key discourses of public participation across a range of media contexts, from callers to radio phone-ins, to members of the studio audience in talk shows and, finally, the web-based audience for the UK prime ministerial debates. In the extracts presented throughout the chapter, we have seen how participants in these broadcast environments structure their contributions to public debate as knowledgeable and warranted, orienting to locally relevant identities and establishing their own situated expertise. In contrast, I have shown how in the shift of participatory framework to a web-based audience, opinion-giving and argument results in a different kind of discursive activity. On-line, participant identity was not oriented to as a local concern in posts that expressed opinions and generated arguments, nor in those posts that commented on the live debate as it was taking place. The opinions in posts after the televised debates were equally tied to their contextual environment, but no longer seem to be tied to specific social identities, while the posters who commented on the live broadcast were primarily evaluating it as a performance, rather than contributing to the debate.

In the next chapter, I will continue to examine the role of argument as a key component of public participation broadcasting, but within a different set of mediated contexts and participation frameworks, where conflict becomes personal and narrative discourse becomes more fragmented. As we will see, argument takes a different shape in programmes in which evaluation and judgement become the primary discourses of participation, and public engagement gives way to personal confrontation and competition.

Notes

1 For example, during a journey on the London Underground, I once witnessed a man expressing his extreme opinions to fellow passengers. These opinions were abusively racist and often directly targeted at other travellers near him in the carriage. The collective response to it was silence, until one female passenger came to the defence of another, saying 'leave her alone, she's done nothing to you'. In this public context, the response to the unsolicited expression of extreme views was to ignore it and not respond at all until the activity became overtly threatening.

2 *The Big Issue* is a weekly magazine sold by homeless people on the streets of UK cities.

3 The BBC Radio 4 *Election Call* phone-in of 2010 was interesting in terms of the production team's decision to revert to taking telephone calls only, rather than include texts and emails as they had done in previous election years (Thornborrow and Fitzgerald, 2013).

4 Tim Montgomery, while not positioned as an 'expert' on the show, was nevertheless an institutional voice and his name appeared on the screen (unlike the names of the beggars and homeless people who arguably represented a different kind of expert).

5 BBC News (2010) 'Prime ministerial debate: Your reaction', web forum. Available at http://www.bbc.co.uk/blogs/haveyoursay/2010/04/prime_ministerial_debate_your_2.html (accessed 21 July 2011).

6 The user IDs of all posters have been redacted to preserve anonymity. However, I have left the first and last letter of the usernames so that their contributions can be distinguished in the exchanges.

7 BBC News (2010) 'Prime ministerial debate: Your reaction', web forum. Available at http://www.bbc.co.uk/blogs/haveyoursay/2010/04/prime_ministerial_debate_your_1.html (accessed 21 July 2011).

6 Discourses of participation
Conflict and judgement

Introduction: from debate to dispute

I make a distinction in this book between two types of argument found in public participation media, each of which can be considered as a different form of discursive activity. The first is the type of argument we found in some of the examples in the previous chapter, produced as a form of mediated debate based on participants' generally orderly, generally reasoned, though occasionally heated and confrontational expressions of opinion within the context of a phone-in or talk show discussion. The second is the type of argument that arises as an interactional dispute, where participants are engaged in some form of much more personal conflict with one another. In this kind of argument, reasoning and orderliness is often less salient and confrontation becomes the dominant key of the event, where participants often talk in overlap, engage in aggravated face threats and sometimes display overt aggression. It is this activity of dispute, rather than of debate, that is at the heart of many arguments in talk shows at the 'trash' end of the spectrum, but which is also increasingly found in other reality TV formats where participants are involved in the production of competing evaluations and judgements of one another. The mediation of these conflicts as a performance for the audience is built around a different participative framework altogether from the mediation of argument as debate with a participating audience, and how this is accomplished in a range of different media genres will be the focus of this chapter.

First of all, we examine the way in which confrontational arguments are built up in talk shows that are structured around personal disputes between participants. These disputes are designed to be played out and performed onstage in front of a largely non-participating (in the sense of being involved in the production of talk) yet highly responsive (in terms of reacting to the talk and action unfolding onstage) studio audience (e.g., *Jerry Springer* in the USA, *Jeremy Kyle* in the UK). This discussion is followed by an analysis of two episodes taken from the talk show *Jeremy Kyle*, broadcast on ITV, as an illustration of how these kinds of arguments are produced as a spectacle for the audience rather than as a debate to include the audience. The next part of the chapter will address the issue of how conflict on the one hand is being linked with judgement on the other, to produce some of the most pervasive discourses of performance in many current formats of reality TV. In such programmes, participants are placed in various kinds of conflictual, often competitive situations where they are primarily engaged in activities that involve 'other' evaluations and judgement. The examples are taken from *Love It or List It* (Canada/USA) and *Come Dine With Me* and *Four in a Bed* (UK). In analysing these shows, I return to the concept of reality TV as an arena for the 'middle-space performances' discussed in Chapter 3. This concerns the ways in which participants are positioned by and through the discursive frameworks of these programmes not as 'ordinary', but as 'someone who' displays particular forms of social identity or 'character' traits, and how these identities are brought into play for the production and performance of conflict. To conclude the chapter, further consideration is given to the points of interface between broadcast media and social media, this time focussing on Twitter sites as a new environment for the construction of an interactive, web-based audience within which these shows are topically discussed and evaluated.

Confrontational discourse as spectacle

The genre of issue-based talk shows dealing with personal and social crises, where participants are presented as being already bound up in a situation of conflict, have been on our TV screens for some time now. In these shows, sometimes referred to as 'trash' TV (Haarman 2001), the main discursive activity often takes the form of a series of aggravated personal confrontations, which are sometimes physically embodied as well as verbally pursued. Participants are presented as being caught up in chaotic family feuds and as having highly dysfunctional social relationships, and, onstage, they take up oppositional, often aggressive stances towards one another (and sometimes towards the host, too). The main business of these confrontations is to produce a performance of conflict as a dispute, rather than the expression of conflicting views in a debate. To this end, the different 'sides' to the argument gradually unfold onstage through the mediation of the host and in front of a studio audience, members of which mainly take up the role of bystanders and spectators to the event rather than contributors to it. In these shows, unlike in the other media contexts for argument I discussed in Chapter 5, some form of resolution of the conflict *is* routinely offered (in the form of the results of a DNA or lie detector test, or through third-party intervention such as an expert counsellor or, sometimes, by hosts themselves, as with 'Jerry's final thoughts' on *The Jerry Springer Show*). Such resolutions provide a form of satisfactory ending, or closure, to the conflict that has just been played out onstage for the studio and viewing audience – another key feature that distinguishes these kinds of shows that produce argument as public spectacle from those that produce argument as public debate. One could posit that these performances of conflict are framed for the viewers as a form of modern morality tale, stories of feuds and human failings with which we can all in some way identify, from which we can all learn, and which, as stories, can be in some way resolved.

In his analysis of confrontational episodes on *Jerry Springer*, Myers observes that talk shows 'present a genre in which topics that might end conversation, with other participants and in other settings, instead open it up [. . . .] talk shows elaborate on topics to make them something participants – and audiences – can talk about' (2001: 174–175). This is accomplished through a sequence of staged activities in which oppositional stances are elicited, made first controversial and then dramatic. One participant is questioned by the host about their behaviour, producing a particular stance in relation to the topic at hand. Then another is introduced who problematises this behaviour (i.e., makes it into a controversial issue) by taking a different, opposing stance, after which the two participants are brought into direct interaction with each other as the conflict is enacted onstage in front of the audience. Below is a short example taken from Myers' account of the process, in which he also gives information in the transcript about the on-screen, visual presentation of these stages, which are framed by different types of camera shots (see also the Appendix of this book, which features a guide to transcription conventions and symbols):

Extract 6.i: Making it controversial on *Jerry Springer*

| MS OF JS | JS: | ok . when you started dating him you were sixteen he was how old? |

Kenny is shown in an inset with the caption OUTSIDE STUDIO

MS OF DIANE	D:	twenty-eight
	AUD:	ooo (4.0)
MS OF JS (LOOKS AT CARDS)	JS:	let's bring out your sister Tina and sister-in-law Christina
	AUD:	(xxxxxxx)

T and C shown from side, walking onto stage. Applause continues until they are onstage

MS OF DIANE FROM FRONT,	C:	how could you do this?
LS OF T AND C FROM FRONT		look how pretty you are . he's twenty-nine he doesn't own anything
MS OF D	D:	do you think I care?

(Transcript from Myers 2001: 179)

Myers describes this sequence as a framed series of embodied stances in which the participants enact the dispute between them. He explains the lack of continuity between Christina's first utterance and the host's previous one as a result of its production 'onstage': the lack of greeting or acknowledgement of the audience, the fact that 'this' is deictically recoverable by the studio audience via on-screen visuals as Kenny and Diane's marriage, while the audience react, laugh, applaud and take sides in the dispute. It is through these repeated, framed sequences as the participants are brought onstage to engage directly with one another, without any acknowledgement of the camera or the audience, that the performance of conflict is produced, with its moments of drama, tension and occasional outbreaks of violence. The framing work done by the camera – from the close-ups of the stage to the long shots of the studio audience and the broadcast frame with split screens showing reactions from participants backstage – is also central to the way conflict is produced as a spectacle for the audience. Myers concludes that the performance of such disputes onstage is also made relevant for the viewing audience through Jerry's 'final thoughts', during which he invites us, within the broadcast rather than the stage frame, not to distance ourselves from these 'freaks and misfits' (2001: 191), ne'er-do-wells whom we consider to be *not like* us, but, rather, to reflect on ways in which they *might* be like us.

'Belligerence' in broadcast talk

Alongside the continuing popularity of the confrontational talk show, in recent years, a new generation of reality TV has emerged that is based around situations of conflict or competition and in which aggravated confrontation between participants is often foregrounded as the predominant discourse of the broadcast programmes. Examples of such shows might include *Hell's Kitchen* in the USA and *Gordon Ramsay's Kitchen Nightmares* or *The Apprentice* in the UK. Higgins et al. (2011) have described the interactions between participants in these shows as primarily characterised by a high level of belligerence and the routine production of aggravated face threat. Arguing that there has been 'an identifiable shift in the tenor of public discourse [. . .] which can be seen across the spectrum of television programming from news interviewing to competitive reality shows, from talent shows to lifestyle makeovers' (Higgins et al. 2011: 511), they suggest that forms of politeness in operation in media discourse are no longer governed by the conventional factors of power, social distance and the level of imposition of a face threat (Brown and Levinson 1987), but, rather, by an overriding orientation to plain speaking. This practice of what we might call 'in-your-face telling it like it is' eschews indirectness and mitigation, and is constituted largely by speech acts that are overtly critical, judgemental and confrontational, including, in some cases, recourse to personal insult and the use of taboo language. Interestingly, they suggest that this is being done for reasons of 'immediacy, authenticity, truth and understanding' (Higgins et al. 2011: 516) across a whole range of current media genres. These range from news programming, such as Jeremy Paxman's adversarial interviews with politicians on the current affairs discussion programme *Newsnight* (BBC Two) or the extreme antagonism of *The O'Reilly Factor* (Fox News) (Hutchby 2011), to reality shows in which participants appear to lose control of their tempers and engage in full-blown rows, such as Jade Goody's aggressive attack on Shilpa Shetty in *Celebrity Big Brother* (Tolson 2007). Belligerence can also be seen in the forms of aggressive behaviour found on talk shows like *Jerry Springer* and *Jeremy Kyle* as well in entrepreneurial competition genres such as *The Apprentice* or *Dragon's Den*.

Whether or not this argument can hold across all these contexts, it does seem to be the case that such moments of confrontation produce television that is spectacular and eminently watchable. Furthermore, it is these moments of conflict and confrontation that provide much of the content of clips from mainstream television that are uploaded to YouTube, and can be watched again, weeks, months and even years later, extracted from their original broadcast context and reproduced in another media entirely as performances of conflict that stand alone in their own right. We will return to a more in-depth discussion of the significance of conflict and judgement as the primary discourses of middle-space performances later on in this chapter, but, first, we examine in more detail how private arguments work as performances in the UK talk show *Jeremy Kyle*.

Narrative, evaluation and performance: disputes on *Jeremy Kyle*

The production of a dispute as a public spectacle tends to involve a shift in participants' actions away from talk that is primarily narrative based and into talk that is much more evaluative and judgemental, and which has the potential to increase the performance value of personal conflicts onstage. This shift was evident in Extract 6.i, quoted above, where the host's elicit of narrative orientation information 'you were sixteen when you started dating him he was how old?' is followed by Christina's evaluative question, 'how could you do this?' In comparing the two extracts below, one of which is much more spectacular and highly performed than the other, we will see how the role of the host, as well as the actions of the participants, is key to the performance of conflict.

As we saw in Chapter 4, telling stories constitutes a fundamental discursive activity across a range of media contexts for public participation, and, in Chapter 5, I argued that narrative is also key to the development of argument as debate in discussion-based talk shows. In shows based on the drama of interpersonal conflicts, once again, we find that participants' stories are often central to the staged event, but that the distribution of participant roles in the telling, and, consequently, the way that the story gets told, results in a different kind of narrative event from the stories we have been dealing with so far. The tale is often fragmented, with an array of different co-tellers, and with conflicting versions and conflicting evaluations of the story being produced at different moments.

The role of the talk show host in transforming participants' stories of personal experience into mediated performances has been well documented by scholars of broadcast talk. In a previous analysis of stories told in talk shows from the UK and the USA, I argued that narrative discourse on these shows has to be worked up into a performance, with the host playing a key part in the dramatisation of a participant's story (Thornborrow 2001a). This dramatisation can involve various discursive actions, including the hosts co-telling a story, as well as evaluating and problematising the narratives they elicit, actions which produce a telling that is designed for its mediated context in front of the studio (and for the viewing) audience. The way in which confrontation is produced as a spectacle in such shows has also been addressed by Ian Hutchby (2001b) in terms of the interactional dynamics of participation through which confrontation is locally accomplished by participants during live interaction in the studio. Hutchby shows how, in *The Ricki Lake Show*, the presence of a studio audience becomes a primary element in this dynamic, particularly in the way different sides to a dispute are established and evaluated in alignments that are built between host, participants and the audience as primary recipients of the talk. And as already mentioned above, Myers (2001) has shown how the disputes that are played out onstage in these confrontational talk shows are highly organised events, in terms of the structure and framing of the various sides to the argument as they are made into what he calls 'talkable issues'.

Many of the organisational features of *Jerry Springer* can also be found in *Jeremy Kyle*, particularly in the way that opposing stances are elicited from participants who are brought into direct conflict on a stage in front of a studio audience. The format is similar: one of the feuding parties is first invited on the stage to give their side of the story, while the other is shown on screen 'backstage' in the green room, reacting to the version of events emerging onstage, elicited through the host's questioning. The other party is then brought 'front-stage' to tell their version of the story, which will initiate a confrontation between the two. However, whereas host Jerry Springer generally positions himself at a distance from the feuding parties – as invoked by Myers (2001) in the title of his chapter, 'I'm out of it, you guys argue' – host Jeremy Kyle frequently takes a much more central role in the developing confrontation, particularly through his personal evaluations of the different sides to the story.

The dispute in the next example exhibits the same kind of stance-producing format involved in the production of conflict identified by Myers, with a shift in the role of the host who is not only acting as story elicitor, but also as problematiser and dramatiser.

'You don't seem to be bothered about that'

This episode features a number of participants involved in an ongoing conflict (they have already appeared previously on the show), at the centre of which is a complex relationship between a mother, her pregnant daughter

Stephanie and a man, Mick, the mother's fiancé. The on-screen strapline 'Did my ex sleep with you, your daughter and my stepmum?' poses the problem shortly to be solved by DNA test results, and, in his introduction to Stephanie, the host briefly summarises the conflicting accounts of the various protagonists. Mick and the mother are onstage, as well as two young women, while Stephanie's reactions backstage in the green room are visible on-screen. The extract below precedes Stephanie's arrival on the stage and consists of an exchange between Jeremy Kyle and the mother, in which her display of apparent indifference to this situation is worked up into a controversial stance – at key points, the studio audience can be heard reacting first with laughter and then with sounds of shock, while the camera frames shift between stage, studio and broadcast as the scene is played out.

Extract 6.ii: 'You don't seem to be bothered about that' (1), *Jeremy Kyle*

1. MS M AND MI	JK:	We haven't yet met your daughter
2.		Stephanie.
3. CU ST		Stephanie is an interesting one to
4.		me because,
5. LS STAGE		Stephanie says she didn't sleep with
6.		you? >to my researchers<
7.		but you say you=
8. CU MI	MICK:	=yeah
9.	JK:	=did sleep with your (.) fiancée's
10.		daughter and you don't seem
11.		(to be bothered about) that still
12. CU M		(3.0)
13.	AUD:	((begins to laugh))
14. LS JK	JK:	I think I think I just (.) y'know
15.		we're gonna do a DNA
16. FACING STAGE		on her kid as well. (.) how would
17.		you feel if he was the father of
18.		Stephanie's (.) baby.
19. CU ST BACKSTAGE	M:	he's not.
20.	JK:	you definitely know that.
21. CU ST RAISES HANDS	M:	yep

In this opening exchange, we find a different participation framework from the essentially narrative eliciting role of host Jerry Springer in Extract 6.i. Host Jeremy Kyle summarises the conflicting versions of the story in his opening turn (lines 1–6), then problematises the mother's reaction to this situation: 'you don't seem to be bothered about that still' (line 11). The camera shows a close-up shot of the mother, her face impassive, saying nothing. After three seconds of this silence, the studio audience laughs at her non-verbally embodied stance of 'not being bothered'. JK pursues this line with a direct, stance-eliciting question: 'how would you feel if he was the father?' (lines 16–17). Her answer, a declarative 'he's not', denies the validity of the question, and we see Stephanie raising her hands in a triumphant gesture backstage. The host reframes the question, and, again, the mother resists giving a direct answer by challenging its validity, as we see in line 24:

Extract 6.iii: 'You don't seem to be bothered about that' (2), *Jeremy Kyle*

22. MS MI AND M	JK:	would it change your view of this situation
23.		if he was?
24. CU M	M:	nah. (2.0) why should it?
25. CU JK	JK:	because it's not normal?
26.	AUD:	((laughter))
27. CU M	M:	and? next question?
28. MS GIRLS	AUD:	((loud intake of breath))

Here, it is the host's problematising action (line 25) that gets a response of laughter from the audience; his evaluation of the mother's emerging stance as 'not normal', which she again challenges: 'and? next question?' (line 27). The work of making her stance controversial is now underway: the audience reacts to the mother's failure to condemn her fiancé with an audible collective intake of breath, and JK offers an evaluative re-formulation of her stance:

Extract 6.iv: 'You don't seem to be bothered about that' (3), *Jeremy Kyle*

29. CU MI	JK:	basically the message you're putting out there
30.		is
31. LS JK IN FRONT		it's alright (.) for your kids to sleep (.) with
32. OF STAGE		your [partner
33.	M:	[it's happened

A brief dispute between JK and the mother then follows. Each utterance is characterised by the turn-initial tokens of opposition 'yeah but', with the host's accusation (line 36) and the mother's candidate justification, a narrative of what happened 'on the last show' (lines 38–39), interrupted by JK in line 41:

Extract 6.v: 'You don't seem to be bothered about that' (4), *Jeremy Kyle*

34. LS JK POINTS AT GIRL	JK:	yeah, but why is it <u>her</u> fault
35.	M:	did I say it was her fault.
36. MS GIRLS	JK:	yeah but you came out here all
37.		ranting and raving at her
38. MS GIRLS	M:	yeah but it was her what lied on the

39.		last show n telled-gone round telling
40. CU M		[(x x x x x) Mick
41. LS JK FACING STAGE	JK:	[but this is my point about this story
42.		((starts increasing in volume))
43. JK WAVING ARMS		I'm gonna come on the Jeremy Kyle
44.		show and say what a fine upstanding
45.		man Mick is
46. JK TURNING ROUND		he doesn't do this he doesn't do that.
47. JK JUMPING UP AND DOWN		BUT HE <u>DOES</u> <u>SLEEP</u> WITH MY
48.		<u>DAUGH</u>TER

The host's last turn in this sequence (lines 47–48) is an even more explicit re-formulation of the mother's stance, in which he shifts his footing into first-person animator of her attributed position: 'I'm going to come on *The Jeremy Kyle Show* and say . . .'. His speech gets increasingly louder, and, to mark the close of his turn, he jumps up and down on the three key stressed syllables of the last utterance: <u>does</u>/<u>sleep</u>/<u>daugh</u>ter. The camera pulls back to give a long shot of JK, facing side on to the stage and the audience as he delivers this judgement of the mother's stance as both controversial and morally reprehensible.

This sequence reframes an on-going dispute for the studio and viewing audiences around a controversial issue. There are references to 'the story', its protagonists and to various previous tellings, but the narrative here is fragmented: the 'tale' is not produced as a complete narrative event. On the other hand, what the host does is to work up its dramatic potential through a series of evaluations and problematising actions directed at the mother: an accusation that she's 'not bothered', his assessment of this stance as 'not normal' and, finally, his judgement of her as morally at fault. In addition, the performance of stance in this sequence is marked in the non-verbal embodiment of the mother's passivity, contrasted with the host's increasingly animated evaluation of this passivity. These actions are nevertheless closely tied to the evaluation potential narratives offer. Here, the host's incremental judgements about the mother 'not being bothered' set the scene for the next stage of dramatic confrontation between the feuding participants: on cue, Stephanie will rush onstage, verbally and physically attack one of the young women with the accusation, 'You are one lying, dirty, disgusting little cow!', and have to be restrained by the bouncer. And, as Myers points out, no introduction or further contextual information is necessary as the confrontational positions are already out there, established and being enacted onstage. The story is thus worked up through a series of evaluations and judgements by different participants into a dramatic spectacle of conflict for the studio audience, whose responses and alignments become a part of the spectacle, as well as through the broadcast framing of the event for the viewing audience.

The format of shows like *Jerry Springer* and *Jeremy Kyle* has the potential to reproduce individual disputes time and time again as a routine performance of conflict. We might argue that the mediation of such disputes alone heightens their performance value, since the 'communicative focussing' that Coupland refers to (2007: 147–148) is present on several levels: in the particular configuration of the confrontation as a bounded event, in front of an audience and accomplished through a repertoire of discursive actions, and with some kind of conclusion or resolution of the dispute. And yet, as we will now see in another episode taken from *Jeremy Kyle*, argument is not performed as a spectacle in every conflict onstage to the same extent.

At this point, it will be useful to recall Blum-Kulka's (1993, 1997) three narrative components of tale (the story materials), teller (the story narrator/s) and telling (the occasion/s on which a story is told). In contrast to discussion-based talk shows, where stories often function to construct positions from which a 'teller' can argue a particular point at that specific moment of 'telling', in the extracts below, it is the 'tale' itself that provides the material of dispute – in other words, the story events are at stake, since the couple disagree on what happened. The story appears to be about an incident of alleged domestic violence. However, the characteristic features of conflicting accounts that we encountered in Chapter 4, where participants shifted into the conversational historic present tense to produce not just different but increasingly dramatic versions of the same events, are absent from this 'telling'. It is also accomplished through a particular configuration of participant roles in which JK is the story elicitor and primary recipient, Fiona the primary narrator and protagonist, but Mike is the primary problematiser, which has particular consequences for Fiona, as we will see. Sitting in one of the two armchairs on the stage is Mike, who has already given his side of the story. JK is facing them, from a position just below the stage. Fiona is then invited to join them and sits down in the other armchair.

Extract 6.vi: 'Did you beat him up?' (1), *Jeremy Kyle*

1. LS F WALKS	JK:	let's cut to the chase
2.		Fiona ladies and gentlemen
3. ON STAGE	AUD:	((8 seconds applause))
4. F SITS DOWN	JK:	Fiona welcome to the show
5. MS JK FACING		I want. and need. the truth (.) okay?
6. F AND M ON STAGE		what (.) is (.) the truth.
7.		about this relationship.
8. CU M	FIONA:	well basically everything he's saying
9.		is a load of rubbish
10. CU F	JK:	did you beat him up.
11. CU F	FIONA:	no. I caught him in his jaw and I did
12.		apologise for it

13.	CU M	MIKE:	so that makes it alright
14.	MS M AND F	FIONA:	no it doesn't make it alright but I
15.			don't know what else
16.	CU JK		[to say or do Mike
17.	CU M	JK:	[how did you catch him (on the jaw)
18.	CU F	FIONA:	we got into a (.) pretty bad argument
19.			and then (.)
20.			I don't know
			it happened so fast (.)

The host, JK, asks Fiona for 'the truth about this relationship' (line 6), a narrative-eliciting turn. Her first response to this is, however, to dismiss Mike's previous version of the story with an evaluation: 'well basically everything he's saying is a load of rubbish' (lines 8–9). JK follows with another, more targeted elicitation, 'did you beat him up?', and Fiona provides her short version of the story in lines 11–12. This account is then problematised by Mike (line 13), 'so that makes it alright?', which shifts the talk into a different participatory frame, as Fiona then responds to him directly, with a justification of her action. JK follows with a third, more specific question, 'how did you catch him on the jaw?' (line 17), re-establishing his position as primary recipient and bringing her back to the details of the story and the allegedly violent relationship between her and Mike. Following this, more problematising/justifying talk ensues as Mike continues to contest Fiona's version of what happened, and Fiona has to deal with both telling her story to JK and responding to Mike's ongoing challenges with justifying turns, as illustrated in this short example below.

Extract 6.vii: 'Did you beat him up?' (2), *Jeremy Kyle*

1.	LS STAGE	FIONA:	[yeah right I had the internet and TV in my
2.			name in <u>his</u> flat
3.	CU M		I weren't <u>living</u> there I weren't <u>wiv</u> him
4.	CU F		and he still expected me to keep it on
5.			in my name
6.	MS F AND M	MIKE:	no you lived with me for a year yeah
7.	MS F AND M		and I didn't expect you to pay one bill
8.	CU M		the only bill you had to pay was that
9.		FIONA:	[so-
10.		MIKE:	[and you got it cut off=
11.	MS F AND M	FIONA:	=no (.) no no no
12.			I paid for <u>everything</u> (.) Mike (.)

The problem here is that, in fact, a 'talkable issue' does not emerge. In terms of the way the camera shots frame this interaction, we see mainly close-ups of the speaking participants, with mid shots of Fiona and Mike but no shots of the audience and their reactions. This seems to be basically because there is nothing for them to react to: unlike the sequence from *Jerry Springer* analysed by Myers above, the talk unfolding onstage here is being made neither dramatic nor controversial, and there is no discernable point. The discursive activity taking place is more like a private quarrel between the two participants, rather than a performance of conflict for the audience. In the final segment of this sequence, the host attempts to bring the activity back to the narrative detail and elicit a more controversial topic (in line 2):

Extract 6.viii: 'Did you beat him up?'(3), *Jeremy Kyle*

```
 1. JK:     [we've talked about that already
 2.          I mean did he ever hit you
 3.          let's talk about that
 4. MIKE:   [yeah let's talk about that
 5. FIONA:  [yeah he did right we went to the park right?
 6.          and we had a bit of an argument and everything and
 7.          then he goes to me oh I should get you back
 8.          for what you done to me in the flat
 9.          which was catching him in the jaw
10.          I so I turned me head and he hit me in the side of the face
11.          so I punched him back
12.          and that's exactly what happened Jeremy Kyle
13. MIKE:   (x x x xi pushed you x x you hit me)
14. FIONA:  that's exactly what happened Mike (.) you are a liar
15. MIKE:   (x x x)
```

Fiona tells her story, this time in a longer narrative sequence with orientation details (the park, the argument); then the complicating action, where we see a shift into the conversational historic present tense, 'then he goes' (line 7); and there is a resolution (line 11) and coda, 'that's exactly what happened Jeremy Kyle' (line 12), which returns us to the context of this occasion for telling it, the initial host demand for 'the truth about this relationship'. But, there is no evaluation on the part of the host. Immediately after the coda, Mike intervenes with yet another challenge to Fiona's version of the tale, and the quarrelling activity between them is thus resumed. Fiona repeats the coda, this time directly to Mike as recipient, but her final declarative 'you are a liar' (line 14) seems to be tied more closely to this repetition of the coda, which refutes his version, and to her initial claim that Mike's version of the story was 'a load of rubbish' (Extract 6.vi, line 9), than to function as a new, confrontational accusation. Delivered in this way, the story gives the audience very little to respond to and we are largely left with the question 'so what?'

So, although this sequence clearly contains a conflict, it seems to be falling short of the kind of 'middle-space performance' that has come to be associated with this kind of talk show. This is because the dispute develops within a participatory framework that remains essentially 'telling'-based: one protagonist's account of 'what happened' addressed to the host, persistent problematising challenges to that emerging narrative addressed to the teller by the other protagonist (rather than by the host) and challenges to which the teller responds in a series of justifying turns. Significantly, in this narrative sequence, there is no evaluation in the form of problematising or dramatising work done by JK, whose role here remains one of story elicitor. Storyteller Fiona shifts constantly between an orientation to the host as primary story recipient, and an orientation to Mike as problematiser of her version of events. Note, too, her frequent use of first-name direct address, 'Mike', which displays a particular orientation to him, rather than to any of the array of other participants present in the studio. The key features of dispute as a performance, in terms of the production of clear participant stances and the building of controversy by the host, are absent, and there is no heightened, dramatic engagement between the participants. What is more, here is a situation where one might argue that the people onstage do seem to be doing being 'ordinary', in the sense that they are essentially engaged in conducting a two-party quarrel that, in its structure, tends to exclude the host and studio audience, rather than in producing a performance of conflict for that audience.

It seems, therefore, that it is when the tale itself becomes the backdrop to a set of more confrontational discourses that the onstage interaction achieves a heightened level of performance. The evaluations of a story, and the production of explicit stances, give rise to audience reactions of laughter, of expressions of surprise or disapproval, as they align with one participant or against another, and it is through the heightened focus on discourses of evaluation and judgement that personal conflicts onstage are successfully transformed into spectacle.

So, what happens when conflict is taken out of the talk show arena, away from the studio audience, and into the domain of reality TV? Removing the studio audience from the participation framework of mediated confrontation opens up another set of performance repertoires that operate within different frameworks of interaction, and this will be the topic of the next part of the chapter as we turn to conflict and judgement as some of the primary discourses in a fast-growing genre of public participation broadcasting: the competition format of reality programming.

Conflict and judgement in competition-based reality TV

A particularly pervasive trend in reality TV formats involving 'ordinary' people over the past decade has been the introduction of variations on a theme of competition, or challenge-based game show, from the first *Big Brother* series to spin-offs like *Survivor* or *I'm a Celebrity . . . Get Me Out of Here!* where contestants are gradually voted off by one another, or by the viewing audience, or both. There is always a category of 'winner' and correspondingly less successful categories such as 'runner-up' or 'first to be voted off the island/out of the house'. But competition also exists in other domains of reality television in a whole range of programmes, often with highly successful viewing ratings, and it is to these that we now turn our attention.

There are currently four main configurations of the basic competition reality show format. The first is where competing participants, whether celebrities or members of the public, are judged on their performance by a panel of professionals or experts in the context of the competition. Examples include *Strictly Come Dancing*, where the panel as well as the audience judge a dance performance; *MasterChef*, where culinary innovation and expertise is evaluated by professional chefs; or *America's Next Top Model*, where aspiring young models are put through their paces by a team of experts from the fashion world. A second variation on this theme is when the competition is not just between participants but also between members of the panel, often 'expert' celebrities who are competing with one another in their role as coaches or trainers of the non-professional performers (as, for example, in *The X Factor*). Thirdly, there are shows in which competing participants are judged by their peers, fellow participants on the show rather than a panel of experts or the viewing audience. These would include *Come Dine With Me*, where contestants rate one another's hospitality, or *Four in a Bed*, where four sets of bed-and-breakfast owners spend a night in each of the competing establishments and then give scores for hospitality, cleanliness, the breakfast, and so on. Finally, there are shows where competing teams of professionals have to convince participants to take one course of action or another – for example, to renovate their house or buy another one in *Love It or List It* (OWN Canada), or competing with each other in taking risks as seen in HGTV's *Property Brothers*.

I will focus on examples taken from the last two configurations, as they feature people who are not media professionals or celebrities. They also constitute an environment in which evaluation and confrontation are foregrounded as discursive activities that provide much of the basic material for the final, edited broadcast. The content of these programmes is developed around moments of tension created through participants' evaluations of each other, which then appear to lead to conflicts between them. In *Four in a Bed*, the competitive element of the broadcast is realised not just through the final scores, which produce winners and losers, but through a series of scenes where 'other' assessment, criticism and, occasionally, direct confrontation provide the momentum for each week's contest. In *Love It or List It*, much of the broadcast version also consists of arguments about what the featured couples do or don't like, do or don't want, as well as occasional disputes between the experts tasked with the makeover of the home, leading up to the programme's final outcome: the decision to stay in their house (i.e., love it) or sell (list it).

Love It or List It is a hybrid reality show where makeover meets real estate. In the episode I focus on here, a couple disagree about what to do about their home: Joe wants to stay and improve the house (on an agreed budget), while Lyn wants to sell it and buy another, more suitable house for their family's needs (again, with a limited budget). The competition dimension is played out between the consultant estate agent and home designer who each have to try to convince the couple to decide one way or the other. This format provides a framework for conflict to take place on various levels – between the couple, between the two individual members of the couple and the professional consultants and, sometimes, between the consultant teams themselves. What kind of discourses then emerge as the salient forms of talk in the edited broadcast?

'What am I getting?'

As Higgins et al. (2011) found in their analysis of *Ramsay's Kitchen Nightmares*, the trailers for the show regularly feature confrontational utterances from participants as a frame for the upcoming programme – from the outset, we are invited to see the relationships between participants as problematic and confrontational. Here is a continuity introduction to *Love It or List It*, where Joe and Lyn disagree about whether to let designer Hilary go ahead with her plans for making over their house:

Extract 6.ix: Joe and Lyn (1), Introduction, *Love It or List It*

1. JOE: It's like the first meeting we said we we would
2.   give her a shot (.) and it's like [(xxx)
3. LYN: [all right you wanna give her a shot
4.   give her a shot I'm (.) you know (.)
5.   I don't wanna talk to her again g<u>o</u>
6. HIL: hi
7. JOE: actually that was pretty easy was pretty smooth so uh
8. HIL: oh ha ha ha

The brief exchange between Joe and Lyn hints at a potential upcoming rift between Lyn and Hilary ('I don't want to talk to her again'), quickly followed by another brief exchange between Joe and Hilary, with an ironic comment from Joe on his conversation with Lyn ('actually that was pretty smooth'). A further continuity shot before an ad break shows the real estate agent, David, showing Lyn and Joe around a house:

Coming up
LYN: now the tour really <u>is</u> over this kitchen is <u>aw</u>ful

The use of this negative evaluation is a frame for the upcoming problems and arguments that will inevitably ensue between Lyn and David at some point in the next part of the broadcast. In the following extract, we find the difficult moment predicted in the trailer between Lyn and Hilary played out, as Hilary presents the couple with her remake of their recreation ('rec') room:

Extract 6.x: Joe, Lyn and Hilary in the new rec room, *Love It or List It*

1. HIL: this is the new rec room
2. LYN: yeah
3. JOE: I <u>like</u> it
4. HIL: good
5. LYN: what's there to like. we asked for open concept
6.   where's the ↑openness
7. HIL: did you not notice that opening is (.) three times
8.   as wide as it was
9. LYN: it's <u>s</u>lightly larger, Hilary,
10. HIL: it's actually [a lot
11. LYN: [it's not open

Joe's approval (line 3) is quickly followed by Lyn's negative evaluation of the changes, 'what is there to like?' (line 5), her disagreement with Hilary about the details and her interruption with an oppositional declarative statement, 'it's not open' (line 11). Thus, the predicted expectations of conflict are fulfilled, and, as a consequence, produce a further problem, as Hilary seems ready to abandon the project:

Extract 6.xi: Joe, Lyn and Hilary argue about the rec room, *Love It or List It*

1. LYN: I don't think that taking down (.) part of this wall
2.   I think that makes enough of a difference
3.   for me to wanna [stay
4. HIL: [well why don't we just stop
5.   I really <u>wish</u> I had listened to my instincts at the outset
6.   told you it wasn't enough money
7. LYN: Hilary you <u>chose</u> to spend our money down here
8.   you <u>said</u> it would be better spent down here than upstairs.
9. HIL: I still maintain it's the right choice

The conflict between Lyn and Hilary is taken to a dramatic moment – 'why don't we just stop' (line 4) – and is followed by an exchange of accusations between the two women: 'I told you X', 'you chose to Y' and 'you said Z'.

Through the disputes that develop on several levels during this show, as the participants argue the toss with one another, the edited broadcast presents us not just with the drama of such conflicts as 'lively' events, where talk between participants is argumentative and judgemental, but it also develops the situated roles of the participants as characters within the show. Joe's utterances tend to be positive actions (we see him agreeing, approving, reconciling), while Lyn's utterances are generally negative actions (we see her disagreeing, judging and criticising). Whatever other kinds of inter-action between the participants may have taken place during the filming, the development of character roles is achieved through the selection of inter-actions that are primarily evaluative in their function and confrontational in their key, and in which participants are routinely shown behaving in predictable ways in relation to their character's role.

In addition to segments showing disputes and conflictual situations as direct exchanges between participants, the edited broadcast also consists of other frameworks for talk. These include voice-over sequences, where one participant's voice is used as commentary on the (on-screen) behaviour of another, usually in some action of evaluation or judgement, and sequences of talk spoken directly 'to camera', as well as the talk that is produced 'for camera' but directed to a member of the production team rather than directly to camera. (The distinction between these two frames is shown in the transcripts as either 'to camera' or 'for camera'.) Below is an example of a typical edited sequence containing various rapid footing shifts in which different forms of address are spliced together with extracts from the interactional exchange and talk direct to camera.

Extract 6.xii: 'What am I getting?', *Love It or List It*

Exchange

1. JOE: you know what I think you're being a little harsh
2. LYN: uh I'm being harsh? now you are ea::sy to impress

To camera

3. HIL: I was telling her the truth when I said to Lyn that
4. I feel like walking off right now (.) cos I do

Exchange

5. LYN: I don't know why you're on her side
6. when clearly you can see
7. she's done absolutely nothing with our money

To camera

9. HIL: what I <u>really</u> understood was that Lyn (.)
10. did not want to be in this house
11. and there was virtually <u>nothing</u> that I could come up with
12. if it wasn't <u>every</u> <u>single</u> thing that was on her list
13. to make her even consider staying

Exchange

14. LYN: I mean I'm not getting open concept upstairs
15. JOE: ((raises hand))

16. LYN: and now I find out I'm not getting open concept (.)
17.   downstairs either?
18. JOE: ((raises hand))
19. LYN: what am I GETTING?

This sequence is structured around evaluations and judgements: it moves from mutual other evaluation (Joe and Lyn) to self-evaluation (Hilary), then Lyn's other evaluation of Hilary and Hilary's other evaluation of Lyn, and, finally, another evaluation of the situation by Lyn. In many contexts for social interaction, other evaluations and assessments can be highly face-threatening discursive acts (Brown and Levinson 1987). Because of this potential for face threat, evaluative discourse can vary tremendously, from highly mitigated attention to a speaker's positive face to none whatsoever, which produces bald, on-record or even aggravated criticism. Like advice-giving, as we will see in the next chapter, the way evaluations are handled in interaction depends crucially on the situated context and on the relationship between the participants. Here, Joe's evaluation of Lyn is mitigated, 'you know what I think you're being a little harsh' (line 1), but Lyn's evaluation of Joe in response is not: 'you are so easy to impress'. In her next turn, she manages to combine accusation (of Joe) and criticism (of Hilary), and her final turn is a rhetorically designed and delivered negative assessment of the situation that ends with, 'what am I getting?'. Meanwhile, interspliced with these exchanges between Joe and Lyn, we have Hilary's to-camera evaluation of her own position, and of Lyn's, which serve as a double framing for the development of Lyn's character role as petty and difficult.

An intriguing aspect of *Love It or List It* is the way the relationships between the professional team members are also sometimes represented as conflictual. In the next extract, we find Hilary and Fergus, the builder, arguing about what changes to make in the house, each of them wanting to do different things:

Extract 6.xiii: Fergus and Hilary, 'It's totally not', *Love It or List It*

1. FER: =so why don't we leave this (.)
2.   this is a perfectly good opening
3.   [>why don't we leave it like this<]
4. HIL: [it's totally <u>not</u>] no it's not an option
5. FER: okay well let's scratch the closet systems (.) on the top floor
6. HIL: no don't be ridiculous that's ke::y to this <u>stor</u>age is <u>ev</u>erything
7. FER: you're so frustrating right now
8. HIL: know what maybe you're just getting a little taste
9.   of what I put up with with you (.) <u>all</u> the time
10. FER: there's no way I'm (missing) that
11. HIL: here's a possible solution
12.   take this wall back I dunno four four and a half feet

13.   as far as we can go give me a seven, eight foot opening
14.   right here
15. FER: that's actually not a bad idea
16. HIL: oh well what do you know
17. FER: cos then I can switch the beam to wood (.)
18.   and I'm gonna save a bundle of money there
19. HIL: at least one of us has you know (1.0) a brain that's
20.   functioning?
21. FER: that wasn't a meeting of the minds?
22. HIL   no
23. FER: felt like a meeting of the minds to me.
24. HIL: yeah (.) right

Although it is supposed to be an argument, apart from a short stretch of overlapping speech between the first two turns, there is no evidence of any of the typical interactional features of argument in this exchange. There are no turn-initial opposition markers ('yes but'), no raised volume, increased speed of delivery or repeated interruptions and overlapping speech. In fact, the overlap in lines 3 and 4 is not really 'violative' at all (Hutchby and Wooffitt 1998), because it occurs at a possible transitional relevance point for speaker change, rather than cutting them off in mid turn. The turn-taking is remarkably orderly, in spite of the potentially face-threatening content of the turns – the initial disagreement between Fergus and Hilary, his suggestion and her marked rejection of it ('it's totally not'), followed by the negative 'other' evaluations in lines 6–10. From line 11, after Hilary's second suggestion, they shift seamlessly into agreeing with each other, and share the joke about 'a meeting of the minds' (lines 21–24). As a result, this sequence thus comes across as an unconvincing, inauthentic argument; it is performed (and possibly rehearsed) as a confrontation, but interactionally it does not come off as one because it bears none of the features of disputatious talk.

   This begs the question, why do it? Indeed, one of the YouTube comments on this episode of *Love It or List It* draws attention to this very question of inauthenticity, asking 'why the faux rudeness?' One answer to this question may be that, because conflict and judgement have become so pervasive as the primary discourses of reality television genres that now, in order to produce spectacular (in the sense of watchable) broadcasts, editors must manufacture arguments wherever possible. Without confrontations, without the production of oppositional stances, without arguments between partici-pants and without evaluations and judgements, we might well ask, along with Lyn (in Extract 6.xii), 'What am I getting?'. Reality television has moved a long way from the live streaming of hours and hours of 'televised reality', available on the web and E4 in the early days of series such as *Big Brother*, where, if you watched for long enough, you might catch something interesting happening in the house. Now, a great deal of reality broadcasting comprises the non-live packaging of conflict as both the norm and the goal, and this is particularly evident in competition-based formats in which one participant, or team, is pitted to win against the other(s).

'Everything is personal'

This brings us to the final example of conflict and judgement as discourses of middle-space performance in *Four in a Bed*. As I have already mentioned above, this programme sets up a competition between B&B owners in the UK who have to evaluate one another's businesses on aspects relating to welcome, comfort, cleanliness and the quality of the breakfast they are given. Over the course of a week, they all go and stay in one another's B&Bs, and, at the end of each stay, they fill in a feedback sheet on which they have to give a score of one to ten, and make any comments they feel necessary about the quality of the experience. They also leave a sum of money in an envelope that corresponds to their professional estimation of what the cost of a night's stay should be in each place. The envelopes are opened at the end of the week, when, as the programme's website blurb puts it, 'the B&Bers come together for one last time to find out what they've been paid and to settle some scores'.[1]

There are very similar editing practices in *Four in a Bed* to those we have just seen in *Love It or List It*. The voice-over introduction to the broadcast states that 'when your home is your business, everything is personal', and the opening sequences contain a series of evaluations that frame the upcoming clashes between participants. They also function as framing devices for the character 'roles' of individual contestants, as will be seen in the following extracts. In this particular episode, three of the competing couples – Peter and Terry, Tony and Dawn Ann and Cherry and Graham – are on their way to their second destination of the week, 'Happy Donkey Hill' in North Wales, which is the B&B run by Katie and Andy.

The programme's continuity introduction consists of various extracts spliced together, showing retrospective shots from the previous episode as well as some short prospective sequences from the upcoming one. Most of these contain evaluations of one sort or another, and, in the shifts between scenes from the previous stay and those in their current location, each participant is attributed a character role that is developed in various ways throughout the week, as the participants go about making judgements not just regarding the standard of the B&B, but also about the personalities of their hosts. Here is the opening sequence:

Extract 6.xiv: Introduction, *Four in a Bed*

VO:	Four proud B and B owners
	((before leaving home, sitting on sofa))
PETER:	without being disrespectful to anybody else (.)
	we <u>are</u> the best bed and breakfast in Oxfordshire

> VO:　　take it in turn to host each other
> 　　　　((sitting at breakfast table))
> TERRY:　yeah white toast I said please

First, we see Peter and Terry in their home doing positive self-evaluation (i.e., boasting), which frames them as smug and superior rather than just 'proud'. Terry's unmitigated complaint about the toast in the next shot shows her being rude and a bit picky about food; this relates back to the previous episode in which she was unable to eat curry and is later picked up in a sequence showing host Katie doing negative other evaluation (i.e., being critical of Terry's pickiness):

> *To camera*　　((sitting on bed))
> KATIE:　　　it's her inability to eat or drink anything (.) without
> 　　　　　　complaining or picking or finding fault (.) and I <u>chall</u>enge
> 　　　　　　her to do that in my house hahaha

The scene is thus set for a confrontation between Katie and Terry. Later, we see the various couples again making critical evaluations of their host Katie and of the 'no children' rule as they drive to their destination; for example, in the following:

Extract 6.xiv: Driving to Happy Donkey Hill (a), *Four in a Bed*

> *For camera*　　((driving to the B&B))
> TERRY:　　　interesting that it's what I would call a family type place
> 　　　　　　to stay and yet they don't have- don't allow children

Extract 6.xiv: Driving to Happy Donkey Hill (b), *Four in a Bed*

> *Exchange*　　((driving to the B&B))
> TONY:　　　I've got a feeling it's gonna be a very interesting place
> 　　　　　　to be (.)
> DAWN:　　　yeah=
> TONY:　　　=the queen of the castle
> DAWN:　　　hh oh she'll be that alright

Extract 6.xiv: Driving to Happy Donkey Hill (c), *Four in a Bed*

> *For camera*　　((in car reading leaflet))
> CHERRY:　　gosh sounds absolutely <u>won</u>derful (.)
> 　　　　　　but they don't take ↑children ↑oh
> 　　　　　　it looks an ideal (.) set-up for children I would
> 　　　　　　have thought

In these extracts, participants are shown making a judgement about one of the others, from which we are invited to infer particular information about their character relating back to the previous episode, but which will also emerge during the current one. Katie is critical of Terry, who is a fussy eater; Katie herself is combative and overbearing; while everyone seems to be critical about the 'no children' rule. Furthermore, Graham's comment:

Extract 6.xiv: Driving to Happy Donkey Hill (d), *Four in a Bed*

For camera	((driving to B&B))
GRAHAM:	we've done our best (.) some people (1.0) have different views and it's quite understandable, and I'm looking forward to seeing (.) <u>oth</u>er B&Bs and picking up ideas

hints at the fact that he is not happy with the scores they received, even though he claims he is willing to 'pick up ideas'. As we saw in the introduction to *Love It or List It* (Extract 6.ix, above), these early sequences set the scene for upcoming issues that will be potential sources of conflict during the course of the episode. For instance, in the next two extracts, we see Katie under strain, getting stressed and snappy towards the end of the episode as she prepares breakfast. But, in Extract 6.xv, we also find evaluations of Katie and Andy spliced in with Graham's voice-over and to-camera comments, and in an exchange between Graham and Cherry:

Extract 6.xv: Breakfast (i), *Four in a Bed*

Exchange	((in the kitchen))
KATIE:	did she mention how she wants her eggs
ANDY:	no
	(3.0)
KATIE:	wearing them might be good

Extract 6.xv: Breakfast (ii), *Four in a Bed*

Exchange	((in the kitchen))
ANDY:	bit more bacon
KATIE:	don't ask
ANDY:	bit more bacon on there (.) sausage ((points at pan))
KATIE:	((throws down utensils)) d'you wanna <u>do</u> ↑it
GRAHAM VO:	Katie herself (.) she's a very strong character ((Katie flustered in the kitchen))
To camera	I would worry (.) from the point of view of running
GRAHAM	(.) a B&B (.) that she actually is going to hh (.) upset a lot of her clients
ANDY (TO KATIE):	that's it mushrooms, tomatoes, sausage,
Exchange	((sitting on the sofa))

CHERRY: I think her husband's a saint (1.0) [heh heh
GRAHAM: [huh that's right poor <u>chap</u>

The scene where Katie and Andy argue in the kitchen is followed by
Graham's VO evaluation of Katie as a 'strong character', which leads into
his to-camera negative judgement of her professional behaviour (her
potential to upset her clients) and Cherry's final evaluation of Andy as 'a
saint', which serves to reinforce the increasingly negative view we are being
given of 'feisty Katie'.

   Earlier in this chapter, I argued that confrontation on talk shows was
made dramatic and spectacular through the onstage performance of
aggravated, face-threatening evaluations and judgements. In the competition
shows, we see the same potential of evaluative discourse, here used to
produce a promise of upcoming drama and spectacle, but this drama is
realised *post hoc* through the editing process rather than framed and
articulated in the talk between participants, or worked up and managed by
a third-party host. The competition frame does, of course, require actions of
evaluation on the part of the participants as they judge the standard of their
accommodation, or the changes made to their home. But what is significant
is the way evaluations are also made on the personal level, and so the
competition is not simply played out as a professional contest between
B&Bs, but as a series of personal judgements and conflicts between the
owners as *characters*.

   The routine sequences at the end of each programme, which show the
host participants reading the anonymous evaluation forms left by their
guests, is an occasion to comment on their scores. In the following extract,
we see Katie and Andy in their kitchen, reacting to their feedback. Katie is
surprised at receiving a '5' for cleanliness:

Extract 6.xvi: Katie and Andy read their feedback forms, *Four in a Bed*

1. *For camera*	((reading form))
2. KATIE:	how clean was Happy Donkey Hill a fi↑ve
3. ((POINTING AT FORM))	we found animal hairs on the bedding
4.	we live on a fa::rm
5. KATIE ((TO ANDY)):	you you moult more than the dog
6.	I know who it was mister Portuguese man
7.	who keeps
8. ((WIPING HANDS))	wiping his (.) clothes and look at me
9.	I'm:: (.) dapper
10. KATIE VO:	and he's just so shot himself in the foot
11.	((Tony and Dawn packing their cases))
12. *For camera*	((reading form))
13. KATIE:	would you stay here again (.) no
14.	if they want to tactically vote or they were
15.	desperate

16.		to win (.) which they obviously are
17.	KATIE VO:	then that was a really really silly move wasn't it
18		((Katie and Andy embrace Tony and Dawn))
19.	((TO ANDY))	because we're going to Tony and Dawn
20.		Ann's next
21.	*To camera*	and I'm gonna pick up on every single fault
22.		I can possibly now

The comment in line 3 about animal hairs on the bedding leads her to the assumption that it was 'Mr Portuguese man' (Tony) who gave her this low score, and then into a critical assessment of him as someone who is over-fastidious and 'dapper' (line 9). More importantly for the momentum of the competition, we next hear her plan how she will take her revenge when it is Tony's turn to host the B&Bers, by picking up 'on every single fault' (line 21). In the next extract, the character judgements become more explicit and negative, where, over the final shots as we see the participants leaving, Katie ups her game and declares she will 'play dirty':

Extract 6.xvii: Leaving Happy Donkey Hill, *Four in a Bed*

1.	KATIE VO:	I think he's a backstabber (.) typical matador
2.		((Tony and Dawn packing the car boot))
3.	KATIE (*To camera*):	get it right between the shoulder-blades
4.		((mimes stabbing))
5.	KATIE VO:	and if that's the best they can come up with (.)
6.		then I'm I'm happy
7.		((Tony and Dawn drive away in their car))
8.	KATIE (*To camera*):	because (.) uhm (.) there's obviously nothing
9.		else that they they could pick up on
10.		((guests saying goodbye and leaving B&B))
11.	KATIE (*To camera*):	my strategy no::w (.) is to play dirty ((laughs))

The competition is now established as a conflict between the two characters Katie and Tony, and the continuity sequence at the end of the programme explicitly frames the next episode as a showdown between them, with the final shots splicing together what are presented as a series of prospective problems for hosts Tony and Dawn:

Extract 6.viii: Continuity sequence, *Four in a Bed*

1.	VO:	Next time on *Four in a Bed*
2.		((two people in yellow waterproofs leaving
3.		a house))
4.	*Exchange*	((in car))
5.	KATIE:	isn't that a terraced house?
6.	ANDY:	huhhum

7. KATIE:	eeoow
8. GRAHAM ((*In room*)):	I think we'll sleep on the floor again
9. KATIE (*To camera*):	he's a snake (.) he's an absolute
10.	snake in the grass
11. DAWN ((*To Terry*)):	are you ok (x x) d'you want to leave the
12.	room that's ok
13. TONY VO:	it is totally (.) unacceptable
14.	((Katie at restaurant table))
15. TONY(*To camera*):	and totally (.) rude
16. KATIE (*To camera*):	bring it on little man ((lying on bed))

The scene is set for another dramatic episode with the B&Bers: we see, first, a couple leaving in the rain, then Katie describing Tony as 'a snake in the grass', Graham saying they will have to sleep on the floor, Tony finding something 'unacceptable' and Katie spoiling for a fight. Once again, it is the evaluations that do the dramatic work here, as the participants are shown expressing dissatisfaction, complaining and making negative comments, while the final shot in the sequence is Katie's confrontational challenge addressed straight to camera. The episode thus concludes with this promise of more conflict and more judgement next time.

In these extracts from two competition format programmes, we have seen how the broadcast episodes are, in each case, saturated with discourses of evaluation and confrontation, seamlessly edited together to provide a framework of narrative coherence to the competition from one episode to the next. By narrative coherence here, I mean the kind of overarching storylines that emerge through the production work of the programme, rather than the oral narratives of personal experience found in other contexts of public participation broadcasting. Similar techniques of narrative construction through character and plot are of course at work in many of the reality television shows I have discussed in this book, from *Big Brother* to *Wife Swap* to *Come Dine With Me*. In one way, this is nothing new. As Jon Dovey noted in his critical discussion of docu-soaps, 'we are positioned not as witnesses to events but as participants in a process of narrative storytelling, moreover this is storytelling of a particularly impoverished kind, robbed of the fiction writer's freedom to truly shape a reality that configures as meaningful dramatic sense' (Dovey 2000: 148). However, in the contemporary reality genres of competition and contest featuring 'ordinary' people, there has been a shift from the dramatised realism of docu-soaps into a more knowingly constructed plotting of events. In programmes like *Love It or List It* and *Four in a Bed*, the narrative coherence hinges on the way that conflict is dramatised between participants with problematic rather than ordinary identities, identities that can be created through the manipulation of a particular set of discourses and developed through selecting specific actions and behaviours, particularly judgemental behaviours, that participants are shown engaging in during the course of the broadcast. In

Love It or List It and *Four in a Bed*, the use of participants' voices in VO segments, as well as their talk to and for the camera, adds a further layer of reflexive commentary and evaluation. The participants' talk thus frames, in various ways, the 'story' of the competition, which emerges primarily as a set of personal conflicts between them. (This is noticeable in comparison to the mocking detachment and fun-poking commentary of the narrator in *Come Dine With Me*, whose voice-over works essentially to produce comic and eccentric character roles for the participants.) And, in the end, it is the spectacle of interpersonal conflict that plays a large part of in making these shows watchable, as we will see in the final part of this chapter.

Conflict, judgement and the web-based audience

If public participation in the form of members of a studio audience with views and opinions is less visible than it used to be, social media sites like YouTube and Twitter provide insights into the way these shows are watched, perceived and interpreted by an audience that is also vocally present on the web. In a small sample of data collected from the official Twitter site for the two programmes, from hashtag term searches, and from YouTube comments, we can see something of what the web-based audience had to say about what its members were watching, and how they were saying it. Some of the key themes I have been discussing in the course of this chapter – performance and scriptedness versus authenticity, as well as discourses of conflict and judgement – are also present in the commenting and tweeting activity of people who participate in the web-based audience.

Although the official Twitter sites for the programmes invite people to 'join the debate' or 'join the conversation', overall, there is little evidence of any interaction between members of the audience on Twitter. The YouTube sites tend to generate more 'conversations' in the form of exchanges, as in the following sequence of six posts where we find a discussion thread commenting on the characters Joe and Lyn in *Love It or List It*. The issue of scriptedness, raised in the post about 'faux rudeness' quoted earlier in relation to Extract 6.xiii, is discussed here:

1. These two are jerks.
2. I hope this is scripted to make viewers hate them.
3. If this is scripting it's WAY over the top – painful to watch.

Who would want to come across as horrible as her. I don't mind the guy but she is a high-maintenance horror show. Doesn't care about her husband's needs and hovers over her children more than necessary. They have a lovely home in a hi-end neighbourhood. No where will ever be good enuf for her. Unless she changes they will be divorced at some point.

4. I cant figure out how the husband proposed to Lynn in the first place..seeing her oj this show alone made me feel bad for her children . . . such a miserable person . . . . . (my opinion base on this show only)
5. why the faux rudeness? Are all the episodes like this?
6. Can you please repost part 3? It's out of order and most of it has not audio. And after listening to this couple be so rude for the first two parts I want to see the final decision/results.

The first post evaluates the characters, while the second introduces the possibility of scripting and manipulated, inauthentic behaviour. In contrast, however, the next two posts (3 and 4) contain quite elaborate evaluations and predictions based on character judgements, which seem to indicate that the participants are being perceived as authentic and situated as real people in a real couple in the real world. The last two posts return to the topic of rudeness, and to the final outcome of the competition. We see here, once again, the articulation of 'like us/not like us' – these are people whose actions are seen to have consequences in the world ('they will be divorced at some point'/'such a miserable person'), yet, at the same time, are seen as 'not like us', in performance, doing things that viewers can disapprove of and judge as 'a high-maintenance horror show'.

The tweets about the programmes fall into various categories, but viewer comments tend to be less about questions of authenticity, and more about their own current status as fans who are currently watching, as well as about the broadcasts' inherent watchability, as in the following:

One of my favorite shows right now is love it or list it. Am I really a 20 year old college student or a 36 year old house wife. #hgtv

I'm watching love it or list it Vancouver. Nobody is changing the channel Wide awake thank god love it or list it's on ☺

I'm trying to start my day but how do I just walk away from Love It or List It. I don't have the strength. #HGTV

#fourinabed – yes.i love this

Reasons to love Sundays – Four In A Bed Omnibus! #fourinabed

I've had the most amazing lamb dinner, going back to bed now to watch the last #FourInABed #lazysunday

Others contain a form of meta-commentary on the genre overall:

> #FourRooms #fourinabed I'd like to see these 2 shows integrated somehow. Tamara running a B&B while trying to sell you a Banksy.

> They should make a #LoveItorListIt show for relationships. Hillary will try to update a mate and David will find a new mate. #youdecide2013

> And who here would watch a show on HGTV about Hilary's assistant Desta from Love It or List It? Maybe called Desta-Nation? Who's with me?

By far the most common postings on YouTube and Twitter in relation to these programmes were about the characters, as we saw in the first post above ('these two are jerks'). In posts about the episode of *Four in a Bed* on YouTube, the comments were all short, evaluative and targeted at Katie. One of the milder versions of these negative evaluations was:

> that woman irritates me

but one poster did show their appreciation of this show as a performance:

> epic evil laugh at the end

The tweets contained equally negative judgements, some addressed directly to the participants:

> "The bed creaks every time you move" WELL IT WILL WITH YOU, YOU FAT, OLD, UGLY BEACH WHALE! #FourInABed

> Watching #FourInABed and I must say the loud mouth cow on here needs a slap! And a gastric band!

> owner of fatbasturd donkey hill would have to pay me to stay me to sleep in her dog bed bitter & vile @happydonkeyhill #fourinabed #4inabed

There are also posts that combine assessments of the participants and places shown on the programme with their status as real people in the world running real businesses:

> Deserved winner on #fourinabed think one couple could have really damaged their business, horrid people.

> #fourinabed this fat woman is absolutely VILE!!! Boycott her b and b

> I would never pay £99 for a b&b. #fourinabed

In sum, this sample of posts on YouTube and Twitter suggests that evaluation is also a dominant discourse in the environment of the web-based audience. While some people comment on the scripted (or not) nature of exchanges on *Love It or List It*, and others make meta-comments on the genre and generic developments, what the participating audience on these websites primarily do is evaluate and judge the characters presented to them in the shows.

Summary: discourses of dispute and evaluation

The discourses of public participation – conflict and judgement – discussed in this chapter are situated in very different kinds of mediated environments from the argument and opinion-giving I focussed on in Chapter 5. From the arguments, discussions and debates of the issue-based talk show and the radio phone-in, we moved to the arena of confrontational talk shows and the highly personal disputes that are played out on the stages of programmes like *Jerry Springer* and *Jeremy Kyle*. We then examined extracts from the developing genre of competition reality shows, where, again, the evaluation and judgement of others is an essential part of the format's generic structure and has an important dramatising function in the production of conflict between participants.

Through the comparison of two separate episodes of *Jeremy Kyle*, we saw how a particular kind of narrative participatory framework is necessary for disputed events to be performed as a spectacle of conflict. Two people quarrelling onstage does not necessarily constitute a performance in the sense we are talking about here – that is, in the middle-space performances of tele-factuality, where there needs to be some attention paid to the production of conflicting stances for the co-present studio audience to align with, or against. In order to achieve this performance, a 'talkable issue' has to emerge from the story before the dispute can be made dramatic. The organisation of the talk is crucial to the successful realisation of that issue, and the story itself then becomes the background to the evaluative work of the host as dramatiser and problematiser of participants' conflicting positions.

In competition formats such as *Love It or List It* and *Four in a Bed*, conflict is again at the heart of a programme's dynamic, since the development of a dramatic 'plot' that will take the series from one programme to the next hinges on there being a potential for confrontation and disputes between the participants. The shows are framed as conflict saturated; participants' talk is recycled in evaluative voice-over commentary, and in talk to camera and for camera that is judgemental and critical of the others, not just of their bed-and-breakfast businesses. The personality and character of competing B&Bers are constantly under scrutiny, and episodes are edited to foreground potential areas of conflict between them.

Finally, in all the mediated contexts examined in this chapter, ordinariness is once more called into question. The people who take part in these shows, whether as protagonists in the performance of stories of social crisis, or as contestants in some form of competition or game show, are positioned through the middle-space environments of reality television as people with very specific identities, and, most crucially, identities that can be brought into opposition and conflict with one another. In his discussion of first-person media and the rise of reality television, Dovey argues that there is an important connection between broadcasting and society, since how people speak in the public domain 'forms the landscape of the common culture' (2000: 155); seeing people increasingly speaking subjectively and emotively on television thus brings about a shift in that public culture. In the kind of competitive programmes examined in this chapter, there does seem to have been a shift in the discourses of public participation broadcasting towards increasingly pervasive personal disputes and confrontations, performed or constructed as people are brought into conflict through the middle spaces of tele-factuality. So, it is not just in talk show studios that conflict between 'ordinary' people is transformed into spectacle for the audience and viewers, but also in competition show formats, where participant identities are deliberately constructed as specific 'characters' through highly edited sequences of evaluative talk. 'Ordinary' people are thus represented as recognisably 'someone who is like X' or 'someone who does Y', but not necessarily as someone who is 'like us'. 'Doing being ordinary' is not very watchable, as the low performance value of Mike and Fiona's appearance on *Jeremy Kyle* demonstrated. A 'high-maintenance horror show', as one of the tweets described Lyn in *Love It or List It*, clearly is.

Note

1 *Four in a Bed*, Channel 4. Available at http://www.channel4.com/programmes/four-in-a-bed/4od.

7 Discourses of participation
Advice and makeover

Introduction: advice-giving as a discursive activity

Advice-giving of one sort or another has become one of the routinely established discourses of broadcasting in a range of contexts and genres, whether through the radio phone-in format or, increasingly, on television in various forms of makeover and lifestyle programming. Interactions between advice-seeking participants and designated 'expert' advice-givers are usually mediated through programme hosts, but mediated advice-giving has been evolving – particularly on radio – to expand participation in the use of interactive media such as text and email. Radio phone-in programmes can be found across all networks, dedicated to offering callers advice on specific topics, from what to plant in their garden or financial problems to health and relationships. On TV, the rapid growth in lifestyle and makeover programming also involves forms of advice-giving, or 'coaching', with experts explaining how to redesign practically every aspect of life: your home, your wardrobe, your business, your body. Members of the public who take part in such programmes are therefore usually positioned as advisees – people with a problem that needs solving, a wardrobe that needs making over or a life that needs changing in some way. In other words, they are on the receiving end of advice-giving as a mediated discursive practice.

This chapter begins with a brief account of pragmatic theories of advice-giving as a discursive activity, and its associated interactional issues of face, particularly in relation to institutional contexts. A range of broadcast contexts will then be examined, including those where advice-giving is the programme's explicitly acknowledged, principal activity, as well as programmes in which forms of advice-giving are recast in the discourses of makeover, coaching and instruction. The focus will be on the design and delivery of this advice within different participatory frameworks for talk, and on the way the interactional roles and situated identities of programme hosts, expert advice-givers and advisees shape and are shaped by these different media contexts.

In pragmatic terms, giving advice is a directive speech act, in that it belongs to a family of utterance types where 'the words are aimed at making the hearer do something, such as commanding, requesting, inviting, forbidding, suggesting and so on' (Cutting 2002: 17). It is a speech act that is generally intended to benefit the hearer or 'recipient' of the advice, rather than speaker as advice-giver, and this distinguishes it as an activity from other directive speech acts such as requests or commands, which generally work the other way around. Requests involve getting someone to do something for the speaker's benefit, while advice involves getting someone to do something for the hearer's benefit. However, the above definition does not capture the complexity of advice-giving as a situated interactional accomplishment, which is always sensitive to the local context in which it occurs: the relationship between the adviser and advisee, the nature of the advice being given and the level of face threat (both positive and negative) which that advice may contain.

For these reasons, advice-giving is not a straightforward matter. Advice can be requested or offered, self-initiated (e.g., 'I'd like some advice') or other-initiated (e.g., 'Do you mind if I give you a bit of advice?'). The design of advice will inevitably depend on the configuration of the particular interactional context in which it is produced. To the question, 'should I go to the party, or stay at home?', the reply might be in the form of a direct, unmitigated, agentless imperative (e.g., 'Go to the party!'), which is functionally closer to a command. Or, it might be delivered in other more or less mitigated forms, from the explicit speech act ('my advice would be to go to the party') to the more mitigated 'I'd stay at home if I were you' or 'you might want to think about staying at home'. These are all constructed examples, rather than naturally occurring instances of advice, however, and all of them could be interpreted as potentially face threatening, depending on the local, interactional context of the utterance. The degree of directness or mitigation of the advice, as well as how it is received, will be contingent on all of the above factors in any naturally occurring talk where advice-giving takes place.

When advice is delivered within a professional, institutional context, where participant roles are likely to be asymmetrical, additional sensitive issues around face threat and levels of explicitness often come into play. This can be illustrated with a brief example of situated advice taken from a specific institutional context: health care offered to first-time mothers in Scotland. In his study of how these women reacted to advice given by health visitors, McIntosh (1986) found that they were often unhappy about the way that advice was delivered:

'I don't like the health visitors. I mean, it's no' like help or advice – they *tell* you. It wisnea, "Maybe you should do this," it was "you *should* do this," it was "you should do this". Y'know, "You're doing it all wrong." That's how I never went to the clinic. I was sick o'bein' bossed about.'

'She keeps tellin' me, "Do this, do that." It makes ye feel like a moron, that yer no' capable o' lookin after yer baby. It undermines yer confidence. Ah always feel guilty after she's been as if ah've been doin' everything wrong. It makes me mad. Ah don't say anything at the time, ah just mutter a few oaths when she's gone.'

(McIntosh 1986; quoted in Heritage and Sefi 1992: 410)

The women in this study reported that they felt the advice they were given was not only demeaning, it made them feel incompetent and even 'guilty'. They found the direct imperatives ('do this', 'do that') particularly problematic; as one of the mothers observes, 'they tell you'. As a result, the advice-giving was experienced by the women more as being 'bossed about'. In a later study in the same context of health visitors talking to first-time mothers, Heritage and Sefi (1992) found that advice was indeed mainly delivered in strongly prescriptive terms:

I would <u>recommend</u> giving her a bath every day
The hospital <u>recommend</u> that she shouldn't start solids until she's four months
<u>Well</u> <u>my</u> <u>advice</u> <u>to</u> <u>you</u> <u>is</u> that you firmly put her down

(Heritage and Sefi 1992: 368)

It was often imperative '<u>always</u> <u>be</u> <u>very</u> <u>quiet</u> at night', and often expressed using verbs of obligation:

and <u>I</u> <u>think</u> <u>you</u> <u>should</u> involve your husband as much as possible now and when you're leaving her <u>you</u> <u>ought</u> <u>to</u> <u>put</u> <u>her</u> on her tummy really

Heritage and Sefi (1992) concluded that the advice was often delivered 'without any indication that it was wanted'; that is to say, advice was other initiated by health visitors whether or not mothers asked for it, and it was 'not accommodated to individual mothers', since little attempt was made to fit the advice-giving to specific contextual situations. They also found that three quarters of health visitor initiated advice was met with either passive or active resistance (1992: 409–410).

Both these studies clearly demonstrate the conversational delicacy of advice-giving – regardless of the benefit to hearers, advice can be tricky to give and is not always positively received by those to whom it is delivered. In the next section, I turn to broadcast contexts for advice-giving, where one of the main differences to the above examples is that the advice tends to be self-initiated; in other words, that, unlike the women in the examples above, participants in occasions for mediated advice-giving have usually requested the advice, and this, in turn, affects its design as well as the way it is received.

Advice-giving on-air

There have been a number of studies dealing with the phenomenon of broadcast advice across a range of different programmes – particularly call-in radio shows that are either dedicated to a specific topic, or that feature more general helplines for emotional or social problem-solving. For example, Hudson (1990) analysed the grammatical structure of advice addressed to callers phoning in to *The Garden Show*, an Australian radio programme where callers can ask an expert, 'the Garden Lady', about their horticultural problems. Hudson found that there were three stages of advice-giving, consisting of a caller request or instruction from the host to provide advice, followed by some direct conversational interaction between the expert as advice-giver and the advisee, and then the completion of the advice, which was usually projected and atelic; in other words, to be carried out at some unspecified time in the future. In the design of her advice-giving turns, the expert sometimes used direct imperatives (e.g., 'check out the roots!'), but also other forms, which seemed particularly tied to the local context of expertise. For instance, advice was found in what Hudson called 'knowledge statements', such as:

> 'A lot of people that are growing exhibition roses and things for show or just want to have the ultimate perfect rose for cutting will prune roses extremely hard.'
>
> (Hudson 1990: 286)

This kind of statement was interpreted as an advice directive; that is, do what the experts do. He also found a routinely consistent alternation of first- and second-person pronouns ('I'/'you') in utterances where first the advice-giver and then advice-recipient were positioned as agents of the projected action. So, for instance, while the advice-giver was in the turn-initial agent position in the following utterance:

> The first thing I would do is prune out anything that looks really bad

in the next two examples, it is the advice *receiver* who becomes the agent of the projected action in the final clause:

I wouldn't feed it until spring no matter what you do
I wouldn't break up the root ball unless you have to

(Hudson 1990: 286)

What appears to be happening, then, in these advice-giving turns is a construction of joint expertise, where the expert occupies the first agent position, then transfers it to the recipient in the second. This positioning of the recipient as agent in advice-giving turns is also evident in the next two examples, each with a variation of future projected doing, or not doing, something ('you will', 'you don't want to') where second-person 'you' is the advisee:

and then you'll start working from the outside
you don't want to prune heavily on a citrus, especially this time of year

(Hudson 1990: 287)

The potential scope of reference for 'you' can be generic as well as particular in these examples, and we will return shortly to the issue of how experts make advice relevant not just to the advisee, but to anyone listening to the broadcast who may also be a potential ratified addressee – that is, able to benefit from advice on the same issue. But, first, we can look at three short examples from another radio programme, based on the same topic of gardening, but with a different participation framework in so far as the advice-seekers are not telephone callers, but present as an audience. Some interesting differences emerge in the way the advice is designed and delivered by a panel of expert horticulturalists who answer questions from members of that audience on a pre-prepared topic.

Advice-giving as performance

In comparison with the examples of advice-giving from the radio phone-in above, the long-running *Gardeners' Question Time*[1] (BBC Radio 4), recorded in a different geographical location in the UK (or, sometimes, outside it) each week, includes requests for advice from co-present members in the programme's local audience. The co-presence of host, a panel of experts and members of the audience constitutes a participatory framework where direct interaction can take place between the person asking for advice and the panel of experts who provide it. This local interactional context plays an important part in both the development of the advice-giving sequence and the design of advice-giving turns.

Although some of the advice shares similar structural forms to those identified by Hudson (1990), much of it does not, as will be shown in the following extracts. First, the advice-giving itself is often framed by a light-hearted key, or jokiness, in its style of delivery. For example, immediately noticeable in Extract 7.i, below, is the humorous keying of the two direct unmitigated imperatives on how to shape a hedge:

Extract 7.i: *Gardeners' Question Time*, BBC Radio 4, February 2011

> so <u>break</u> <u>away</u> from these strict verticals and horizontals
> and just <u>allow</u> it to- to bulge with age like the rest of us

There is also an alternation of first- and second-person agents, but not as agents of the same type of actions. In Extract 7.ii, below, which consists of an extended advice-giving turn by another expert on the panel addressing the same question about hedges, it is the expert who is agent of all the projected actions (shown in ***bold italics*** in the transcript below), while the recipient benefits from the results (underlined in the transcript).

Extract 7.ii: *Gardeners' Question Time*, BBC Radio 4, February 2011

1. EXP: ***I would let it get established*** for the first year and then
2.   I would come in and I would cut it (.) at the height
3.   <u>you</u> <u>want</u> the goblet-shaped branches to form
4.   which is <u>what you're</u>
5.   <u>after</u> isn't it a more open shape
6.   and so ***I would cut it back*** to a bud that's pointing out
7.   just above it and then it will throw out other branches
8.   and <u>you'll get</u> that open shape
9.   and I think they're beautifully shaped trees
10.   I've got four in my courtyard and ***I actually sort of lightly***
11.   ***shape them*** and cut- cut quite a lot out of them each year
12.   and I've got these lovely gnarled knobbly shapes
13.   and they are a really beautiful winter outline

Here, the advice develops in a series of recommended actions that will produce the desired results: 'you'll get that open shape' (line 8). But, rather than constructing a relationship of joint expertise between the advice-giver and the recipient, this advice is delivered entirely through first-person agency as a more one-sided display of expertise, ending with an evaluative sequence describing those results from personal experience (lines 10–13) – 'I've got four in my courtyard' and 'I've got these lovely gnarled knobbly shapes' – that provides a warrant for the advice just given.

The final *Gardeners' Question Time* example is a complete advice-seeking/advice-delivery sequence. It begins with a question from Carol in the audience about what to plant on a river bank, which produces a non-serious answer from one of the panel members. The host then selects another expert, Bob, to answer the question (line 10). Further interaction between expert and questioner serves to elaborate the kind of advice being sought, in terms of what it is exactly that she wants for her river bank (lines 11–14), and another joke (lines 19–20). This is followed by a lengthy advice-giving turn and acknowledgement by the recipient.

Extract 7.iii: *Gardeners' Question Time*, BBC Radio 4, February 2011

```
 1. CAROL:   [—] and my question is (.) we have about two hundred
 2.          metres of river bank (.) which occasionally floods (.)
 3.          what does the panel suggest that we plant on it
 4.          to provide interest (.) uh and which will survive
 5. EXP:      you thought of rice?
 6. CAROL:    uhhuh =
 7. AUD:             =hahahaha
 8. CAROL:    I do have the odd (.) willow.
 9. AUD:      uhahahahaha
10. HOST:     um Bob (.) what d'you think.
11. BOB:      well Carol you said you want interest d'you mean
12.           you want (.) interest in flowers and foliage?
13.           to bring in more wildlife or you want
14.           something tasty that will grow there.
15. CAROL:    um more like shrubs and small trees we do get swans:
16.           a:nd we do get (.) quite a lot of wonderful birds
17.           including kingfishers so anything that attracts the birds
18.           would also be (.) very useful.
19. BOB:      well if you want to attract birds I can't think of anything
20.           more effective than redcurrants (.) um ahuh
21. CAROL:    huhuhu=
22. AUD:            =uhuhhuh[huh
23. BOB:                    [I mean (s)=
24. CAROL:                  [uhuh↑
25. BOB:      =uh possibly cherries but they won't grow so well there
26.           however (.) if you want to fill up the bank with something
27.           then the the flowering redcurrants (.) which of course
28.           give you that very early um flowers and there's not just
29.           the ordinary pink ones don't forget there's (.) white ones
30.           (Tidesman's White) there's a dark red one there's
31.           a whole range of those (.) and then *I would also go with*
32.           *the brambles* because again (.) providing it's not totally
33.           waterlogged all the time you get the flowers (.)
34.           (again there's) a range of flowers some of them qui:te
35.           attractive smaller leaf but the amount of butterflies (.)
36.           the amount of bees they bring in (.) is unbelievable
37.           plus the brambles will really help to hold the bank together,
```

38.		improve your security and they're <u>won</u>derful havens
39.		for wildlife so *I would go in that direction* rather than
40.		look for something more exotic.
41.	CAROL:	thank you
42.	HOST:	right let's take another one

Two further points about how advice is designed can be made in relation to this example. First, once again, we find an orientation to the same light-hearted, playful keying of the activity as in Extract 7.i, above. The host's question, 'what does the panel suggest' (line 3), indicates no specific, selected next speaker, and the first response is a self-selection by one of the panel members (line 5) who suggests rice. This gets a response of laughter from the audience. Another joking exchange occurs in lines 19–20 where the first advice Bob offers also produces a response of laughter, first from the recipient then from the audience. Second, within the long advice-giving turn in lines 25–40, where various suggestions are made in the form of a list of different plants, we find two occurrences of the advice-giver as projected agent: 'I would also go with the brambles' and 'I would go in that direction' (lines 31–32, 39). As in Extract 7.ii, the recipient is positioned as recipient of a desired outcome (lines 19 and 26) – 'if you want to attract birds' and 'if you want to fill up the bank' –while the agency position is taken up by the expert for all the projected actions.

To summarise, in the context of this particular programme and its partici-pation framework of co-present host, audience and panel of experts, the activity of advice-giving is being produced as a performance. Significantly, one of the affordances of this participatory framework of a co-present panel and audience is that the interactional relationship between advice-givers and recipients is locally established within a staged, bounded event, rather than within the framework of a phone-in where caller and expert are not physi-cally co-present. Furthermore, this relationship also constitutes one of in-group membership: experts do not simply give advice, but deliver it with a repertoire of jokes that work through shared topical knowledge and life experience frames between the panel and the audience (in these examples, making jokes about rice or redcurrants, or the implication of a shared age identity in 'allow it to bulge like the rest of us').

In *Gardeners' Question Time*, the situated performance of expertise in front of an audience is as salient as the advice itself. In all the above examples, several features of the 'communicative focussing' in performance events at the higher end of the scale (Coupland 2007: 147–148) can be identified; in particular, the humorous keying of the experts' turns that produces meanings which are designed to be both informative and amusing, and which serve to frame the delivery of the expert advice itself. The advice is addressed to one specific recipient, but it is designed for the collective audience (both co-present in the studio and listeners to the broadcast) by gardening experts who are also media professionals, and whose display of expertise is keyed as both knowledgeable and entertaining, at least for the specific in-group community of listeners it principally targets. As such, it is 'listenable to' in terms of its performance value, as well as being topically informative. The participatory role of the audience is collectively to represent that community and respond to the jokes, as well as individually to provide the questions, and, in that specific role, their most relevant interactional identity is oriented towards being (a) someone who has a garden, however tiny, and (b) someone with a particular problem relating to that garden.

In the next section, we return to advice-giving in the context of radio phone-in programmes where the advice is more explicitly distributed in terms of its target addressees to include not just the person seeking advice but others in the listening audience who may have similar issues and problems. Once again, the participatory frameworks of the broadcast, and the interactional identities of the participants, play an important part in shaping the local design and delivery of the advice that is given.

Calling for advice

In radio phone-ins offering advice, whether on a specific, pre-selected topic or in response to caller-initiated topics, it is routine for hosts and experts to design their talk in such a way as to address the audience as well as the current caller. In their study of advice-giving on talk radio in the USA, DeCapua and Dunham observed that 'a basic similarity among all radio talk shows is that the interactions taking place are not occurring solely for the benefit of the interlocutors, but are instead functioning as entertainment and sources of information for a wider listening audience' (1993: 528). Hutchby (1995) also analysed distributed advice-giving on call-in radio, and the specific ways in which experts design their advice for the wider constituency of the listening audience as well as for the advice-seeking caller. In these calls, shifts in footing occur within advice-giving turns where the expert is no longer addressing one particular caller with a problem, but anyone who might have a similar kind of problem. Hutchby also noted how the host displayed an orientation to the wider listening audience by acting as 'proxy questioner', asking further questions on behalf of the caller or on behalf of other people in similar situations who may be listening. Advice-giving is thus often designed for more than one recipient, although this can sometimes be interactionally problematic for the actual caller, as Hutchby showed in the following extract:

Extract 7.iv

```
1. E:   but I would always say to people if you're
2.      gunna do that, .hh yih must go into an advice
3.      centre, .h an sit dow:n with an advice giver
4.      in a C.A.B. or somethin' like that,
```

5.		.h an' go through the figure work. .h
6.		an' go through whether, it's (.) all<u>ow</u>able
7.		in your particular case. .hh because if yuh
8.		<u>don'</u>t do that an' just go into it b-
9.		yihknow, .h er because you've 'eard
10.		there's been a change in the rules yih
11.		<u>c</u>an come uns<u>tuc</u>k.
12.		(0.6)
13.	E:	okay?
14.	C:	<u>I</u>: see

(Transcript adapted from Hutchby 1995)

Here, having broadened out the target addressees to include 'people' and continued to use a more generic second person 'you' in lines 1–2 ('I would always say to people if you're gunna do that yuh must go into an advice centre'), Hutchby notes that it is only after the expert produces an understanding check in line 13 that the current caller responds, having failed to recognise that they are also a targeted recipient of this advice-giving sequence and thus the selected next speaker at the end of the expert's turn (lines 11–12). Further ways in which hosts and experts work towards making an individual caller's problem relevant to the wider audience are discussed in the next section, taking examples from a popular UK radio broadcast offering help and advice called *The Surgery*.[2]

'How can we help?'

In phone-ins where callers are seeking advice about problems such as relationship breakdown or other complex social issues, the problem has to be first established ('the diagnostic stage') before the expert can suggest what the caller should do about it ('the directive stage') (DeCapua and Dunham 1993). The role of the caller is thus to recount their problem, sometimes in the form of a narrative, while the role of the host is to elicit the background to the story and arrive at the clear identification of the problem. The role of the expert is to provide the advice. The following extract illustrates how these different roles are played out, how the problem gets to be identified and how subsequent advice is designed for an array of potential listeners. BBC Radio 1's *The Surgery* features a host, an expert psychologist and callers phoning in for advice, often on thematic issues. This particular show is dealing with problems of confidence. Aled is the host, Matt is the expert on the show and Mark is the caller:

Extract 7.v: 'Kind of closeted' (1), *The Surgery*

1.	ALED:	er let's go to the phone lines line one hello Mark?↑
2.	MARK:	hi there

```
 3. ALED:   hey Mark how can we help tonight?
 4. MARK:   erm so (.) yeah basically my problem is one
 5.         that should have been eradicated years ago
 6.         but it's still a bit of an issue (.) erm I'm gay erm
 7.         I'm ki::nd of closeted er cause I go to church and stuff
 8.         erm a::nd a lot of people are still kind of divided within
 9.         the church about that but also my mum and dad
10.         are from Africa and so people are still kinda
11.         getting loads and loads of hate about something
12.         that's not really their fault↑ and something that
13.         they probably wouldn't choose
14. ALED:   yeah
15. MARK:   I'm totally comfortable in myself↑ er I've been to uni
16.         an' stuff e::rm and my uni friends know and it's not even
17.         an issue↑erm but er my mum and dad obviously
18.         I love them to bits I'm just wondering (.)do I need
19          to rock the boat and if so erm (1.0) why (.) and (1.0)
20.         just [just getting the confidence to do that [because it=
21. ALED:        [hmmm                                    [well
22. MARK:   = could cause massive divisions (x x x)
23. ALED:   before we talk to Matt then I suppose I would say Mark
24.         that you're the only person that can actually answer
25.         whether your parents need to know
26. MARK:   yeah
27. ALED:   when we have people calling up talking about coming out
28.         normally its err (.) I'm I- I'm worried about it going wrong
29.         I don't know whether I'm going to be accepted
30.         but you sound completely sort↑ed in who you are
31.         and your life and your friends accept you and (.)
32.         you sound like you're in a very good place?
33.         (2.0)
34.         is that the case?
35. MARK:   yeah definitely yeah yeah yeah definitely erm loving life
36.         at the moment I'm on my way to an Easter egg hunt party
37.         (x x )
38. ALED:   ((laughing)) so when it comes to your parents then
39.         what why is it↑you tell me why do you want
40.         your parents to know?
```

This extract begins with the host's problem-eliciting question: 'how can we help?' Mark then gives an account of the background to his problem, with extensive details of context and identity that serve to ground his request for advice on coming out to his parents delivered in lines 18–19 ('I'm just wondering (.) do I need to rock the boat') and the possible outcome of this action ('it could cause massive divisions'). Having produced two typically disaffiliating tokens in line 21 ('hmm', 'well') as Mark nears the completion of his request for advice, the host's first response in lines 23–25 is interesting as it almost appears to be challenging the relevance of this caller's request: 'I suppose I would say Mark that you're the only person that can actually answer whether your parents need to know'. Just as Fitzgerald and Housley observed in their discussion of the relationship between opinions and social membership categories (see Chapter 2), where certain opinions are often assumed by hosts to be tied to specific identities, we can see here that experiencing particular problems seems to be tied to social identity categories. Mark has just self-presented as someone who appears to be very confident, rather than expressing his problem in terms of being 'worried' which the host associates with callers who have 'coming out' questions:

when we have people calling up talking about coming out
normally its err (.) I'm I- I'm worried about it going wrong

The host pursues his assessment of the caller as 'someone who is com-pletely sorted' (line 30) with a request for clarification of this from Mark at the end of the turn in line 32: 'you sound like you're in a very good place?' This is followed by a two-second pause as the caller does not immediately take up the next turn here to respond, and the host has to reframe his assessment as a direct question: 'is that the case?' (line 34). The two-second delay (line 33) may well be caused by the host's assessment of Mark as someone who doesn't appear to have a problem. Having called in to ask for help, Mark finds himself being re-categorised as someone who seemingly doesn't need any. The host then goes on to elicit more information about the problem with a directive-framed question in line 39: 'what why is it↑ you tell me why do you want your parents to know?'

As can be seen in the above sequence, the host's role is not simply to elicit a putative problem from the caller, but to do some considerable work in establishing that there is in fact a problem and then clarifying exactly what that problem might be. In the next extract, following on from the host's directive 'tell me why you want your parents to know', Mark represents himself as 'just a little bit worried' in line 3:

Extract 7.vi: 'Kind of closeted' (2), *The Surgery*

1. MARK: Well just because (.) I dunno I've got kind of an-
2.   an unconditional love at the moment between me and my
3.   parents and I'm just (.) a little bit worried
4.   that it is conditional
5.   and I guess (.) just to kind of

6.   move on from this point in my life
7.   erm my Dad has often kinda said about (.) about people
8.   that gay erm he kind of lumps us in with all sort of other
9.   [different kinds of people
10. ALED: [yeah
11. MARK: and [I'm just thinking does he really love me do-does=
12. ALED: [yeah
13. MARK: =my mum really love me and I'm sure they do erm
14.   but if they were just confronted with this knowledge=
15. ALED: =yeah=
16. MARK: =about it it might take them a bit of [time or ( )
17. ALED: [is there any chance they know?

From this point onwards in the call, the host moves into more of an alignment with the caller through his minimal response turns ('yeah'; lines 10, 12, and 15) as Mark elaborates his 'worries' in more detail: 'I'm just thinking does he really love me do- does my mum really love me' (lines 11–13). Further elaboration of these worries ensues, with a more explicit alignment developing between host and caller, culminating in the host's rhetorical question seen below in line 1, the beginning of a transition sequence in which the host hands over the floor to Matt, the expert on the show:

Extract 7.vii: 'Kind of closeted' (3), *The Surgery*

1. ALED: =what is it about coming out to dads eh?
2.   I don't think that ever gets any easier does it so Matt (.)
3.   Mark a refreshing [caller when it comes to coming out=
4. MATT: [yeah
5. ALED: = clearly [sorted in who he is=
6. MATT: [absolutely yeah
7. ALED: =see he doesn't need to do this because
8.   as in he doesn't live under his parents' roof or or anything
9. MATT: no
10. ALED: =but he just wants to↑
11. MATT: and I can completely understand why he does because
12.   everyone (.) w- wants to feel that that people
13.   understand them completely especially their loved ones
14.   y'know you want to live freely you want to live your life
15.   a- as you are you don't want to hide things from people
16.   that you love and and who love you back
17.   so I can I can totally understand that (.)
18.   and I think he's thought this through really well
19.   and he's at a really good place now because he's he's

20.	he's weighing up
21.	you know whether he should
22.	or whether he shouldn't what I would say is
23.	he just has to consider the consequences and whether
24.	he can live with those consequences whatever they are
24.	and only he he is going to know what that might be

The rhetorical question in the host's turn (line 1) generalises Mark's particular problem as a recognisable, shareable experience, and functions as a pivotal move into the expert advice-giving section of the call. Directly addressing the expert in line 2, the host quickly summarises Mark as someone who is 'refreshing' and 'clearly sorted', referring to him in the third person and shifting into a new footing in which Mark becomes the topic of the advice-giving, rather than its direct recipient. We then find a further orientation to his specific situation as a generalised one first in lines 12–13 ('everyone wants to feel that people understand them completely') and also as expert Matt continues using the third-person generic 'you' in lines 14–15 ('y'know you want to live freely, you want to live your life as you are'). When he finally delivers the advice itself, it is addressed to the host rather than directly to Mark: 'what I would say is he just has to consider the consequences and whether he can live with those consequences' (lines 22–24).

In this sequence of advice-giving, the host and caller do a considerable amount of work to identify and elaborate the problem, which involves repositioning Mark from being someone who is confident to a more relevant caller identity as someone who is worried. The expert then reframes his specific problem as a recognisable and generalisable one, moving the caller from the participant role of directly addressed recipient to that of ratified overhearer of talk between the host and the expert. In this sequence, Mark and his problem become topicalised and evaluated – in a sense, 'modelled' by the expert as the right way to start thinking about how to come out to your parents. The stages of a call for advice identified by DeCapua and Dunham (1993), and the participatory framework and associated footings of a call identified by Hutchby (1995), are reproduced in this extract, with the advice itself eventually being delivered on this occasion as a mitigated directive to an indirectly targeted third-person addressee. Unlike the experts giving gardening advice in the extracts discussed previously, however, the expert here does not project himself as agent of the suggested course of action, but remains in the position of advice-giver, leaving the caller as agent ('what I would say is he just has to consider the consequences . . .'), thus pragmatically maintaining a degree of distance between adviser and advisee, yet without the explicit advice-giving and strong modal forms of obligation found in the advice from health visitors discussed earlier (Heritage and Sefi 1992).

'Get ready to text': the audience as advice-givers

As discussed in earlier chapters, one of the ways in which broadcasting has developed public participation through the use of interactive modes of communication is by regularly inviting listeners to text, email or comment in online forums. This has had varying consequences, depending on the activity engaged in. In the context of debate and discussion, such as during the BBC's Asylum Day or *Election Call*, the introduction of text and email produced a different set of affordances that proved to be ultimately less satisfactory than those of interactional engagement in co-present face-to-face, or telephone voice-to-voice, talk between members of the public and politicians or other experts. In the narrative context of *Changing Tracks* examined in Chapter 4, texting and online chat enabled listeners as story recipients to do the evaluating work, which displayed their alignment and affiliation with the protagonist of the narrated tale.

In the context of advice-giving, *The Surgery* also features an altogether different framework of participation and shift of roles, when people listening to the show are invited to provide advice requested by a caller either by sending texts and emails, or joining in the chat room discussion online. This regular slot within the programme is called *Second Opinion*, and, in contrast to the mediated participatory framework of one-to-many in the previous examples, where advice is designed for the listening audience as well as for the recipient, the advice here is delivered through an advice-giving framework of many-to-one.

As with Extracts 7.v–vii, the example below also deals with a caller's problem of 'confidence'. The expert joins the host in the role of problem elicitor, identifying the problem through questions that establish the narrative background to the situation, and the specific need for advice, while listeners take up the role of advice-givers as selected texts and emails are read out on-air by the host and expert. How this new framework affects the formatting of the advice, as it is delivered in the written modes by advice-givers, and how this advice from ordinary members of the public is mediated by the host and expert as they read it out on-air, is examined in this next section.

Extract 7.viii, taken from the show when it was still called *The Sunday Surgery*, shows an opening sequence of the *Second Opinion* feature by host Letitia, with instructions to listeners to 'get ready' as the advice-seeking caller Rachel is brought on-air. The expert is Mark:

Extract 7.viii: 'Get ready to text' (1), *The Sunday Surgery*

1. LETITIA: ok guys it's your turn to give the advice
2.   so listen really closely and get ready to text
3.   on 081199 or you can email the surgery at bbc.co.uk
4.   to help out Rachel hi Rachel
5. RACHEL: hi↑i↓

6.	LETITIA:	hello darling d'you wanna tell us what's going on.
7.	RACHEL:	um well yeah basically um I just got out of a <u>very</u>
8.		horrible relationship
9.		[uh
10.	LETITIA:	[did you say horrible or long
11.	RACHEL:	uh horrible (.)
12.	LETITIA:	ok
13.	RACHEL:	it wasn't a very nice relationship he basically got
14.		a little bit violent with me?
15.	LETITIA:	oh no
16.	RACHEL:	he wasn't very nice.
17.	LETITIA:	no:.
18.	MARK:	how d'you get out of it then (x x)
19.	RACHEL:	uh basically it just turned (.) one night it just got really
20.		ba::d and I just walked then

The host's first question turn in line 6 elicits the background narrative. Rachel initially provides an abstract ('I just got out of a very horrible relationship'), then continues her story with some evaluation and the complicating action ('he basically got a little bit violent with me'; lines 13–14). The expert's first question turn, in line 18, elicits the resolution: 'basically it just turned (.) one night it just got really ba::d and I just walked' (line 19). At this point, there is a story but not yet a problem as such. In the next extract, from a little later in the sequence, further information about the exact nature of Rachel's problem is made explicit to the listening audience as the host retells the story and details the kind of help needed, while the expert identifies precisely why advice is required and models the work of the listeners as potential advice-givers. This invitation to listeners to participate as advice-givers is delivered in a very similar way to that in which radio phone-in hosts model the kind of participation invited in discussion-based shows, such as in the opening to *Election Call* (as noted in Chapter 5 in relation to callers as people with particular kinds of views and opinions).

Extract 7.ix: 'Get ready to text' (2), *The Sunday Surgery*

1.	MARK:	I can see some coming through already (.)
2.		some good ones here
3.	LETITIA:	alright well guys (.) you've heard from Rachel (.)
4.		she's feelin- by the sound of it she's feeling really low
5.		and she's come out of a really violent and horrible
6.		relationship her friends aren't believing (.) you know
7.		aren't believing her (.) they're believing her boyfriend
8.		and that's just horrible when it happens .hh

9.		she needs help (.) with building her confidence and
10.		what else would you say Rachel just the confidence?
11.	RACHEL:	it's j- confidence really like trying to find new friends
12.		like I live in a very small town
13.	LETITIA:	mm
14.	RACHEL:	there's no one new coming into the town at all (.)
15.		um and it's trying to find people to actually go out with
16.		and trying to get the confidence to get myself out
17.		to meet new people
18.	LETITIA:	right and you need you need some tricks on
19.		how to meet some friends some tips on I should say
20.	RACHEL:	yeah
21.	LETITIA:	on how to make some more (.) new friends okay
22.		well Rachel you know what go and make yourself
23.		a cup of tea
24.	RACHEL:	haha thank you
25.	LETITIA:	and try not to cry listen to the radio and there'll be
26.		lots and lots and lots of advice coming in for
27.		when we call you back next alright?
28.	RACHEL:	brilliant thank you very much guys
29.	LETITIA:	you're welcome
30.	MARK:	so hang on there Rachel we'll be with you soon
31.		so before Rachel goes to the doctors does I mean
32.		she says she feels that low she's gonna go
33.		to the doctors soon she's come to this surgery
34.	LETITIA:	that's right
35.	MARK:	so this is your chance it's a Second Opinion texts
36.		on 081199 if you've been in a similar situation
37.		if you've got any advice whatsoever for Rachel
38.		you can also call us 08700100100 s .hhh
39.		what's it gonna be Second Opinion it's up to you
40.	LETITIA:	okay

This sequence inviting listeners to send in their advice to the caller via text, email or a phone call is followed by an interlude during which a song is played, and the advice arrives. Both host and expert discursively construct the 'surgery' as a physical environment, a deictic centre and point of connection for the advice-givers and recipient. The expert Mark's comment in line 1, 'I can see some coming through already', refers to the material presence in the studio of these texts and emails from listeners, and later, in line 33, he also refers to Rachel's call as if she was in the studio as a physical space: 'she's come to this surgery'. The extracts below are further illustrations of this kind of discursive work around the studio/surgery as the deictic point of contact within which caller Rachel will receive her advice:

> MARK: listen listen to the pages Rachel loads of them still I can't go through them all but- [x x x x
>
> LETITIA: there's loads of really touching ones coming in people telling you to do stuff that you've never done before
>
> MARK: and then this one just popped in (.) just in the last few seconds there and it's anonymous it just says for the girl who phoned up about the uh domestic violence
>
> LETITIA: we've got loads like that Hannah says uh she should take up evening classes or something to make new friends

As these examples show, this reference to the materiality and quantity of the advice arriving in the studio that is being sent in by listeners via texts and emails is consistently reinforced by the host and expert. Also, as we saw in Chapter 4, in relation to when listeners send texts or emails with their evaluations of *Changing Tracks* stories, the host and expert here frame the content of the messages they read out as coming from an individual who is named and usually located in some way. The locations vary depending on the technology used and information provided by the advice-givers, so host prefaces to the advice itself range from a simple name ('Hannah says uh she should take up evening classes'), or, indeed, the lack of any name ('and it's anonymous it just says'), to more elaborate location details, as seen in these next examples:

> Carrie says . . .
> Claire on uh I think from the chat room says . . .
> Tanya in Scarborough says (.) she's cleaning her house but she says . . .
> That's from David in Belfast . . .

Here, again, we find the same practice of identifying participants by name and location, even if it is a virtual location like 'in the chat room' or, as we saw with *Changing Tracks*, a transitory one such as 'on the A14'.

Designing advice in texts and emails

Given what we know about the pragmatics of advice-giving as a delicate interactional activity that may require a certain amount of face management, what is striking about the way advice from listeners is formatted in these various communicative modes is their level of directness, and the predominance of direct imperatives and of deontic forms of modality such as 'she should' and 'you need to'. As mobile SMS technology lends itself to brevity, and mitigation takes time, it is perhaps not surprising that many of the text messages read out contain short, direct imperatives addressed to the caller, such as:

> <u>Try</u> new sporty activities
> <u>Try</u> to be happy
> <u>Do</u> <u>not</u> resort to a doctor
> <u>Don't</u> let him run your life
> <u>Make</u> a list of things you want then go for it
> Concentrate on you

However, much of the advice-giving also contains modal forms of obligation that are structurally longer, and, sometimes, like the advice given by the expert, Matt, in Extract 7.vii, refer to the advice-seeker indirectly in the third person, as in the following:

> She <u>should</u> take up evening classes or something
> She <u>should</u> go out to a party wearing a stupidly risqué outfit to get her used to attention again
> What she <u>needs</u> <u>to</u> <u>do</u> is be honest with her friends
> She <u>needs</u> <u>to</u> get out and do more social activities

Furthermore, at one point, the expert comments on the length of a text message as he is reading it, so the choice of media does not necessarily determine the design of the advice. The message in question in fact contains a whole series of direct, unmitigated imperatives:

Extract 7.x: 'This is all on text', *The Sunday Surgery*

1.	MARK:	and then this one just popped in (.)
2.		just in the last few seconds there
3.		and it's anonymous it just says for the girl who phoned up
4.		about the uh domestic violence and the manipulation
5.		of her friends
6.		I have been there do u resort to a doctor
7.		you will end up on another roll of problems that you'll
8.		then have to get over you need by practising to learn to look
9.		in the mirror each day and see what you're worth
10.		this is all on text

There are a number of knowledge statements, which, like the examples taken from *The Garden Show* earlier, also function as a form of expertise, for example:

Tanya says yoga's good for therapy (.) a nice warm bath a book and a smile
try to be happy love

Claire [..] says a dance class something like salsa is fun and uplifting you meet new friends

but, in this episode at least, there are no mitigating strategies in the design of the advice offered. It is directly addressed to the recipient, or expressed in terms of obligation ('what she should do is . . .', 'what she needs to do is . . .'). On the other hand, what we do find in the advice-giving messages is a high level of affiliation with the advice-seeker, from the use of familiar, direct address terms ('try to be happy love') to positive endorsement ('she's <u>brave</u> and will be fine') or establishing their own identity as someone who has experienced a similar problem ('believe me I've been there', 'I did the same as Rachel a year ago today'). So, while the many-to-one framework here on the one hand produces advice-giving that is largely direct and unmitigated, on the other, it also displays a high degree of positive face-work in terms of that affiliation. In their emails, texts and messages, advice-givers often draw on their own similar experiences, taking up a position of situated expertise at the same time as displaying empathy and strong alignment with the recipient.

This can be contrasted with the much higher level of mitigation in the design of expert Mark's turn towards the end of *The Sunday Surgery* feature, as he recycles, summarises and evaluates the advice coming in from listeners. Note the frequency of hesitations and disfluencies, of hedging ('I mean', 'maybe') and of expressions known as markers of 'sympathetic circularity' (Montgomery 1986), such as 'you know' (underlined in the extract below), which produce a much more mitigated and indirect packaging of the advice directed to Rachel.

Extract 7.xi: 'You know start from within', *The Sunday Surgery*

1.	MARK:	that's the thing <u>I mean</u> there's that external <u>you know</u>
2.		going out meeting people <u>uh</u> making friends and
3.		that really does boost your confidence but what
4.		a couple of those <u>uh</u> were saying specially the texts
5.		I read out <u>you know</u> start from within realise- <u>you know</u>
6.		you said it was creeping up this violence
7.		and then you left (.) really <u>you know</u> you didn't-
8.		lots and lots of women hang around and hope for the best

9.		and think it's gonna change but you realised it wasn't
10.		gonna change but <u>maybe</u> before that <u>you know</u>-
11.		he sounds like he's very clever he can manipulate people
12.		<u>uh</u> so <u>mebbe</u> he was just trying to get control of you=
13.	LETITIA:	=and he did

The same forms of hesitation, hedging and sympathetic circularity are also found in expert Matt's turn in Extract 7.vii discussed above, when assessing the request for advice on coming out to one's parents:

> and he's at a really good place now because he's he's
> he's weighing up you know whether he should
> or whether he shouldn't

Even though one addresses the caller directly, while the other refers to them in the third person, each is handling the pragmatic delicacy of delivering advice in a similar way that maintains their institutional distance, yet, at the same time, displays an orientation to the positive face needs of the advice-seeker through the use of these dialogic markers of sympathetic understanding.

The analysis of these examples from *The Sunday Surgery* has revealed some significant differences in the way advice is packaged by participating listeners in a many-to-one context compared to the way experts do advice-giving in a one-to-many context. This is not just evident in the way that experts routinely shift footing in order to address potential recipients in the listening audience, compared to many listeners' directly targeted advice to one recipient, but also in other aspects of the design of the advice-giving activity. While experts tend to routinely adopt a footing that maintains them at a sympathetic distance from the advice-seeker, the delivery of advice through texts and emails favours a mode of address which, in those messages that are selected to be read out on air at least, is direct and affiliative. In relation to the established discourse practices of broadcast advice-giving then, the incorporation of online and mobile modes of public participation into the traditional formats of the radio phone-in does in this case seem to create an environment for the expression of 'ordinary' situated expertise, albeit subject to selection, reframing and evaluation by the institutional expert.

The participatory frameworks and roles explored in these extracts from *The Sunday Surgery* show that although the advice-giving from listeners is both direct and directive, it nevertheless constructs a relationship of equivalence between advice-giver and advice-seeker, rather than one of institutional asymmetry that requires the mitigation of expertise. The broadcast 'talk' – or, in this case, the broadcast 'voice' of the public as it arrives via text and email and is relayed to the recipient by the host and expert on-air – seems to work towards establishing a community between advice-givers and the recipient. In these examples, Rachel is addressed through pragmatic choices in relation to face and directness that are primarily oriented towards constructing a mediated relationship of social proximity and affective solidarity between ratified participants, compared to the much more mitigated expert talk that maintains institutional distance and is also oriented to distributed members of a non co-present audience.

From advice to makeover

This chapter began with a discussion of advice-giving as a situated, interactional activity and the ways in which considerations of face are often at stake in the way advice is designed, delivered and received. In institutional contexts, where the social relationship between advice-giver and recipient is asymmetrical, as we saw in the case of the first-time mothers receiving advice from health visitors, the activity of advising can often be perceived as more like instruction, with a strong obligation on the part of the advisee to act on the 'advice' being given. For these women, who often had not asked for the advice in the first place, the other-initiated advice-giving was experienced by recipients as being told what to do, as being 'bossed about' and, in some cases, as being treated as incompetent: 'it makes me feel like a moron' (see McIntosh 1986, quoted above).

In the context of reality television formats, however, members of the public have voluntarily elected to participate in some kind of transformation, whether this be of their home environment (e.g., *Changing Rooms*, *Property Ladder*), their wardrobe (*What Not to Wear*, *How to Look Good Naked*) or their body (*The Biggest Loser*, *You Are What You Eat*), and they are, therefore, in the position of self-initiating advice-seekers, just like the callers to the radio phone-in programmes discussed earlier. The crucial difference between the two broadcast contexts is one of telicity: on the radio, advice is usually atelic, the advised actions are projected into some unspecified future and the uptake of the advice by the recipients is not generally a broadcastable matter; on the other hand, in television makeover programmes, the process of uptake is fundamentally telic. The on-screen transformations of personal behaviour or social environment depend on the uptake of the advice, coaching or instruction being given, and, therefore, generally entail a strong obligation on the part of those being 'made-over' to act on whatever advice or coaching they may be receiving. Experts tell participants what to do and how to do it, and the 'reveal', that 'crucial moment of revelation' (Moseley 2000), is supposed to capture the natural response of participants' emotions to transformation, their reactions to the change and, above all, to make that personal moment visible for the viewing audience. Both the process that leads towards that transformation as well as the result have become key components of the discourses of public participation in lifestyle and makeover television.

Establishing the problem

Before the process of transformation through expert advice-giving and instruction can begin, the participant being made-over has to be constructed as someone with a problem. The behaviours that need to be changed, whether they are in relation to your dress sense or your parenting skills, need to be publicly displayed. In her analysis of the fashion makeover show *What Not to Wear*,[3] Angela Smith (2009) characterises the way this is accomplished by the programme's two female presenters as a discursive practice of 'bullying' involving positive face threat whereby 'ordinary' members of the public are routinely humiliated. 'Bossy' fashion experts Trinny and Susannah inspect participants wearing their own choice of clothes in a room with all-round mirrors so that they (and the viewers) can see what they look like 'from all angles'. The presenters then use aggravated forms of threat to positive face in order to criticise this choice, as in the following example:

> 'Do you know what (.) if I'm going to be completely frank which I will (.) you look like a hunchback in that'
>
> (Smith 2009)

In this particular episode, explicit criticism is followed by a sequence during which Trinny and Susannah select a skirt for participant Hannah to wear – but she doesn't like it:

Extract 7.xii: *What Not To Wear*

H: It doesn't do anything for me at all
T: It does so much for you I can't tell you
H: I know but it doesn't for me
    it doesn't for me
T: I know but this is your perfect shaped skirt (.)
    perfect length and shape (1.0)
S: But if we're not going to persuade you
    we are not going to persuade you (.)
    it's your loss

(Transcript adapted from Smith 2009)

In this sequence, presenter Trinny uses a series of declarative, strongly evaluative statements to express the opinion that the woman looks good in this new skirt, while she continues to maintain her own opposing view. This serves not just to establish her lack of judgement, but also to construct her as difficult and stubborn ('but if we're not going to persuade you we are not going to persuade you'). The fact that she is rejecting their advice about what to wear provides further work for the presenters – part of this particular makeover will involve persuading her that they are right and she is wrong.

Smith argues that this kind of ritual humiliation is still present in many makeover shows, even when an expert presenter takes up a less directly face-threatening stance towards participants, since the process of transformation still requires participants' tastes and behaviours to be visibly, publicly decried before changes can take place. Taking the case of Gok Wan,[4] Smith describes the way the presenter of *How to Look Good Naked* often aligns with his participants (who, as she points out, are 'female, straight and nearly always middle aged'), as illustrated in the following extract, where he stands with his arm supportively around the woman, looking at her clothes hanging up on a washing line stretching all the away across a public park:

GW:	we're going to be ruthless (.) if it doesn't fit you
AM:	yeh
GW:	it's going
AM:	yeh

The need for transformation has to be established on-screen, and, in this particular episode, Smith argues that this is accomplished through the more humorous but nevertheless humiliating public spectacle of her ill-fitting and undesirable items of clothing strung up across the park.

A similar technique is used in many makeover shows. While it is not always treated as a humorous matter, the nature of the problem has to be established visually, through shots of the participants in their pre-makeover state, as well as verbally, through the statements they make to the presenter or direct to camera about how the problem is affecting their daily lives. For example, in programmes devoted to the makeover of families with parenting issues, the extent and nature of the problem is established by showing scenes of the children behaving badly and of their hapless parents' manifest inability to control them. The parents are then shown inviting experts like Jo Frost (*Supernanny*) or Tanya Byron (*Little Angels*) into their homes in order to help them regain control of their children and their family lives by changing their own behaviour. In the weight-loss competition and makeover show *The Biggest Loser*,[5] we are introduced to participants at home, displaying their overweight bodies while, in voice-over sequences, they explain how they are struggling to cope with day-to-day activities. At the end of the show, having spent weeks doing rigorous fitness training and weight-loss programmes, the transformed participants express their satisfaction with their new, made-over body and life.

The next example is taken from *Little Angels*: Jo and her husband Jason have called on expert Tanya for help in managing their two older children's problematic behaviour. In this short extract from near the end of the programme, they reflect on how they have been 'taking Tanya's advice and everything' and how this has changed not simply their parenting behaviour but also the quality of their family life:

Extract 7.xiii: 'More coaching', *Little Angels*

VO: After a week by themselves, Tanya's back to give Jo and Jason some more coaching . . .

JO: What I think has come to light from doing the programme and taking Tanya's advice and everything is that it's a parent's behaviour and attitude towards the children that can make them better behaved they haven't necessarily become any better behaved from doing this we have been able to manage what we like and what we don't like.

JASON: We've now got Luke and Elliot into bed a lot earlier (.) a lot less fuss which means that we have more free time in the evening and therefore a better night and it's excellent

In a similar vein, a participant from *The Biggest Loser* in the following extract comments on how, after training and successfully losing weight, she can now do things she couldn't do before:

Extract 7.xiv: 'Trying on clothes', *The Biggest Loser*

PAULA: I would never try on the clothes at home that I tried on here today (.) I would never have the confidence just because I think straight away (.) ya know it won't suit me

The discursive processes through which these transformations are accomplished can take several forms. First of all, the kind of expert 'coaching' and 'advice' (as Jo puts it in Extract 7.xiii) given to parents with problem children is generally unmitigated and direct, and often delivered in situations where the use of imperative forms requires participants to instantly carry out that advice. Similarly, in the weight-loss programmes, participants are given personal trainers who coach them in physical workout sessions. In these contexts, the coaching activity becomes a form of explicit instruction rather than advice: participants are shown doing what they are told to do, acting on the directives there and then, for the camera, with the results of their efforts given in the weigh-in sessions each week. In the next extract, taken from one of these scenes in the gym, the trainer is making two participants compete against each other in a fitness workout:

Extract 7.xv: 'Push each other', *The Biggest Loser*

TRAINER:	I need you guys to push each other (.) three. two. one. Let's go!
TRAINER (*To camera*):	I know that Jessie and Sarah are both quite competitive so I used that to really get the most of the pair of them and it worked
TRAINER:	right up with those elbows Jess (.) don't lock them up each time it's neck and neck (.) come on (.) get right down

In front of the camera, and under the eye of their personal trainer, who is using need/want statements as directives ('I need you guys to push each other') as well as direct imperatives ('right up with those elbows Jess'), the participants do as they are told, carrying out instructions as they engage in the processes that will result in the visible transformation of their bodies. This work in the gym is perhaps not so very different discursively from the kind of work being done through instructions in family makeover programmes, as we will now see.

Direct instruction about what to do and how to behave is also evident in the episode from *Little Angels* already quoted above, where, while shopping in a department store, the mother Jo (wearing an earpiece) is seen pushing a pushchair through the aisles while expert Tanya watches from a distance. Using a miked headset, she instructs Jo in what to say to her children, modelling exactly the words she needs in order to keep them under control as she does her shopping:

Extract 7.xvi: 'In the store', *Little Angels*

1. JO:	right (.) boys
2. VO:	first up keeping the boys occupied
3. JO:	come on then lambs (.) Elli?
4. TANYA:	ok lots of distraction and <u>ooh</u> look what's down this way
5.	and <u>who's</u> gonna help mummy
6.	and who's gonna find it first
7. JO:	was it that one she wanted (.) do you think
8. TANYA:	that's a lovely choice what a clever boy for helping me
9. JO:	that's great that's a brilliant one
10.	ooh that looks funny look at those funny people
11. TANYA:	thank you for helping mummy
12. JO:	thank you for getting that
13.	Elli ((Elliot picks up a pair of huge green glove
14.	hands and puts them on))
15. TANYA:	you need to tell him now
16.	take them off him and bring him
17.	he needs to do as he's told now

18. JO: Elliot can you take them off now (.) quick quick
19. TANYA: just- don't ask him take them off that's it brilliant
20. JO: come on then
21.   good job ((puts gloves back on shelf)) good boy
22. TANYA: Jo your five minutes is up (.) so you could regroup
23.   and do a sticker each and tell them how good they are

As we see from line 4 here, Tanya first instructs Jo about how to approach her shopping trip, giving her prompts in the form of candidate utterances in order to achieve the goal of keeping the two boys under control. Lines 7, 9, 10 and 12 are Jo's implementation of these prompts – not necessarily repeated word for word, as she does not refer to herself in the third person, except in line 7 ('is that the one she wanted'). When things start to go wrong and one of the boys starts to do his own thing with a pair of gloves, Tanya uses direct imperatives and the modality of obligation in her instructions ('you need to tell him now', 'take them off him', 'he needs to do as he's told now'; lines 16–18), correcting Jo at her first attempt to get Elliot to remove the gloves: 'don't ask him take them off' (line 19). This remote controlling of the mother's actions and utterances by the expert, with immediate, visible, telic effect, forms part of the discourse of transformation and makeover; in this case, of bad parenting habits into successful ones – at least on this occasion.

A further example of the same practice of instruction can be seen in the next extract taken from *Supernanny*.[6] Expert Jo Frost is telling a father (Paul) how to get his very angry nine-year-old daughter (Megan) to apologise to him. Megan is in trouble for having thrown her sticker chart with crowns for good behaviour into the bin. As a consequence, she has been sent to the 'reflection room' to calm down – in this case, the family dining room – where her father and Jo will join her. In the first part of this sequence, Jo explains to Paul how to manage the conversation with Megan before they go into the reflection room. The two direct-to-camera segments and the voice-over function as a frame for the ensuing interactional exchange:

Extract 7.xvii: 'I want an apology' (1), *Supernanny*

Jo (*to camera*):
1.   Megan usually gets away with this kind of behaviour (.)
2.   ((Megan is shown lying across dining room table))
3. JO VO: but this time (.) I told Paul (.) to give her a warning (.)
4.   and when she didn't listen (.) she ended up
5.   in the reflection room
6. JO: when you (.) go into the room (.) after her time (.) explain
7.   why you put her in there (.) oka:y?
8. PAUL: yup

9.	JO:	and say to her you want an a<u>pol</u>ogy (.) for that behaviour
10.		(.) and (.) if she delivers a sorry (.) that's <u>angry</u> (.)
11.		SORRY (.) and she's really <u>rude</u> (.) say to her
12.		<u>no</u> that's not good enough (.)
13.		I want an a<u>pol</u>ogy <u>prop</u>erly which is (.) sorry (.) and if she
14.		doesn't then she stays in there
15.	PAUL:	okay
16.	JO:	okay

Paul (*to camera*):

17.	certainly someone like Megan it's (.) get an apology so she
18.	understands (.) <u>why</u> (.) cos- cos you (.) you when you get
19.	the apology you (.) you say to them why (.)
20.	do you understand <u>why</u> you are in the reflection room

In the sequence, lines 6–14, the expert uses a series of direct imperatives to instruct Paul in what he needs to do, and ends with a statement of what should happen next if Megan does not comply:

> <u>explain</u> why you put her in there
> <u>say</u> to her you want an apology
> <u>say</u> to her no that's not good enough
> and if she doesn't she stays in there

She delivers these imperative directives with an understanding check ('okay') in line 7, which Paul acknowledges in line 8 and again in line 15. Then, in a segment direct to camera, he explains his understanding of what he has to do and why before going into the room to talk to Megan. In the second part of this sequence, the following exchange takes place in the dining room between the three participants (Jo, Paul and Megan):

Extract 7.xviii: 'I want an apology' (2), *Supernanny*

((Paul and Jo go into the dining room))

21.	PAUL:	the behaviour you're (.) you're showing is (.) rea::lly
22.		unacceptable (.) and I want an apology
23.	MEGAN:	((head on table)) <u>so::::rry</u>
24.	PAUL:	I want (.) a heartfelt sorry not just a [sorry]
25.	JO:	((sitting on other side of table)) [but how] how does (.)
26.		how will Megan (.) know how to give you a heartfelt
27.		sorry unless you have to show her (.) say to her=
28.	PAUL:	[Mega::n]
29.	JO:	[=look] at me [and say I'm sorry]

30.	PAUL:	[look at me (.) look] at me
31.	JO:	so that she kno::ws otherwise she won't know
32.	PAUL:	you need to look at me (.) and sa:::y I'm sorry (.) properly
33.	MEGAN:	((inaudible))
34.	PAUL:	as if you mean it
35.	MEGAN:	I don't mean it cause I DON'T (X X)
36.		((jumps onto table/hits Jo's arm))
37.	PAUL:	Mega::n (.) no ((pulls her back))
38.	JO:	s'alright Paul (.) Paul (.)
39.	PAUL:	no we don't hit
40.	MEGAN:	yes I DO
41.	JO:	Paul (.) just [follow through]
42.	MEGAN:	[she's not] a member of the household so I can do it
43.	JO:	follow through
44.	PAUL:	Megan (.) start (.) with a proper apology to me (.)
45.		and then we can go and get you a glass of water
46.		we can get the picture out the bin (.)
47.		and then we can start (.) again

Here, Paul attempts to carry out the instructions given by Jo, and Megan does indeed say 'sorry' (line 23). However, this is taken by Paul to be 'an angry sorry' and he proceeds with the next stage of Jo's instructions, requesting 'a heartfelt sorry' (line 24). At this point, Jo intervenes to model how this should be done (lines 25–31), again with the use of very direct directives ('you have to show her', 'say to her'), and then she shifts footing into first-person animator of the utterance, projecting Paul's next turn and giving him exactly the words she thinks he needs to get the kind of apology he wants: 'look at me and say I'm sorry'. In overlap with Jo and again in line 32, Paul carries out the instructions, repeating what Jo has said practically verbatim (lines 30 and 32) but without the desired effect. Megan launches across the table shouting, attacks Jo and continues to behave very aggressively towards her. In voice-over, Jo explains that it takes another hour of leaving Megan in the reflection room before Paul gets the apology he wants from her. The final extract from this episode shows the moment of transformation where the furious child eventually co-operates:

Extract 7.xix: 'I want an apology' (3), *Supernanny*

1.	PAUL:	right I need you to look at me first (.)
2.		right I want an apology
3.	MEGAN:	((sniffing)) sorry
4.	PAUL:	alright a little bit louder please
5.		((Megan looks at Paul))
6.	PAUL:	a little bit louder I'm going a bit deaf come on

7. MEGAN: you're not deaf ((smiling))
8. PAUL: come on
9. MEGAN: ((looking at Paul)) sorry
10. PAUL: good girl ((leaning over to Megan)) give us a cuddle

The discursive environments in which these exchanges take place, and the meta-commentary that frames them, are interesting on several counts. First, the contextualising scenes of the child's extremely aggressive behaviour serve to embody the problem for viewers, preceding the expert's advice on how to transform this unacceptable behaviour, which is given in various explicit ways – not just by using direct, unmitigated forms, but also by modelling what the specific content of a parental turn should be. Just like the participants in the gym and the mother in the department store, the father here is essentially in a position where his actions are under the direct scrutiny of, and being directly controlled by, the expert. The process of transforming his daughter into a compliant, well-behaved child depends on him putting into practice the 'advice' he is given, which, in this context, means immediately doing what Supernanny tells him to do. The desired result is at last achieved (albeit with a touch of humour and without her in the room) and the family is seen to be a step further along the makeover road towards harmony rather than constant conflict. Just like the competitors in *The Biggest Loser* have to be seen to be losing weight, the process of transforming this family's behaviour has to be seen to be taking place, and both depend crucially on the participants acting on instructions.

Another point to make here is that, very much like the families who appear on conflict-based talk shows, the families on parenting makeover programmes are shown to be in a state of extreme crisis. The children behave spectacularly badly, and the parents display a lack of control in the pre-transformation stage that goes beyond the realms of what might be taken to be 'ordinary' family interactions. The construction of participant identities on such programmes thus depends on the viewer's complicit recognition of such social behaviours as deeply problematic. Whether they are 'like us' or 'not like us', these families are watchable precisely because they are people who are categorised and perceived as being in a critical social situation. As the embodiment of what happens when parental control breaks down, in this role, they perform in a very dramatic manner the kinds of conflicts that result from such breakdown: they are, in effect, being what we do *not* want to be like. For a reality makeover programme, however, the situation also has to be shown to be fixable – by the end of the show, the lessons delivered are seen to be working through participants' compliance, not just in inviting and accepting the expertise offered, but also in acting on it, modifying their own behaviour, which, in turn, improves their lives.

'The new me'

The people who participate on *The Biggest Loser* are also constructed as being in socially problematic situations, out of control of their lives as well as their weight. The transformation that takes place during the course of the show relates not just to their bodies, but also to their sense of personal identity. In the moment of the reveal on this show, the participants' reaction to their physical transformation is realised on-screen by a rhetorical performance in which they acknowledge that some kind of personal transformation has also occurred. The final part of this chapter focuses on the performance of 'the new me' on this successful game show-meets-makeover format, which combines many of the features of both 'game-doc' reality TV genres and the lifestyle makeover show. Participants live together, away from the rest of the world, in a constructed environment; they compete against one another as individuals or in teams, and there is voting and/or elimination of one of the contestants each week. At the same time, through a series of fitness and workout challenges, they are also transformed from people with serious weight problems into slimmer, healthier and also more stylish versions of their previous selves. The show has a host, a team of professional trainers (as we saw in Extract 7.xv, above) and, at the end, a team of expert fashion and hairstylists who give the contestants a new look – clothes, hairstyle, etc. – that is commensurate with their new, slimmer bodies. The extracts below illustrate the way in which participants react to their physical makeover:

I've finally closed the book on the old Bobby

This is who I was searching for
and I've found her

just to feel like a new person and to feel
so refreshed (.) and strong

on my way to see my loved ones and I am dying to see who is here
tonight
it's a new me and I feel ~totally~ different now and I know whoever is
here is gonna be just blown away

Each one of these contestants refers to the emergence of a new 'self' as the product of the process of transformation: 'this is who I was searching for and I've found her'. Feeling like a new person, and 'closing the book' on the old self, is part of the rhetorical performance of identity change, and is a recurring theme at the moment of the show's reveal. As participants come out of the dressing room wearing their new outfits to meet the approving eye of fashion expert Tim and look at themselves in the mirror, they all display an emotional reaction to their new identity, as illustrated in the next two extracts:

Extract 7.xx: 'The new me' (1), *The Biggest Loser*

1.	RACHEL:	I'm in such a more positive area now in my life so
2.	(*To camera*)	I'm nervous to try it on but I'm hopeful
3.		to create a new sparkly black dress
4.	TIM:	the dressing room's right in there (.) ok
5.	RACHEL:	((in dressing room))
6		I- I think I'm ready to come out
7.	TIM:	well come on ↑out.
8.		((Rachel walks out, music plays))
9.		good heavens (.) well come over here
10.		look at you
11.	RACHEL:	((tearful, sniffing, raises hand to wipe eyes))
12.		(2.0)
13.		wow (1.0) and it's such a <u>sh</u>ock

Extract 7.xxi: 'The new me' (2), *The Biggest Loser*

1.	TANYA:	((tearful, sniffing))
2.		it's me ((raises hands to face, wipes eyes))
3.	TIM:	what are you thinking
4.	TANYA:	I've made so much progress on this [journey
5.	TIM:	[look at you
6.	TANYA:	and I feel amazing I look (1.0) amazing
7.	TIM:	and this person is staying
8.	TANYA:	((nodding))
9.	TIM:	yeah=
10.	TANYA:	=yes this person is staying

In these extracts, we can note a similar pattern in the behaviour displayed as each participant, having gone into the dressing room as one person, emerges as a different one. In these moments, they produce the same kind of gestures (Rachel and Tanya wipe away their tears), both mention a change of state – being in a different place now (Rachel in line 1), having gone on a journey (Tanya in line 4) – and Tim repeats 'look at you' to each one, where the 'you' who comes out of the dressing room is significantly different from the 'you' who went in. The made-over Tanya is 'this person', different from 'that person' she was before, while Rachel expresses 'shock' at the change in her appearance. In Extract 7.xxii, below, Bobby expresses the same kind of shock and surprise when he stands in front of the mirror:

Extract 7.xxii: 'The new me' (3), *The Biggest Loser*

1.	TIM:	holy smoley (.) come over h↑ere.
2.	BOBBY:	((stands in front of mirror))
3.		wow
4.	TIM:	wow is right (.)
5.		how do you react to this when you look in the mirror
6.	BOBBY:	I'm a little shell-shocked (.) be honest like I haven't
7.		seen myself like this <u>ever</u> (.) and I feel freer than (.)
8.	(*To camera*)	I've come out to my dad
9.		there's so many things I've gone through on here
10.		on the ranch and the biggest thing you know is
11.		coming out to my dad and being an openly gay man
12.		and I feel like a com<u>plete</u>ly different person
13.		on the inside and <u>now</u> makeover week (.)
14.		what's shown on the outside
15.		((turns in front of mirror))
16.		is reflective of what's on the inside
17.		I've kind've closed the book on the (.) old Bobby

The initial expressions of shock – 'wow' (line 3), 'I'm a little shell-shocked' (line 6) – as he comes out of the dressing room shift seamlessly into a voice-over edit in which he explains his metaphorical coming out, using another metaphor of transformation and change of state ('so many things I've gone through here on the ranch'), and, like the others, referring to himself as 'a completely different person on the inside' (line 12).

The discursive display of emotion, of shock and the reference to 'a new me' present in all three extracts produces a rhetorical performance of identity makeover that I would argue is as important in this show as the change in weight. The significance of participant identity is not simply a matter of being an 'ordinary' person, it is about the mediated production of transformation from one particular kind of person into another; from someone who was overweight and had lost control of their life to someone who is slimmer, smarter and back in control. In makeover broadcasting, the processes of transformation, realised through shared discursive practices of expert instruction, and the participants' positive reactions to the final results are thus very similar across a whole range of contexts for public participation.

It has already been argued that makeover TV involves 'educating audiences in judgements of taste rather than disseminating skills or knowledge' (Giles, 2002: 607), but, in the contexts I have discussed here, it now also involves educating audiences in judgements of social behaviour. In order to do this, the members of the public who elect to take part in makeover shows have to be people whose lifestyles and behaviours are perceived to be outside the norms. They are then put in a situation where they have to comply with instructions, which enables them to be seen to be transformed into people whose control over their lives, their children or their bodies also involves a transformation of their identity. This is part of doing the work of being watched, to be someone who changes from their former problematic identity into a new, unproblematic, better one.

Summary: advice, telicity and transformation

In this final chapter on discourses of participation, I have brought together various media genres where public participation involves the requesting and the receiving of advice and instruction. By examining different contexts for advice and makeover, each with their particular framework of participation, I have argued that the pragmatics of mediated advice-giving is closely tied to the institutional relationship between advisers and advisees, the kind of advice being sought, as well as the framework through which it is delivered. Thus, on the radio, advice about gardens given in front of an audience is designed differently in terms of its form and its key from advice about personal issues given to a caller. Advice given by institutionally ratified experts who interact directly with a caller in a radio phone-in is more hedged and mitigated than advice texted or emailed from members of the audience, since the discursive management of affiliation and solidarity with the advice-seeker needs to be handled in different ways. The introduction of mobile and email technology in this context offers new participatory identities and sets up new interactional relationships between radio hosts, callers, listeners and the active members of the audience who text, message and email. The ratified recipients of advice-giving can thus shift from one-to-many to many-to-one frameworks, but the reconfiguring of advice for the listening audience remains the discursive role of the expert.

When we turn to advice-giving in the context of lifestyle and makeover broadcasting, the participants are very much in the hands of the experts, with whole rafts of psychologists, dieticians, designers, instructors and trainers undertaking the transformation of 'ordinary' members of the public on-screen. The advice-giving in these contexts is telic, and needs to be shown to be effective, so the pragmatics of advice as a discursive activity moves much closer to direct instruction, as participants are seen acting on the advice they are given and carrying out instructions. Since this transformation has to be discursively as well as visually achieved (the visual construction of the problem and its resolution is, as I have argued, accompanied by the transformation of a participant identity from one that is chaotic, miserable and out of control into a new, improved and happier self), the discursive performance of 'the new me' has become a routine rhetorical performance of the make-over.

Notes

1 *Gardeners' Question Time* has been aired in various formats on BBC Radio 4 since 1947.
2 BBC Radio 1's *The Surgery* (formerly called *The Sunday Surgery*) has been running since 1999 with a number of different celebrity hosts, including Sara Cox, Letitia SD, Kelly Osborne and, since 2009, Aled Haydn Jones.
3 Launched by the BBC in 2001, the reality makeover show *What Not to Wear* ran for seven series, with Trinny Woodall and Susannah Constantine as hosts of the first five.
4 Gok Wan has hosted several Channel 4 fashion makeover series: *How to Look Good Naked*, *Gok's Fashion Fix*, *Gok's Clothes Roadshow* and *Gok's Style Secrets*.
5 *The Biggest Loser* started in the USA in 2004 (NBC), and is now franchised worldwide – it is shown on ITV in the UK. It has been hosted by Kate Garraway in the UK, and Alison Sweeney in the USA.
6 *Supernanny* originated on Channel 4 in 2004, and was also shown in the USA on the ABC and Style networks.

8   Conclusions

The debatable state of being 'ordinary'

Reaching the end of a book, one is tempted to think about how it might have been different, and about all the things that have been left out. This ending has been no exception, and so, in the final pages of this short concluding chapter, I would like to spend a little time considering what has not been done, and some of the questions that have been left unanswered, as well as reflecting on what have been the book's main themes and lines of argument.

Throughout the book, I have been engaging in a critical reappraisal of ordinariness in discourses of contemporary public participation broadcasting, and making the argument that we need to re-examine what being an ordinary person on television or on the radio actually involves. I have based this argument on an analysis of locally situated participatory identities that are closely tied to the discursive practices and locations in which people known as 'ordinary' participate in mediated interactions. Drawing on theoretical concepts that have enabled me to address the relationship between talk, identity and performance, I have focused on two main issues that seem to me to be at the heart of these debates about what we mean by 'ordinary' in broadcast contexts. The first relates to how participants' social identities are displayed and constructed within the contexts of reality TV genres and makeover programming, on the one hand, as well as in discussions, debates and arguments on radio and television on the other. The second relates to how the introduction of mobile and web-based media and technology – chatting, emailing, texting, tweeting – has changed and continues to change the public's access to, and participation in, forms of broadcast discourse. Some final reflections on these issues have been grouped into three broad headings below: (1) the material selected for discussion, (2) the people who participate in broadcast discourse, and (3) the method of analysis.

The material

In selecting the data for each of the chapters, and in the accompanying discussions and analyses, I have inevitably worked with a small sample of what has been of interest to me out of what is currently available as broadcast material. Generic evolution means that, while some popular series can run for several seasons, others that do not attract the same viewing figures are quickly dropped. New ideas are introduced, and successful formats are developed in different directions, often with a 'celebrity' version or with ever more complex scenarios for participation and competition. There will always be much more to say about forms of public participation in broadcast media that are in a state of constant flux. The data examined here are therefore presented as a snapshot of contexts for public participation media.

As an example, since my focus has been on non-scripted forms of broadcast talk, I have not introduced any discussion of the current highly popular, second-wave reality TV formats such as *The Only Way is Essex*, *Made in Chelsea* or *Jersey Shore*. These shows are scripted and storyboarded, and, as such, offer a different kind of opportunity for middle-space performances by participants who are selected, cast and directed to perform a version of themselves as a character in their own social and relational dramas. Second-wave reality shows generate just as much debate as the first wave did: whether cynical and exploitative of a celebrity-obsessed generation or simply 'just another way of telling stories' (Flynn 2011), they raise a new set of questions about 'ordinary' participant identities and contemporary broadcasting that are outside the scope of this book, but which will deserve much further attention in others.

The articulation between broadcast interaction and digital interactivity opens up new frameworks for participation in broadcast talk, and I have discussed some of these participatory roles and activities in selected media contexts. However, the relationship between broadcast media and the participating, online public raises broader questions of public engagement with political and social issues that need still further exploration. From the evidence in the material discussed here, it would seem that including platforms for interactivity in many broadcast contexts tends paradoxically to limit rather than extend public participation in discussion and debate on-air; on the other hand, this is not to say that debate and discussion are not taking place online. They clearly are. But, one of the most significant changes in the discourses of public participation broadcasting since the introduction of web-based and mobile technology, and as the locus for public debate and discussion moves onto the web, has been a gradual silencing of the television studio audience. For example, *The Wright Stuff*, a social and current affairs chat and panel discussion show broadcast on the UK's Channel 5, and recorded in front of a studio audience, invites calls, tweets and texts (shown on-screen) from the viewing audience. But, while the callers exchange views and opinions with the presenter, and texts are shown on-screen, the members of the studio audience are occasionally seen, heard laughing, but don't speak. This brings me to the next theme – people – and the changing role of members of the public as participants.

The people

It is undoubtedly the case that our television screens are increasingly popu-lated by people who are not actors, or journalists or other types of media professionals, such as hosts or presenters. Given the ubiquity of reality TV formats, and the continual need to recruit members of the public to feed the ever-increasing market for tele-factuality, it is more than likely that most people reading this book will know somebody who has been auditioned for or has actually been 'on telly': for example, recruited for *Dinner Date*, com-peted on *Come Dine With Me*, auditioned for *Britain's Got Talent* or been in the audience of a talk show like *Trisha* or *Jeremy Kyle*. Official Twitter sites are full of recruitment advertisements and posts with the current casting dates and locations. The opportunities for public access to the media are, in some ways, more numerous than ever before – television is on our streets, in our homes and in our communities.

Furthermore, being on-air, or being on-screen, in one way or another puts people into a discursive context where identity matters, where it is made relevant and where displaying that identity is something that participants do, routinely and predictably. On talk radio, participants who call in are members of the general public, but they will have been selected out of a number of potential callers because they have something to say and reasons for saying it. It is also worth noting that establishing who you are in relation to what you have to say – that is, the personal grounding of participant identity and situated expertise that is so routinely produced by participants in radio phone-in interaction and audience participation debates and talk shows – is largely absent from the web-based posting and commenting activity tied to broadcast debates and discussions that I examined here.

In reality and makeover shows, participants are often selected precisely because they seem to have a certain kind of character, or a very specific social identity. As Frances Bonner notes, this means that they can be represented as 'the embodiment' of a particular social issue or problem (Bonner 2003). Participants who are selected thus tend to be categorised as a distinctive 'someone who' – someone who will draw attention to them-selves in some way, as posts on the *Come Dine With Me* Twitter site have commented:

Former university flatmate is going to be on Come Dine With Me. He might be the first person to serve crisps for each course

I would definitely be that person on "come dine with me" that, on the second day, had forgotten everyone's name

So, is it the case, as Bignell (2005) suggested, that people who take part in these programmes are ordinary people, are just like us in some ways, but not like us in others because they are on television? Or is it more that they possess 'the capacity to perform a particularly spectacular version of ordinariness in public', as Turner (2010) claims? The answer may lie somewhere else: these are participants whose social identities and personal characteristics can be worked up as watchable material through middle-space performances of reality television. Just being ordinary can't do the same thing.

As I argued in relation to *Wife Swap,* the success of the series owes much to the selection of participants whose differences and specific identities are made salient through their middle-space performance, rather than to their ordinariness. These differences are also potential generators of conflict, and, again, *Wife Swap* has all the ingredients for producing moments of tension and drama on screen. Substituting one element of a functioning domestic system for another produces a shock to that system, and this frequently results in a confrontation that is highly watchable, as viewing figures proved. Also, as we saw in the rhetorical performances of 'the new me' in *The Biggest Loser,* the display of a specific identity as 'someone who' is also at stake for participants in makeover and lifestyle broadcasting, where particular social identities and behaviours can be represented as problematic and in need of fixing, but also as material for a visibly emergent transformation through the discursive processes of makeover (i.e., advice and instruction).

The method

In focusing on talk as the principal communicative object of analysis, I have not made use of multi-modal or visual analytical theory and method, even though, at times, I have included details of visual aspects of the TV data I represent in the transcripts. The immediacy of talk, as a form of social interaction, for me remains the primary mode through which broadcasting can still most successfully directly engage, and engage with, its participating audience. I have used a discourse analytic approach also because it has enabled me to draw out similarities and differences between talk on radio, on television and on the web (which, although a written mode of communication, is commonly and conventionally treated as if it were a form of talk), and to make comparisons across these different media by looking in close detail at what people are saying and how they are saying it in each discursive context and framework for public participation.

However, the construction of a web-based audience, through online comment and discussion forums, and through the invitation to join in 'conversations' on Twitter, opens up a different kind of discursive environment for participation. Interaction – in the conversational analytic sense of a sequential exchange locally organised between one speaker and the next around a shared orientation to conditional relevance – tends to be replaced by a different kind of sequence, one that is much more like a form of paratactic commentary. This is not to say that exchanges do not occur between participants on the web forums or Twitter; they do. But, the interactional exchange is not the dominant form of discursive activity for posters and tweeters in this particular discursive space.

Choosing to focus on the analysis of talk has also enabled me to examine how different discursive environments for public participation have produced shifts in the most pervasive forms of mediated discursive activity. From the days of TV talk shows, when narrative was the primary discourse of participation for members of the public (as documented in Chapter 4) and the basis from which other activities could then be developed, such as debate and argument, this kind of storytelling on TV seems to have all but disappeared. The increase in reality formats has produced a shift in narrative discourse, a shift that puts the stories into the hands of the media professionals rather than into the voices of 'ordinary' people. As suggested above, this is a different way of telling stories.

In conclusion

This brings me to a final observation about discourses of public participation media. As I have just noted, personal narratives told by people claiming their own particular, relevant and situated identities were generally considered to be the core discourse of audience participation broadcasting in the genres of TV talk shows like *Oprah* and *Kilroy* from the mid 1990s onwards. With the emergence of reality and makeover programming, and the development of the interactive web-based audience, the primary activity in which audiences now engage is one of evaluation, rather than narration. I think there are three main reasons for this. First, the interactive audience is often called on to vote, and voting involves making judgements about identities and performances, judgements that are often bound up with evaluations of character and social behaviour. Secondly, online sites like YouTube and the social media network of the Twitterverse have provided a space for a type of discursive activity in relation to broadcast material that is primarily evaluative rather than narrative; it is a space for commenting and judging, not for storytelling. And, thirdly, the presence of a studio audience is now increasingly found within a participation framework where members of that audience are ratified to react as spectators, rather than to speak as debaters. In the end, it is perhaps popular radio that has, to some extent, and in certain contexts, been so far most able to broaden the ratified participatory roles for its audience through online chat and mobile technology, inviting and incorporating messages from listeners into some of its current forms of broadcast talk. Future research will need to keep exploring these complex interconnections of the discursive spaces of broadcasting, the web and social media, and what members of the public are doing there.

Appendix
Key to transcription symbols

The following transcription conventions have been used in the process of transcribing talk for use as data:

square brackets	[say]	[overlapping talk starts and ends]
equals sign	=say	latching, no break between turns
numbers in parentheses	(0.5)	timed pause to nearest .5 second
dot in parentheses	(.)	very brief pause
underlining	<u>say</u>	emphasis or stress
colons	sa:::y	stretching of prior sound
up and down arrows	↑say↓	indicate marked pitch movement
full stop	say.	falling intonation
comma	say,	continuing intonation
capital letters	SAY	very loud talk, shouting
degree signs	°say°	quiet talk
'greater' than	<say>	slowed down speech
'less' than	>say<	speeded up speech
. preceding h	.hhhh	marked in breath
no . preceding h	hhhh	marked out breath
laughter particles	huh huh huh	laughter
tilde each side of word	~say~	'smiley' voice
parentheses with xxxx	(x x x x)	stretch of untranscribable talk
double parentheses	((sits down))	contextual information

In addition, for television transcripts, the following conventions have been used to indicate different types of shots:

CU	close up
MS	mid shot
LS	long shot

and to differentiate different forms of address:

To camera	talk spoken directly to camera
For camera	talk for but not directly to camera
VO	voice-over segments
Exchange	talk between participants

NB: In transcripts that I have quoted from other work rather than from my own data, there may be occasional minor differences in the use of some symbols.

References

Andrejevic, M. (2004) *Reality TV: The Work of Being Watched*. Lanham, MD: Rowman & Littlefield Publishers.

Androutsopoulos, J. (2013) Online data collection. In C. Mallinson, B. Childs and G. Van Herk (eds.) *Data Collection in Sociolinguistics: Methods and Applications*. London, UK: Routledge, pp. 236–250.

Benwell, B. and Stokoe, E. (2006) *Discourse and Identity*. Edinburgh, UK: Edinburgh University Press.

Bignell, J. (2005) *Big Brother: Reality TV in the Twenty-First Century*. Basingstoke, UK: Palgrave Macmillan.

Billig, M. (1991) *Ideology and Opinions: Studies in Rhetorical Psychology*. London, UK: Sage.

Blum-Kulka, S. (1993) 'You gotta know how to tell a story': Telling, tales and tellers in American and Israeli narrative events at dinner. *Language in Society*, 22: 361–402.

Blum-Kulka, S. (1997) *Dinner Talk: Cultural Patterns of Sociability and Socialisation in Family Discourse*. Mahwah, NJ: Lawrence Erlbaum.

Bonner, F. (2003). *Ordinary Television: Analyzing Popular TV*. London, UK: Sage.

Brown, P. and Levinson, S. (1987) *Politeness: Some Universals in Language Usage*. Cambridge, UK: Cambridge University Press.

Bruner, J. (1990) *Acts of Meaning*. Cambridge, MA: Harvard University Press.

Carpignano, P., Anderson, R., Aronowitz, S. and DiFazio, W. (1980) Chatter in the age of electronic reproduction: talk television and the 'public mind'. *Social Text* 25, pp. 33–55.

Chafe, W. L. (ed.) (1980) *The Pear Stories: Cultural, Cognitive and Linguistic Aspects of Narrative Production*. Norwood, NJ: Ablex.

Chouliaraki, L. and Morsing, M. (eds.) (2010) *Media, Organizations and Identity*. Basingstoke, UK: Palgrave Macmillan.

Clayman, S. (2010) Address terms in the service of other actions: The case of news interview talk. *Discourse & Communication* 4(2): 161–183.

Clayman, S. and Heritage, J. (2002) *The News Interview: Politicians and Public Figures on Air*. Cambridge, UK: Cambridge University Press.

Corner, J. (2002) Performing the real: Documentary diversions. *Television & New Media*, 3: 255–269.

Coulter, J. (1990) Elementary properties of argument sequences. In G. Psathas (ed.) *Interaction competence*. Washington, D.C.: University Press of America, pp. 181–204.

Coupland, N. (2007) *Style: Language Variation and Identity*. Cambridge, UK: Cambridge University Press.

Cutting, J. (2002) *Pragmatics and Discourse*. London, UK: Routledge.

DeCapua, A. and Dunham, J. F. (1993) Strategies in the discourse of advice. *Journal of Pragmatics* 20: 519–531.

Dersley, I. and Wootton, A. J. (2001) In the heat of the sequence: Interactional features preceding walkouts from argumentative talk. *Language and Society* 30: 611–638.

Dovey, J. (2000) *Freakshow: First Person Media and Factual Television*. London, UK: Pluto Press.

Drew, P. and Heritage, J. (eds.) (1992) *Talk at Work: Interaction in Institutional Settings*. Cambridge, UK: Cambridge University Press.

Fairclough, N. (1995) *Media Discourse*. London, UK: Arnold.

Fitzgerald, R. and Housley, W. (2002) Identity, category and sequential organisation: The sequential and categorical flow in a radio phone-in. *Discourse and Society*, 13(5): 579–602.

Flynn, P. (2011) Do TV's 'scripted reality' shows fuel regional prejudice? In J. Raeside and P. Flynn, 'The debate' series, *The Observer*, Sunday, 17 July, 2011. Available at http://www.theguardian.com/commentisfree/2011/jul/17/scripted-reality-tv-shows-debate (accessed 10 March 2014).

Freed, A. and Ehrlich, S. (eds.) (2010) *'Why Do You Ask?': The Function of Questions in Institutional Discourse*. Oxford, UK: Oxford University Press.

Gee, J. P. (1990) *Social Linguistics and Literacies: Ideologies in Discourses*. London, UK: Falmer Press.

Giles, D. C. (2002) Keeping the public in their place: Audience participation in lifestyle television programming. *Discourse and Society* 13(5): 603–628.

Goffman, E. (1959) *The Presentation of Self in Everyday Life*. Garden City, NY: Doubleday.

Goffman, E. (1963) *Behaviour in Public Places: Notes on the Social Organization of Gatherings*. New York, NY: Free Press.

Goffman, E. (1981) *Forms of Talk*. Oxford, UK: Blackwell.

Goffman, E. (1983) Felicity's condition. *American Journal of Sociology* 89(1): 1–53.

Goodwin, M. H. (1990) *He-said-she-said: Talk as Social Organisation among Black Children*. Indianapolis, IN: Indiana University Press.

Haarman, L. (1997) Argument style and performance in the audience discussion show. In G. Bussi, M. Bondi and M. Gatta (eds.) *Understanding Argument: La logica informale del discorso*. Conference publication. Bologna, Italy: CLUEB, pp. 71–90.

Haarman, L. (1999) Performing talk. In L. Haarman (ed.) *Talk about Shows: La parola e lo spettacolo*. Conference publication. Bologna, Italy: CLUEB, pp. 1–53.

Haarman, L. (2001) Talking about talk. In A. Tolson (ed.) *Television Talk Shows: Discourse, Performance, Spectacle*. Mahwah, NJ: Lawrence Erlbaum, pp. 31–64.

Habermas, J. (1989) *The Structural Transformation of the Public Sphere*. Cambridge, UK: Polity Press.

Hall, S. (1997) The spectacle of the 'other'. In S. Hall (ed.) *Representation: Cultural Representations and Signifying Practices*. London, UK: Sage Publications in association with the Open University Press, pp. 223–279.

Hartley, J. (1982) *Understanding News*. London, UK: Methuen.

Hartley, J. (2009) Less popular but more democratic? *Corrie*, Clarkson and the dancing Cru. In G. Turner and J. Tay (eds.) *Television Studies after TV: Understanding Television in the Post-Broadcast Era*. London, UK: Routledge, pp. 20–30.

Heritage, J. and Sefi, S. (1992) Dilemmas of advice: Aspects of the delivery and reception of advice in interaction between health visitors and first-time mothers. In P. Drew and J. Heritage (eds.) *Talk at Work*. Cambridge, UK: Cambridge University Press, pp. 359–417.

Higgins, M., Montgomery, M., Smith, A. and Tolson, A. (2011) Belligerent broadcasting and makeover television: Professional incivility in 'Ramsay's Kitchen Nightmares'. *International Journal of Cultural Studies*, 15(5): 501–518.

Hill, A. (2002). *Big Brother*: The real audience. *Television & New Media* 3(3): 323–340.

Holmes, S. (2004) 'But this time *you* choose': Approaching the interactive audience in reality TV. *International Journal of Cultural Studies*, 7(2): 213–231.

Hudson, T. (1990) The discourse of advice giving in English: 'I wouldn't feed until spring no matter what you do'. *Language and Communication* 10(4): 285–297.

Hutchby, I. (1995) Aspects of recipient design in expert advice-giving on call-in radio. *Discourse Processes* 19(2): 219–238.

Hutchby, I. (1996) *Confrontation Talk: Arguments, Asymmetries and Power on Talk Radio*. Mahwah, NJ: Lawrence Erlbaum.

Hutchby, I. (2001a) Witnessing: The use of first-hand knowledge in legitimating lay opinions on talk radio. *Discourse Studies* 3(4): 481–497.

Hutchby, I. (2001b) Confrontation as a spectacle: The argumentative frame of the *Ricki Lake Show*. In A. Tolson (ed.) *Television Talk Shows: Discourse, Performance, Spectacle*. Mahwah, NJ: Lawrence Erlbaum, pp. 155–172.

Hutchby, I. (2006) *Media Talk: Conversation Analysis and the Study of Broadcasting*. Maidenhead, UK: Open University Press.

Hutchby, I. (2011) Doing non-neutral: Belligerent interaction in the hybrid political interview. In M. Ekström and M. Patrona (eds.) *Talking Politics in the Broadcast Media*. Amsterdam, The Netherlands: John Benjamins, pp. 115–134.

Hutchby, I. and Wooffitt, R. (1998) *Conversation Analysis*. Cambridge, UK: Polity.

Jefferson, G. (1978) Sequential aspects of storytelling in conversation. In J. Schenkein (ed.) *Studies in the Organization of Conversational Interaction*. New York, NY: Academic Press, pp. 219–248.

Jones, A. (2004) Emerging platform identities: *Big Brother* UK and interactive multi-platform usage. In E. Mathijs and J. Jones (eds.) *Big Brother International: Formats, Critics and Publics*. London, UK: Wallflower Press, pp. 210–231.

Labov, W. (1972) *Sociolinguistic Patterns*. Oxford, UK: Basil Blackwell.

Leith, D. (1995) Tense variation as a performance feature in a Scottish folktale. *Language in Society* 24: 53–75.

Levinson, S. (1983) *Pragmatics*. Cambridge, UK: Cambridge University Press.

Livingstone, S. and Lunt, P. (1992) Expert and lay participation in television debates: An analysis of audience discussion programmes. *European Journal of Communication*, 7(1): 9–35.

Livingstone, S. and Lunt, P. (1994) *Talk on Television: Audience Participation and Public Debate*. London, UK: Routledge.

Lorenzo-Dus, N. (2001) Up close and personal: The narrativisation of private experience in media talk. *Studies in English Language and Linguistics* 3: 125–148.

Lorenzo-Dus, N. (2009) *Television Discourse: Analysing Language in the Media.* Basingstoke, UK: Palgrave Macmillan.

Macdonald, M. (2007) Television debate, 'interactivity' and public opinion: The case of the BBC's Asylum Day. *Media, Culture and Society*, 29: 679–689.

McIntosh, J. (1986) *A Consumer Perspective on the Health Visiting Service.* Glasgow, UK: Social Paediatric and Obstetric Research Unit, University of Glasgow; Greater Glasgow Health Board.

Maynard, D. (1985). How children start arguments. *Language and Society* 14: 1–30.

Montgomery, M. (1986) *An Introduction to Language and Society.* London, UK: Methuen.

Montgomery, M. (1991) 'Our Tune': A study of a discourse genre. In P. Scannell (ed.) *Broadcast Talk.* London, UK: Sage, pp. 138–177.

Montgomery, M. (2001) Defining authentic talk. *Discourse Studies* 3(4): 397–405.

Montgomery, M. (2007) *The Discourse of Broadcast News.* London, UK: Routledge.

Moseley, R. (2000) Makeover takeover on British television. *Screen* 41: 299–314.

Myers, G. (2001) 'I'm out of it, you guys argue': Making an issue of it on the *Jerry Springer Show.* In A. Tolson (ed.) *Television Talk Shows: Discourse, Performance, Spectacle.* Mahwah, NJ: Lawrence Erlbaum, pp. 173–192.

Myers, G. (2004) *Matters of Opinion: Talking about Public Issues.* Cambridge, UK: Cambridge University Press.

Ochs, E. and Taylor, C. (1992) Family narrative as political activity. *Discourse and Society* 3(3): 301–340.

Oliver, M. (2005) The problem with affordance. *E-learning* 2(1): 401–413.

Polanyi, L. (1979) So what's the point? *Semiotica* 25(3/4): 207–241.

Pomerantz, A. (1975) Second Assessments: A Study of some Features of Agreements/ Disagreements. Ph.D. dissertation, University of California, Irvine.

Pomerantz, A. (1984) Agreeing and disagreeing with assessments: Some features of preferred/dispreferred turn shapes. In J. M. Atkinson and J. Heritage (eds.) *Structures of Social Action: Studies in Conversation Analysis.* Cambridge, UK: Cambridge University Press, pp. 79–112.

Propp, V. (1968) *Morphology of the Folk Tale.* Austin, TX: University of Texas Press.

Richardson, K. (2010) *Television Dramatic Dialogue: A Sociolinguistic Study.* Oxford, UK: Oxford University Press.

Rimmon-Kenan, S. (1983) *Narrative Fiction: Contemporary Poetics.* London, UK: Methuen.

Sacks, H. (1984) On doing 'being ordinary'. In J. M. Atkinson and J. Heritage (eds.) *Structures of Social Action: Studies in Conversation Analysis.* Cambridge, UK: Cambridge University Press, pp. 413–429.

Sacks, H. (1995) *Lectures on Conversation: Volumes 1 and 2.* Oxford, UK: Blackwell.

Sacks, H., Schegloff, E. A. and Jefferson, G. (1974) A simplest systematics for the organization of turn-taking for conversation. *Language* 50(4): 696–735.

Scannell, P. (ed.) (1991) *Broadcast Talk.* London, UK: Sage.

Scannell, P. (1996) *Radio, Television and Modern Life.* Oxford, UK: Blackwell.

Scannell, P. (2002) *Big Brother* as a television event. *Television & New Media* 3(3): 271–282.

Scannell, P. and Cardiff, D. (1991) *A Social History of British Broadcasting: Serving the Nation 1923–1939*. Oxford, UK: Blackwell.

Schegloff, E. and Sacks, H. (1973) Opening up closings. *Semiotica* 7: 289–327.

Schiffrin, D. (1981) Tense variation in narrative. *Language* 57: 45–62.

Schiffrin, D. (1984) Jewish argument as sociability. *Language in Society* 13(3): 311–335.

Schiffrin, D. (1990) Management of a co-operative self during argument. In A. D. Grimshaw (ed.) *Conflict Talk*. Cambridge, UK; New York, NY: Cambridge University Press, pp. 241–259.

Smith, A. (2009) Big sister TV? Humiliation, banter and bullying in makeover programmes. Paper presented at the Ross Priory Seminar on Broadcast Talk – Belligerence in Broadcast Talk, 13–16 September 2009, Ross Priory, University of Strathclyde, Glasgow, UK.

Thornborrow, J. (1997) Having their say: The function of stories in talk show discourse. *Text* 17(2): 241–262.

Thornborrow, J. (2000) The construction of conflicting accounts in public participation TV. *Language in Society* 29(3): 357–377.

Thornborrow, J. (2001a) 'Has it ever happened to you?': Talk show stories as mediated performance. In A. Tolson (ed.) *Television Talk Shows: Discourse, Performance, Spectacle*. Mahwah, NJ: Lawrence Erlbaum, pp. 117–137.

Thornborrow, J. (2001b) Authenticating talk: Building public identities in audience participation broadcasting. *Discourse Studies* 3(4): 459–479.

Thornborrow, J. (2002) *Power Talk: Language and Interaction in Institutional Discourse*. London, UK: Pearson Education.

Thornborrow, J. and Coates, J. (eds.) (2005) *The Sociolinguistics of Narrative*. Amsterdam, The Netherlands: John Benjamins.

Thornborrow, J. and Fitzgerald, R. (2002) From problematic object to routine 'add-on': Dealing with emails in radio phone-ins. *Discourse Studies* 4(2): 201–223.

Thornborrow, J. and Fitzgerald, R. (2013) 'Grab a pen and paper': Interaction v. interactivity in a political radio phone-in. *Journal of Language and Politics* 12(1): 1–28.

Thornborrow, J. and Morris, D. (2004) Gossip as strategy: The management of talk about others on reality TV show 'Big Brother'. *Journal of Sociolinguistics* 8(2): 246–271.

Tolson, A. (1991) Televised chat and the synthetic personality. In P. Scannell (ed.) *Broadcast Talk*. London, UK: Sage, pp. 178–200.

Tolson, A. (ed.) (2001) *Television Talk Shows: Discourse, Performance, Spectacle*. Mahwah, NJ: Lawrence Erlbaum.

Tolson, A. (2006) *Media Talk: Spoken Discourse on TV and Radio*. Edinburgh, UK: Edinburgh University Press.

Tolson, A. (2007) Celebrity Big Bully: Race, rage and retribution in the demise of a 'demotic' celebrity. Paper presented at the Ross Priory Seminar on Broadcast Talk – Privateness, 2–5 May 2007, Ross Priory, University of Strathclyde, Glasgow, UK. Available at http://hdl.handle.net/2086/3885 (accessed 10 March 2014).

Tolson, A. (2010) A new authenticity? Communicative practices on YouTube. *Critical Discourse Studies*, 7(4): 277–289.

Toolan, M. J. (2001) *Narrative: A Critical Linguistic Introduction* (3rd ed.). London, UK: Routledge.

Turner, G. (2010) *Ordinary People and the Media: The Demotic Turn*. London, UK: Sage.

Van Eemeren, F. H., Grootendorst, R. and Kruiger, T. (1987) *Handbook of Argumentation Theory*. Dordrecht, The Netherlands: Foris Publications.

Van Leeuwen, T. (2001) What is authenticity? *Discourse Studies*, 3(4): 392–397.

Vuchinich, S. (1990) The sequential organization of closing in verbal family conflict. In A. D. Grimshaw (ed.) *Conflict Talk*. Cambridge, UK: Cambridge University Press, pp. 118–138.

Index